THEMES AND SOCIAL FORCES IN AMERICAN HISTORY SERIES
Under the editorship of Robin W. Winks

Purpose: To explore major influences
on the development of American society and character.

ANTIDEMOCRATIC TRENDS
IN TWENTIETH-CENTURY AMERICA

Edited by
ROLAND L. DELORME
and
RAYMOND G. MCINNIS
Western Washington State College

ADDISON-WESLEY PUBLISHING COMPANY
Reading, Massachusetts
Palo Alto, California · London · Don Mills, Ontario

To Jeanne and Karen

The editors are convinced that this collection's chief significance derives from the topic's intimate connection with virtually every facet of American history in the twentieth century. The United States' hurried leap into technological maturity; its passage through severe economic crises; its assumption of vast international responsibilities; its confrontation with deep-rooted urban and ethnic dilemmas; even its confused groping for the achievement and sustenance of its own celebrated promise—these are the major themes of the nation's course in this century. They also represent the principal sources of doubt, disillusion, and social upheaval that comprise the challenge to the continuation of popular sovereignty in America. Antidemocracy is a basic undercurrent in recent and contemporary national thought and activities, not a product of false historical analogies or an invention of scholars seeking to delimit a novel "problem area."

A truly important historical movement owes its vitality to its continuing presence as well as to the circumstances of its prior existence. The antidemocratic trend claims a long-neglected past and an increasingly foreboding immediacy. The brave assertion that men shared a basic equality and deserved a social organism reflecting that equality never stood wholly unchallenged, even in the nation's brightest moments. There always have been theorists who scorned human worth and politicians who constructed power bases on such theories. Hysteria generated in times of crisis, mixed with the American fascination with efficiency, has occasionally called into question the lumbering gradualism of parliamentary decision-making. Since the days of Aaron Burr, Americans have tolerated the translation of political differences into sporadic violence. Yet it is in the twentieth century that such fleeting, isolated signs of antidemocratic tendencies have reached a full and terrible growth.

To gauge the influence of this antidemocratic trend, the student need only question his own understanding of, and attachment to, American democracy. As he reads the following selections, he should bear in mind some pertinent questions. Is a democratic structure useful or necessary for a modern state attempting to cope with a maze of complex domestic and world problems? Has the scientific world view rendered any presumption of human rationality and dignity impossible? Are the forms and formulas of political participation in the United States approximations of democratic processes, or do they simply shield a "real government" which remains detached from popular control and responsibility? In a contemporary, pluralistic society, can democratic dissent be defined as programmed violence? Can law become simple suppression? Finally, if democracy is worth preserving, how can its critics be answered, and how can the democratic spirit be restated and reconstituted in order to meet and conquer the adversities that weigh so heavily upon it in this age of furious desperation?

The editors owe a debt of gratitude to Professors Keith A. Murray and J. Gary Kepl of Western Washington State College, Robin Winks of Yale University, Allen Guttmann of Amherst College, and Leslie Decker and David Smith of the University of Maine for their perceptive suggestions. Among the many persons who helped in locating the selections chosen for this book, we wish to thank particularly Mrs. Corine Ackley and Mr. Don Duncan of the Washington State Library and the staff members of the University of Washington and Seattle Public libraries. Through the cheerful cooperation of Dean Herbert C. Taylor, expert assistance in the typing and proofreading of the manuscript was rendered by Jane Clark and Deborah Harris of Western Washington State College's Bureau of Faculty Research. Also helping with the typing were Esther Ericson, Linda Farrell, Kay Adams, and Kay Crocker.

Western Washington State College   R.L.D.
January, 1969   R.G.M.

Contents

Introduction

Nineteenth-century America seemed synonymous with democracy. "In America," Tocqueville admitted, "I saw more than America; I sought the image of democracy itself, with its inclinations, its character, its prejudices, and its passions."[1] The emergent United States, holding sway over a vast area of unexploited land and natural resources, was a nation of hardy yeomen and bustling shopkeepers, free in comparative isolation to grow toward maturity and already aware of its own uniqueness. No hope appeared impossible in that setting. Americans injected a boundless optimism into all their ventures. The American, they were quick to avow, *was* a new man and the United States an apparently successful experiment in self-government. All over the world, men craving release from oppression looked to the New World for revolutionary democratic inspiration.[2]

The sources for the democratic ferment in America were an equation of liberty with natural law, belief in the intrinsic reasonableness of man, and a vague perception of America's role as the missionary of republicanism in a world ruled by tyrants. The supports for divine monarchy were brushed aside by Newtonian science, which posited a world of balance, uniformity of design, and harmony. The new social equivalent was a state in which all men shared in the responsibilities and privileges of power. Democracy was deemed as natural as gravity, and any form of government that placed power before liberty was, as James Madison remarked, "a perversion of the natural order of things."[3] The citizen of the democratic state was enlightenment man—rational, free, infinitely improvable. His dignity issued from his reasonable nature and was nurtured by individual freedom and political representation. The state was a bulwark of, not a threat to, those rights, and as such also bore the burden of exemplar of democracy for a misguided, suffering world tottering on the brink of inevitable revolution.[4]

1

Through most of the nineteenth century, democracy appeared to re-deem its promises. That century was America's bumptious youth, filled with remarkable political and economic achievements that fed a cocky self-assurance. Even sectional turmoil failed to daunt those who, no doubt speaking for the majority, envisioned a future of limitless progress. Yet the turn of the century chronicled the end of adolescence. Deep and persistent problems appeared that could no longer be dismissed as growing pains. An expanding population drove the frontier line to the shores of the Pacific, then moved in inexorable waves upon the chief urban centers of the nation. The rapid concentration and consolidation of national wealth which were unmistakable signs of industrialization posed acute ideological as well as economic questions. A barely mature national identity tested almost be-yond endurance by the Civil War seemed threatened by the immigration from Eastern and Southern Europe that came after 1870. In the span of a century, despite remarkable growth, the land of opportunity had collected a growing residue of failures and discontents. The conditions that had bred optimism faded away and in their place came hesitancy, disillusionment, national self-doubt. Probably most Americans retained a stubborn though blurred belief in democracy, but as one observer noted wearily, "Faith in Democracy has always required a great deal of idealism."[5] Idealism, in the twentieth century, would become increasingly difficult to sustain.

Some degree of disaffection for democracy has never been absent from the United States. A small but distinguished minority which included Alexander Hamilton, John Adams, and Fisher Ames seldom bothered to mask their suspicion of the supposed rationality of man or their disbelief in the naturalness of democracy. "Democracy," Ames sneered, "is an illumi-nated hell . . . . The most ferocious of all animals . . . is man."[6] The denial of the efficacy of majority rule was carried into this century by scholarly aristocrats like Charles Eliot Norton, Irving Babbitt, and Paul Elmer More.[7] Such critics argued that the rise of democracy was, in effect, the "rise of the uncivilized, whom no school education can suffice to provide with intelli-gence and reason," and they proposed to make a virtue of inequality by entrusting leadership to a cultivated minority.[8]

An ancient distrust of popular government was refurbished with vague allusions to economic and social determinism and psychological "proof" of the mental incapacity and irrationality of common men. American political practices, according to prophets of doom like William K. Wallace and Harry Atwood, amounted to dictatorship of, by, and for the mediocre; Atwood defined democracy as "too much participation by the people."[9] Ralph Adams Cram, whose efforts as architect to revive the Gothic style reflected his political preferences, agreed with Henry and Brooks Adams that the twentieth century would witness democracy's end. Also sharing Henry Adams' escapist fantasies about the medieval era, Cram's "Higher Democracy" included the reestablishment of monarchy and knighthood.[10] Few supporters of aristocracy ventured so far. Most were content to demonstrate that the increasing economic stratification of American society presaged the inevitable emergence of an aristocracy of wealth.[11] Herbert Spencer's image of human society as governed by natural selection no longer claimed the allegiance of a majority of Americans, but a few writers persisted in limiting human motivation to a ruthless struggle for survival. These traditional doubters were prepared to wield any ideological weapon to predict or announce the supplanting of democracy by some form of aristocracy.

A new and more dangerous source of antidemocratic sentiment was twentieth-century science. In the age of Newton, the spirit of scientific inquiry had lent its prestige to the affirmation of human rationality and a balanced universe ruled by natural laws. Modern science, however, advanced a theory of evolution that could be interpreted as sanctifying violence, inequality, and domination as natural. Applied to the mental processes of man, moreover, scientific methods appeared to uncover deep reservoirs of irrationality lurking beneath the veneer of reason. Theoretical and applied science, promising stabilization and control through measurement and prediction, tempted men as never before to replace the gropings of free individuals in an open society with efficiency and regulation. The contrast of laboratory with life was painful for some. The average American, Walter Lippmann complained, "does not know what is happening, why it is happening, what ought to happen."[12] The complications of modern living demanded scientific control, another political analyst agreed: "Population is becoming too dense, the resultant inter-relations of interest too complex, the dependence of individual upon individual, of individual upon group, and of group upon group, too great, to permit us to retain the ramshackle methods of an earlier day."[13]

Pioneer research in genetics not only fostered popular interest in scientific plant and animal breeding, but it also inspired nativists to clothe their doctrines of racial or biological superiority in pseudo-scientific terminology. Democracy was unnatural because unscientific; racial differentiations represented inherent inequalities in men. Ascribing American greatness to the physical prowess, intelligence, and social astuteness of the Nordic race, the amateur eugenicist Madison Grant warned that unless immigration were restricted, "the citadel of civilization" would "fall for mere lack of defenders."[14] "This generation must completely repudiate the proud boast of our fathers that they acknowledged no distinction in 'race, creed, or color,' or else the native American must turn the page of history and write: 'FINIS AMERICAE.' "[15] While thoughtful Americans like E. G. Conklin sought to "harmonize . . . democratic equality and hereditary inequality," Alleyne Ireland pictured the dilemma as virtually insoluble and the Eugenics Record Office assigned a committee the task of finding "the best practical means of cutting off the defective germ-plasm in the American population."[16] Though their views were shown to be riddled with fallacies, eugenics advocates succeeded in lobbying efforts aimed at securing federal restrictions on immigration, and a few states also passed legislation authorizing sterilization of criminals and the mentally deficient.

Still more far-reaching were the effects of psychological theories and findings on democratic beliefs. The measurement of human intelligence through testing procedures, first used on a massive scale in World War I, produced results that cast grave doubt on the wisdom of democracy's reliance upon the intelligence of average men. And theories about human behavior, in league with the technology of mass media, focused on and exploited the emotional side of man. As politicians were quick to see, advertising techniques borrowed from the amazingly successful propaganda efforts of the Office of Public Information were ready-made for use in political campaigns. There was somber truth to a later presidential candidate's angry charge that office seekers in twentieth-century America were marketed like breakfast cereals. The whole democratic process stood in danger of becoming just another form of public amusement. No hint of belief in reasonable man was discernible in the campaigns managed by public relations counsel.

Behaviorist and Freudian psychologists affirmed the notion that man was irrational and malleable. They emphatically rejected the portrayal of man as a moral agent in a universe of free choice. Wrote Dr. William A. White: "Man may be prepared to have all of his activities which in the past have been considered as the free actions of myriads of individuals reduced to law . . . ."[17] White's conception of law was a determinism that transformed man into a Pavlovian dog or Freudian dog in heat—a view scarcely compatible with the democratic faith. What basis could there be for trust in the popular will if the public could "act only on the excitement of its pugnacities and its hopes?"[18] What future had American democracy in this critical century if its enlightened citizenry suddenly became "the unformed, exploitable mass of public opinion?"[19] What was the staying-power of democratic rule—"the reign of reason on the most extensive scale"—once the psychologists convinced officeholders "how slender a reed is reason—how recent its emergence in man, how deep the countervailing instincts and passions, how treacherous the whole rational process?"[20] Was modern man unequal to the psychological burden of freedom, as the respected theorist Erich Fromm argued?

According to some writers, the demolition of eighteenth-century democratic precepts by twentieth-century scientific theories represented a clear intellectual advance. If science struck down existing institutions, argued the behaviorist B. F. Skinner, it could also supply new ones. Science measured, predicted, and regulated portions of the physical world; why not use it to devise a human engineering that could resolve all the problems of human conduct and society? Insisting that, "designing a new cultural pattern is in many ways like designing an experiment," Skinner outlined a utopia where experts would condition men to accept "normal" life patterns.[21] The conflict of any scientific regulation of human affairs with democracy was freely acknowledged: "The theoretical structure with which science represents its facts . . . is clearly at odds with the traditional democratic conception of man."[22] Skinner's solution was to depict democracy as a means, and an imperfect means at that, for achieving human happiness. In turning from the democratic faith in man to a science for human control, "we turn from the ill-defined and remote to the observable and manipulable."[23]

Skinner's trust in the inevitability of rule by experts was shared by James Burnham, a rebel from the ranks of orthodox Marxists, who saw democracy as no more than capitalism's facade—doomed like the profit system to fall before a managerial revolution. In spite of ideological differences, capitalism and communism faced an identical fate. As automatically as industrialization bred technical complexity, economic (and thus political) power would be concentrated in the hands of the technicians themselves. Some of the main outlines of Burnham's prediction have been advanced less systematically by Americans driven by recurrent crises to the conclusion that democracy is government by amateurs and thus unadapted to twentieth-century life. Howard Scott's Technocracy, Inc., calling for total social control supervised by technical experts, is an interesting variant of the theory of managerial revolution.

The prolonged economic troubles of the 1930's provided a social context in which imported, frankly authoritarian ideologies could challenge American democracy on native soil. Many confused, frustrated Americans were attracted to the political certainty and security of modern totalitarianism, mistook dialectic for scientific fact, and worshipped Marx and Lenin as chief deities in a cult of scientism.[24] Before 1917, believers in the inevitability of class strife had looked to the disunited splinter groups which comprised the American socialist movement or to the Industrial Workers of the World. The Bolshevik accession to power in Russia provided a dramatic new model and focus for Marxist activities in the United States. Revered for their apparent success, Soviet-inspired and directed communists could pretend, amidst the wreckage of American prosperity after 1929, to have all the answers. "We insisted to our Liberal friends," Benjamin Gitlow recalled, "that pure objectivity was the determining factor in all Communist politics."[25] The science of communism decreed the cause higher than the individual: "We believed it to be an incontrovertible truth . . . that in the Communist movement the individual factor was of negligible, if any, importance. The individual . . . merely reflected social conditions."[26] Those who traveled this road to certainty surrendered their responsibilities as free men to a revolutionary movement under a foreign power's tutelage. They performed "like privates in a military organization. Orders given were carried out. . . . A Communist's life is in and of the Movement. He is like a squirrel in a cage, always running around in circles."[27]

Like the communists, fascists affirmed the existence of class conflict, prophesied an early end for capitalism and democracy, and considered violence a useful and necessary political instrument. Lawrence Dennis expounded American fascism in its most sophisticated form; however, his influence on the general public probably was negligible. Far more widely disseminated and dangerous were the writings and speeches of demagogues who sought to assemble political followings by trading in hysteria, frustration, and hate. The fascists had a clear message for those who doubted a free society's capacity for survival. They offered order in place of freedom, worship of power as a substitute for faith in human reason, and racist myths for equalitarianism.

Americans hypnotized by the dazzle of corporate statism could don the black blouse and trousers, flowing black tie, and tassled overseas cap that comprised the regulation uniform of the one hundred twenty fascios organized in the United States by the Fascist League of North America and greet their hero's name standing stiffly erect, arm upraised with palm forward, chanting, "Mussolini! Eja! Eja! Allala!"[28] They could join the Friends of the New Germany, participate in the parades and mass rallies of the German-American Bund or America First, or enter the ranks of William Dudley Pelly's Silver Shirts ("the cream, the head and the flower of our Protestant Christian manhood"), Art Smith's Khaki Shirts, George W. Christians' Crusaders for Economic Liberty, or Harry Jung's American Vigilantes.[29] In Washington, D. C., a congressional committee heard a retired Marine Corps officer accuse a bond salesman of conspiring to foment a fascist military coup, and in Hollywood, California, screen stars Victor McLaglen and Gary Cooper organized and equipped paramilitary horsemen in preparation for some future time of violence.[30] A Catholic priest, Father

Charles Coughlin, parlayed fascism, anti-Semitism, and a talent for radio oratory into a popular following that rivaled President Roosevelt's. Though his third-party efforts failed, Coughlin's magazine, *Social Justice,* espoused the policies of Hitler and Mussolini until it was suspended by the Justice Department following the outbreak of World War II.[31] Despite the obliteration of the Axis powers, neonazi and fascist publications and political activities reappeared in the United States at the end of the war.

Meanwhile, an even greater threat to democratic processes had developed from native roots—an essentially antidemocratic tendency that issued from the accumulated personal and social anxieties of twentieth-century America. This was the disillusioned wail of those for whom democracy had failed, an ideology of despair suited to forgotten men. The politics of alienation issued from startlingly disparate quarters. Characteristically, it belonged to those suffering from economic inequities or an absence of social status and political voice: a rural-minded Protestant minority, ethnic minorities (particularly Afro-Americans), and intellectuals. All of these groups shared a sense of isolation from, and grievance against, American society. Divided from one another by probably ineradicable differences in viewpoint, they nevertheless agreed (1) that the American political system was failing in some essential way; (2) that there was a break-down of representative institutions traceable to some sort of conspiracy; (3) that desperate action, even violence, was an acceptable corrective.

Embattled defenders of an agrarian myth pieced together a patchwork of oversimplified economic doctrines, social paranoia, racism, and religious fundamentalism—"Americanism"—that they swore to defend against the conspiratorial agents of godless communism. Revived by war-time intolerance and long-nurtured economic complaints, the Knights of the Ku Klux Klan had spread out of the South into other parts of the United States in the 1920's, attaining a potent if temporary national prominence. They were dedicated to white supremacy, secrecy, and violence. Depression transformed the fiery crosses into a political prairie fire that resembled the nineteenth-century farmers' revolt. But this movement of the twenties was a variant of Populism, a shrill, malevolent form of hysteria that cast aside the Bryanite emphases on equalitarianism and democratic processes while magnifying a latent nativism and anti-intellectualism. Louisiana's Huey Long, until stopped by an assassin's bullet, dominated his state and husbanded a national following by preaching his "Share the Wealth" plan, approved, he insisted, "by the law of our Divine Maker. You will find it in the Book of Deuteronomy . . . .You will find it in the writings of King Solomon. You will find it in the teachings of Christ. You will find it in the words of our great teachers and statesmen of all countries and of all times."[32] After Long's death, leadership passed to the durable fundamentalist preacher Gerald L. K. Smith, whose technique—"Religion and patriotism, keep going on that"—made him, in his own words, "a symbol of a state of mind . . . . The people will start fomenting, fermenting, and then a fellow like myself . . . will get on the radio and have the people with him, hook, line, and sinker. I'll teach 'em how to hate."[33]

Although Smith failed to establish a lasting political movement, through his magazine, *The Cross and the Flag,* he was able to promote an alliance between his Christian Nationalist Crusade and the rapidly multiplying rightist organizations of the late 1940's and 1950's. Command of the revitalized assault on civil liberties in the name of anticommunism fell to Wisconsin's Senator Joseph McCarthy. McCarthy's sensational charges of subversive activities within federal government agencies spurred a rash of noisy witch hunts and loyalty oath legislation that, critics claimed, placed new restrictions on the rights of free speech and assembly without appreciably curbing treasonable acts. The most tangible results of the tactics of McCarthy and his allies were heightened suspicion and insecurity. McCarthy's censure and early death only made him a martyr for groups like Carl McIntire's Christian Anti-Communist Crusade and Billy James Hargis' Christian Crusade. These groups publicly attacked the enlargement of federal government, the civil rights movement, and American participation in the United Nations as parts of a communist master plan. Secret societies like the paramilitary Minutemen and the John Birch Society prepared feverishly for a day of judgment. The Birch Society's founder sounded the call for drastic countermeasures, hinting darkly that the age required a man on horseback supported by a million well-drilled followers.

Extremists on the right railed against a liberal establishment: "the Supreme Court of the United States, the political demagogues, the sappy preachers, the insipid educators, the ivory tower intellectuals, the downright traitors, and the Moscow-trained agitators."[34] To some Afro-Americans, on the other hand, the foe was a white establishment: "the man, the police force, the governors that serve the ruling class in America."[35] Here, too, a deep, brooding sense of alienation from the sources of social control resulted in a demand for total redress regardless of the consequences. An almost unbroken history of betrayed promises and silently enforced inequality made it difficult for many Americans to counsel patience once again. A majority no doubt agreed solemnly with civil rights leaders who urged that there could be no compromise with bigotry this time.

The chief point of contention was the method of redress. Could the rights of minorities be realized within existing democratic institutions? Could unjust statutes and institutionalized brutality be erased without jeopardizing faith in law? Could full democracy become a reality—now—before another generation suffered under a double standard, and could this transformation take place without violent upheaval? Many would not be persuaded that these were real possibilities. Armed terrorists plotted organized mayhem. In the tense, corrosive slums of urban America, black nationalists preached their own brand of racism as an antidote to centuries of psychological enslavement, and violence as the solution to racial troubles. A small but influential group of leaders declared their patience at an end: the search for justice through the existing social fabric would be terminated. "We want to play our game according to the new rules," announced Stokely Carmichael, "the rules of the guerilla . . . . We are organizing the urban guerilla in the United States according to the inspired tactics expressed in the maxims of Ché Guevara: i.e., to create various Vietnams in order to overthrow capitalism and imperialism."[36] Henceforth, the justifiable fury of many Afro-Americans would be channeled toward desperate acts of violence that threatened the freedom for which they were committed. "You gave us violence," a new director of the Student Nonviolent Coordinating Committee reminded a white audience, "and this is the only value that black people can use to their advantage to end oppression."[37]

The cult of irrationality had penetrated at last into the sanctions governing dissent in a democracy. Some depicted terror as a bona fide instrument of political change; others, opposed to violence, apparently forgot the image of man as reasonable and free, and urged in reply only an unthinking allegiance to order for its own sake, emphasizing the outer trappings of law and the magic of consensus, as though dissent were subversive and the political structure could no longer bear criticism or modification. Neither faction appeared to think that existing representative institutions could produce rapid political or social change.

Most alarming was the lack of interest displayed by American intellectuals either in defending, or seeking new supports for, the democratic faith. Acute crises in the past had summoned revitalizing interpretations. The brutalization that accompanied the first thrust of industrialization had led to the addition of humaneness to an American definition of progress. Although not without just misgivings, American intellectuals rationalized entry into a world war as an extension of the United States' mission of carrying democracy around the world. Even in the gloomy 1930's, amid the signs of a tragic second global conflict, the bulk of the nation's writers and thinkers remained faithful to the American Dream. But the Allies' failure in World War II to preserve even the pretense of a struggle for worldwide freedom—the halt of the New Deal's domestic reform emphases, a seeming disregard of the Atlantic Charter, the Darlan episode—lent credence, among intellectuals, to a growing sense of separation from the sources of national political power. Former believers in a flexible democracy's ability to survive and progress grew angrily critical. "The truth is," Oswald Garrison Villard wrote Charles Beard, "we have a highly militaristic, lower middle class, back-slapping American legionnaire in the White House, who has given free rein to the militarists . . . ."[38]

Intellectuals found support for their feeling of alienation in a sophisticated adaptation of conspiracy theory: the belief that, despite a facade of self-government, political power is vested in a ruling elite. The new version of this theory had found its way into intellectual circles through the sociological writings of Robert S. Lynd, whose chief premise was the conflict between democracy and capitalism. According to Lynd, a privileged class used democratic forms as a cloak for its manipulation of American society.[39] The idea was restated by C. Wright Mills in the light of postwar concern about the dangers of maintaining a large, permanent military force: "The political directorate, the corporate rich, and the ascendent military have come together as the power elite."[40] By the 1960's this cynical disbelief in democracy spurred a hurried, paranoiac jerry-building of mysterious "establishments" whenever or wherever the political structure responded sluggishly to pressures for change. The theory tended toward self-fulfillment. Champions of the establishment myth declined to engage in the processes of representative government, thus contributing to their possible collapse, but lent support to revolution, "nonviolent" or otherwise.

There could be no doubt that American democracy confronted disturbing problems. Deepening involvement abroad sapped not only the United States' military strength but the national commitment to freedom as well. After two decades of cold war, Americans had grown accustomed to attempts to regiment opinion for the sake of security; government secrecy had become a commonplace, all the more dangerous because it was tolerated complacently. Some observers warned of the approach of a garrison state, the creation, ironically, of a people seeking to defend liberty. "Stalin has really conquered the United States," wrote one worried liberal, "in that he has completed its militarization and has frightened it to death."[41] Yet the real need for anxiety about the future prospects for democracy in America stemmed from another source—the absence of fresh affirmations of the validity of democratic principles in the contemporary age. There seemed no firm resolve to save both freedom and reason, no conviction, indeed, that they should or could be saved. At the historical moment when the American will would face a severe (perhaps supreme) test, that will appeared paralyzed. No unity of purpose or belief rose above the din of clichés. "There must be faith," James Reston noted, "and this, for the present, is what we do not have—neither faith in our common purposes, nor in our old religious and philosophic institutions, nor in our present policies, nor in the men who are making or administering them."[42]

NOTES

1. Alexis de Tocqueville, *Democracy in America* (New York: Colonial Press, 1900), I, p. 14.

2. R. R. Palmer, *The Age of the Democratic Revolution* (Princeton: Princeton University Press, 1959), I, p. 239.

3. Quoted in Adrienne Koch, *Jefferson and Madison: the Great Collaboration* (New York: Oxford University Press, 1964), p. 97.

4. Ralph H. Gabriel, *The Course of American Democratic Thought,* 2nd ed. (New York: Ronald Press, 1956), pp. 12-25.

5. Vida D. Scudder, "The Hidden Weakness in our Democracy," *Atlantic,* 89 (May, 1902), p. 638.

6. David Spitz, *Patterns of Anti-Democratic Thought* (New York: Macmillan Co., 1949), p. 97.

7. Paul Elmer More, *Aristocracy and Justice* (Boston: Houghton Mifflin Co., 1915), *passim;* Lloyd Morris, *Postscript to Yesterday, America: the Last Fifty Years* (New York: Random House, 1947), p. 137.

8. Charles Eliot Norton, in Alan P. Grimes, *American Political Thought* (New York: Henry Holt and Co., 1955), p. 397.

9. Spitz, *Patterns of Anti-Democratic Thought,* pp. 97-98.

10. Grimes, *American Political Thought,* p. 412.

11. T. W. Higginson, "The Aristocracy of the Dollar," *Atlantic,* 93 (April, 1904), pp. 506-513; "Is America Heading for Aristocracy?" *Living Age,* 254 (September 21, 1907), pp. 757-760.

12. Walter Lippmann, *The Phantom Public* (New York: Harcourt, Brace and Co., 1925), p. 39.

13. Pitman B. Potter, "Science in Politics," *North American Review,* 222 (December, 1925), p. 265.

14. Madison Grant, *The Passing of the Great Race* (New York: Charles Scribner's Sons, 1921), p. xxxi.

15. *Ibid.,* p. xxxiii.

16. Eugenics Record Office, *Report of the Committee to Study . . . the Best Practical Means of Cutting Off the Defective Germ-Plasm in the American Population* (Cold Harbor, New York, 1914), *passim.*

17. William A. White, *Twentieth Century Psychiatry: Its Contribution to Man's Knowledge of Himself* (New York: W. W. Norton and Co., Inc., 1936), p. 182.

18. Walter Lippman, "Basic Problems of Democracy," *Atlantic,* 124 (November, 1919), p. 621.

19. *Ibid.,* p. 626.

20. Felix Frankfurter, "Democracy and the Expert," *Atlantic,* 146 (November, 1930), p. 650.

21. B. F. Skinner, "Freedom and the Control of Men," *American Scholar,* 25 (Winter, 1955-1956), p. 50.

22. *Ibid.,* p. 52.

23. *Ibid.,* p. 65.

24. Theodore Draper, *The Roots of American Communism* (New York: Viking Press, 1966), p. 124.

25. Benjamin Gitlow, *I Confess* (New York: E. P. Dutton, 1940), p. 169.

26. *Loc. cit.*

27. *Ibid.,* pp. 287, 289.

28. Marcus Duffield, "Mussolini's American Empire," *Harper's Magazine,* 159 (November, 1929), p. 663, 662.

29. Arthur M. Schlesinger, Jr., *The Politics of Upheaval* (Boston: Houghton Mifflin Co., 1960), pp. 76-82; also E. C. Lindeman, "Fascist Sympathies in the United States," *Nation,* 131 (September 10, 1930), pp. 267-268; and H. F. Ward, "Development of Fascism in the United States," *Annals of the American Academy of Political and Social Science,* 180 (July, 1935), pp. 55-61.

30. Schlesinger, *Politics of Upheaval,* pp. 82-83; Carey McWilliams, "Hollywood Plays with Fascism," *Nation,* 140 (May 29, 1935), pp. 623-624.

31. H. C. Field, "The Fascist Press in America," *Contemporary Jewish Record,* 5 (June, 1942), pp. 291-298.

32. Huey Long, "Our Blundering Government and its Spokesman—Hugh Johnson," *Vital Speeches of the Day,* I (March 25, 1935), p. 397.

33. Herbert Harris, "That Third Party," *Current History,* 45 (October, 1936), p. 84.

34. Gerald L. K. Smith, "The Black Revolution is On," *The Cross and the Flag,* 26 (September, 1967), no pagination.

35. H. Rap Brown, "Speech at the Annual *Guardian* Meeting," in *National Guardian,* November 4, 1967, p. 3.

36. *Diario Las Americas,* August 3, 1967, p. 1.

37. Brown, "Speech," p. 3.

38. Arthur A. Ekirch, Jr., *The Decline of American Liberalism* (New York: Longmans, Green and Co., 1955), p. 323.

39. John H. Bunzel, *Anti-Politics in America* (New York: Alfred A. Knopf, 1967), p. 99.

40. C. Wright Mills, *The Power Elite* (New York: Oxford University Press, 1957), p. 296.

41. Ekirch, *Decline of American Liberalism,* p. 321.

42. James Reston, "Washington: New Policies or New Leaders?" *New York Times,* August 6, 1967, p. 10-E.

Part One

The Traditional Doubters

Part One

The Traditional Doubters

The close of the nineteenth century found a small but influential group of men who shared doubts about the real value of American democracy—doubts which had survived a successful war for independence with its accompanying Tory exodus and had been nurtured through a hundred years of momentous economic, political, and social upheaval. The traditional doubters included sensitive intellectuals who found the Gilded Age an affront, property holders who feared that the growth of industrial strife was a prelude to revolution, and a pathetic patrician remnant which equated democracy with the status revolution which was rendering them powerless and forgotten. The names of the disillusioned included some of the country's most notable educators and writers: Charles Eliot Norton, Henry Adams, James Russell Lowell, Edwin Lawrence Godkin.[1] These men had concluded that democracy and industrialization were irretrievably perverting American social values and political practices. Henry Adams, in particular, utilized his considerable mental powers in fashioning a "dynamo theory" which purported to reveal the rapid, inevitable disintegration of national cohesion through a frenetic expenditure of social energies. Adams died in 1918, but his insistence upon the fatal intertwining of industrial capitalism with popular sovereignty, and with democracy's imminent collapse, was taken up by Irving Babbitt and Ralph Adams Cram, among others.

Babbitt (1865-1933) approached social criticism from the same vantage point from which he surveyed literature. He was a staunch, learned advocate of monistic unity, symmetry, and abstraction.[2] He deployed formidable talents—a "powerful scalpel-like mind; a direct and simple message; an intense urgency; and a passionate, prophetic desire to proselytize"—in order to attack the causes of spiritual and social decay in the twentieth century.[3] Babbitt believed that the United States faced certain doom because it had embraced materialism as a measuring rod of progress, and a popular government as the means for achieving individual liberty. American politics had been lured astray by the siren songs of Locke and Rousseau, with the result that equalitarianism and unregulated passions threatened "the integrity of irreducible individuality."[4] As a leader of an intellectual revolt against democracy, Babbitt wrote countless essays, as well as *The New Laokoon* (1910), *Rousseau and Romanticism* (1919), and *Democracy and Leadership* (1924), insisting upon the absurdity of the doctrines of self-rule and human equality. His remedy comprised a political Buddhism; Babbitt wished to recall Americans to moral regulation and restraint through the application of an inner check to impulse.[5] What he diagnosed as the self-destructive combination of democracy and capitalism had to be supplanted, he argued, by a social peace won by the recognition of the fundamental inequality of men, the training of an intellectual elite, and rule by example, exercised by this self-disciplined, virtuous natural aristocracy.[6]

Ralph Adams Cram (1863-1942) had his own peculiar solutions for the debilitating effects of American democracy. Like Babbitt in his abhorrence of a society ruled, so he thought, by plutocrats pandering to the tastelessness of the proletarian herd, this architect and social critic proposed to eradicate disorder by restoring medieval values and social structure. "The ideals of honor, duty, courage, adventure, heroism, chivalry"—ideals Cram perceived in the Gothic church architecture he championed—would be resurrected by demolishing the twin evils industrialism and democracy, and establishing a new moral aristocracy replete with titles and ceremonial trappings.[7] The United States Senate would be reconstituted as a body of guild representatives elected for life. The chief executive would become a president-king empowered to designate a prime minister and, when necessary, to dissolve a balky House of Representatives. The judicial branch of government would be left with carefully restricted prerogatives.[8] Among Cram's numerous books and articles, *The Nemesis of Mediocrity* (1917) and *The End of Democracy* (1937) stand as testimony to a political philosophy that one writer classified as marking "the zenith of intellectual reaction in the United States."[9]

Ironically, although both Babbitt and Cram scorned and feared the political involvement of men of capital, their wholesale condemnations of popular rule provided one source for an antidemocratic current clearly perceptible in the business literature of the twenties. Their utter contempt for the common man was translated into a blunt credo that rested on simplistic definitions of elitism, natural preeminence, stability, suspicion of the masses, and rugged individualism.[10] Substituting business acumen for sensitive intelligence, one "booster" could write: "Without these great minds, the multitude would eat their heads off, and, as history proves, would lapse into barbarism and die of pestilence and famine. The masses are the beneficiaries, the few, the benefactors."[11]

Babbitt's variety of neo-humanism and Cram's prescriptions for institutional reform did not survive the depression years. But a later generation of malcontents, searching for a foundation for their own doubts about democracy's future, has found a "pressing relevance" in the predictions of the traditional doubters.[12] The efforts of Peter Viereck, Russell Kirk, and others to rekindle a "conservatism" are echoes of the generation of Babbitt, Cram, and Adams, and share a common ground in the doubts of some Americans as to the survival capacity of a uniquely American political experiment.[13]

NOTES

1. Alan P. Grimes, *American Political Thought* (New York: Henry Holt & Company, 1955), pp. 396-397.

2. William G. Carleton, "American Intellectuals and American Democracy," *Antioch Review,* 19 (Summer, 1959), p. 203.

3. John A. Yunck, "The Natural History of a Dead Quarrel: Hemingway and the Humanists," *South Atlantic Quarterly,* 62 (Winter, 1963), p. 35.

4. Henry S. Kariel, "Democracy Limited: Irving Babbitt's Classicism," *Review of Politics,* 13 (October, 1951), p. 440; also, Carleton, "American Intellectuals and American Democracy," p. 188.

5. Kariel, "Democracy Limited," p. 431; Grimes, *American Political Thought,* p. 402.

6. Grimes, *American Political Thought,* pp. 395, 405; M. Morton Auerbach, *The Conservative Illusion* (New York: Columbia University Press, 1959), p. 101; Clinton Rossiter, *Conservatism in America* (New York: Alfred A. Knopf, 1955), p. 167.

7. *National Cyclopaedia of American Biography* (New York: James T. White & Company, 1927), Vol. B, p. 228.

8. Auerbach, *The Conservative Illusion,* p. 102.

9. Rossiter, *Conservatism in America,* p. 168.

10. Grimes, *American Political Thought,* p. 395; James W. Prothro, "Business Ideas and the American Tradition," *Journal of Politics,* 15 (February, 1953), pp. 67-87.

11. Eugene Lombard, "Where the Surplus Value Comes From," *American Industries,* XX (January, 1920), p. 18.

12. Kariel, "Democracy Limited," p. 430.

13. Bernard Crick, "The Strange Quest for an American Conservatism," *Review of Politics,* 17 (July, 1955), pp. 359-360; also, Samuel P. Huntington, "Conservatism as an Ideology," *American Political Science Review,* 51 (June, 1957), p. 472.

Democracy and Leadership
IRVING BABBITT

Judged by any quantitative test, the American achievement is impressive. We have ninety percent of the motors of the world and control seventy-five percent of its oil; we produce sixty percent of the world's steel, seventy percent of its copper, and eighty percent of its telephones and typewriters. This and similar statistical proof of our material preeminence, which would have made a Greek apprehensive of Nemesis, seems to inspire in many Americans an almost lyrical complacency. They are not only quantitative in their estimates of our present accomplishment, but even more so if possible in what they anticipate for the future. Now that we have fifteen million automobiles they feel, with Mr. Henry Ford, that we can have no higher ambition than to expand this number to thirty million. Our present output of fifty million tons of steel a year is, according to Mr. Schwab, a mere trifle compared with our probable output of twenty years hence. In short, an age that is already immersed in things to an unexampled degree is merely to prepare the way for an age still more material in its preoccupations and still more subservient to machinery. This, we are told, is progress. To a person with a proportionate view of life it might seem rather to be fullblown commercial insolence.

The reasons for the quantitative view of life that prevails in America are far from being purely political. This view has resulted in a large measure from the coming together of scientific discovery with the opening up of a new continent. It has been possible with the aid of science to accomplish in a hundred years what even the optimistic Thomas Jefferson thought might take a thousand. The explanation, it has been said, of much that is obscure to us in the Chinese may be summed up in the words "lack of elbow-room." We in this country, on the other hand, have received a peculiar psychic twist from the fact that we have had endless elbow-room. A chief danger both to ourselves and others is that we shall continue to have a frontier psychology long after we have ceased to have a frontier. For a frontier psychology is expansive, and expansiveness is, at least in its political manifestations, always imperialistic.

From Irving Babbitt, *Democracy and Leadership,* Houghton-Mifflin Co., Boston, 1924. Reprinted by permission of the publisher.

If quantitatively the American achievement is impressive, qualitatively it is somewhat less satisfying. What must one think of a country, asks one of our foreign critics, whose most popular orator is W. J. Bryan, whose favorite actor is Charlie Chaplin, whose most widely read novelist is Harold Bell Wright, whose best-known evangelist is Billy Sunday, and whose representative journalist is William Randolph Hearst? What one must evidently think of such a country, even after allowing liberally for overstatement, is that it lacks standards. Furthermore, America suffers not only from a lack of standards, but also not infrequently from a confusion or an inversion of standards. As an example of the inversion of standards we may take the bricklayer who, being able to lay two thousand bricks a day, is reduced by union rules to laying five hundred. There is confusion of standards, again, when we are so impressed by Mr. Henry Ford's abilities as organizer and master mechanic that we listen seriously to his views on money; or when, simply because Mr. Edison has shown inventive genius along certain lines, we receive him as an authority on education . . . .

The problem of standards, though not identical with the problem of democracy, touches it at many points and is not therefore the problem of any one country. Europeans, indeed, like to look upon the crudity and chaotic impressionism of people who are no longer guided by standards as something specifically American. "America," says the *Saturday Review,* "is the country of unbalanced minds, of provincial policies and of hysterical Utopias.". . . If we in America are perhaps preeminent in lack of distinction, it is because of the very completeness of our emancipation from the past . . . . When the element of conversion with reference to a standard is eliminated from life, what remains is the irresponsible quest of thrills. The utilitarian and industrial side of the modern movement comes into play at this point. Commercialism is laying its great greasy paw upon everything (including the irresponsible quest of thrills); so that, whatever democracy may be theoretically, one is sometimes tempted to define it practically as standardized and commercialized melodrama. This definition will be found to fit many aspects of our national life besides the moving-picture industry. The tendency to steep and saturate ourselves in the impression of the moment without reference to any permanent pattern of human experience is even more marked, perhaps, in our newspapers and magazines . . . . It is hard to take a glance at one of our newsstands without reflecting that, though we may not be fools we are reading just the things that fools would read. Our daily press in particular is given over to the most childish sensationalism. "The Americans are an excellent people," Matthew Arnold wrote from Boston in 1883, "but their press seems to me an awful symptom." This symptom was not so awful then as now; for that was before the day of the scarehead and the comic supplement. The American reading his Sunday paper in a state of lazy collapse is perhaps the most perfect symbol of the triumph of quantity over quality that the world has yet seen. Whole forests are being ground into pulp daily to minister to our triviality . . . .

One is inclined, indeed, to ask, in certain moods, whether the net result of the movement that has been sweeping the Occident for several generations may not be a huge mass of standardized mediocrity; and whether in this country in particular we are not in danger of producing in the name of democracy one of the most trifling brands of the human species that the world has yet seen. To be sure, it may be urged that, though we may suffer loss of distinction as a result of the democratic drift, by way of compensation a great many average people will, in the Jeffersonian sense at least, be made "happy." If we are to judge by history, however, what supervenes upon the decline of standards and the disappearance of leaders who embody them is not some equalitarian paradise, but inferior types of leadership. We have already been reminded by certain developments in this country of Byron's definition of democracy as an "aristocracy of blackguards." At the very moment when we were most vociferous about making the world safe for democracy the citizens of New York City refused to reelect an honest man as their mayor and put in his place a tool of Tammany, an action followed in due course by a "crime wave"; whereupon they returned the tool of Tammany by an increased majority. The industrial revolution has tended to produce everywhere great urban masses that seem to be increasingly careless of ethical standards. In the case of our American cities, the problem of securing some degree of moral cohesion is further complicated by the presence of numerous aliens of widely divergent racial stocks and cultural backgrounds. (For example, 4 percent of the residents of New York City are actually foreign-born; if we add those whose father or mother or both were born abroad, the more or less foreign element in its population amounts to 80 percent.) In addition our population is not only about half urban, but we cannot be said, like most other countries, to have any peasantry or yeomanry. Those Americans who actually dwell in the country are more and more urban in their psychology. The whole situation is so unusual as to suggest doubts even from a purely biological point of view. "As I watch the American nation speeding gaily, with invincible optimism down the road to destruction," says Professor William McDougall, an observer of the biological type, "I seem to be contemplating the greatest tragedy in the history of mankind. . . ."

We are assured, indeed, that the highly heterogeneous elements that enter into our population will, like various instruments in an orchestra, merely result in a richer harmony; they will, one may reply, provided that, like an orchestra, they be properly led. Otherwise the outcome may be an unexampled cacophony. This question of leadership is not primarily biological, but moral. Leaders may vary in quality from the man who is so loyal to sound standards that he inspires right conduct in others by the sheer rightness of his example, to the man who stands for nothing higher than the law of cunning and the law of force, and so is, in the sense I have sought to define, imperialistic. If democracy means simply the attempt to eliminate the qualitative and selective principle in favor of some general will, based in turn on a theory of natural rights, it may prove to be only a form of the vertigo of the abyss . . . . One's choice may be, not between a democracy that is properly led and a democracy that hopes to find the equivalent of standards and leadership in the appeal to a numerical majority, that indulges in other words in a sort of quantitative impressionism, but between a democracy that is properly led and a decadent imperialism. One should, therefore, in the interests of democracy itself seek to substitute the doctrine of the right man for the doctrine of the rights of man . . . .

The opposition between traditional standards and an equalitarian democracy based on the supposed rights of man has played an important part in our own political history, and has meant practically the opposition between two types of leadership. The "quality" in the older sense of the word suffered its first decisive defeat in 1829 when Washington was invaded by the hungry hordes of Andrew Jackson. The imperialism latent in this type of democracy appears in the Jacksonian maxim: "To the victors belong the spoils." In his theory of democracy Jackson had, of course, much in common with Thomas Jefferson. If we go back, indeed, to the beginnings of our institutions, we find that America stood from the start for two different views of government that have their origin in different views of liberty and ultimately of human nature. The view that is set forth in the Declaration of Independence assumes that man has certain abstract rights; it has therefore important points of contact with the French revolutionary "idealism." The view that inspired our Constitution, on the other hand, has much in common with that of Burke. If the first of these political philosophies is properly associated with Jefferson, the second has its most distinguished representative in Washington. The Jeffersonian liberal has faith in the goodness of the natural man, and so tends to overlook the need of a veto power either in the individual or in the State. The liberals of whom I have taken Washington to be the type are less expansive in their attitude towards the natural man. Just as man has a higher self that acts restrictively on his ordinary self, so, they hold, the State should have a higher or permanent self, appropriately embodied in institutions, that should set bounds to its ordinary self as expressed by the popular will at any particular moment. The contrast that I am establishing is, of course, that between a constitutional and a direct democracy. There is an opposition of first principles between those who maintain that the popular will should prevail, but only after it has been purified of what is merely impulsive and ephemeral, and those who maintain that this will should prevail immediately and unrestrictedly. The American experiment in democracy has, therefore, from the outset been ambiguous, and will remain so until the irrepressible conflict between a Washingtonian and a Jeffersonian liberty has been fought to a conclusion . . . .

Our present drift away from constitutional freedom can be understood only with reference to the progressive crumbling of traditional standards and the rise of a naturalistic philosophy that, in its treatment of specifically human problems, has been either sentimental or utilitarian. The significant changes in our own national temper in particular are finally due to the fact that Protestant Christianity, especially in the Puritanic form, has been giving way to humanitarianism . . . .

At bottom the point of view of the "uplifter" is so popular because it nourishes spiritual complacency; it enables a man to look on himself as "up" and on someone else as "down.". . . A man needs to look, not down, but up to standards set so much above his ordinary self as to make him feel that he is himself spiritually the underdog. The man who thus looks up is becoming worthy to be looked up to in turn, and, to this extent, qualifying for leadership. Leadership of this type, one may add, may prove to be, in the long run, the only effectual counterpoise to that of the imperialistic superman.

No amount of devotion to society and its supposed interests can take the place of this inner obeisance of the spirit to standards. The humanitarian would seem to be caught here in a vicious circle. If he turns from the inner life to serve his fellow men, he becomes a busy-body. If he sets out again to become exemplary primarily with a view to the benefit of others, he becomes a prig. Nothing will avail short of humility. Humility, as Burke saw, is the ultimate root of the justice that should prevail in the secular order, as well as of the virtues that are specifically religious. The modern problem, I have been insisting, is to secure leaders with an allegiance to standards, now that the traditional order with which Burke associated his standards and leadership has been so seriously shaken. Those who have broken with the traditional beliefs have thus far shown themselves singularly ineffective in dealing with this problem of leadership, even when they have admitted the need of leaders at all. The persons who have piqued themselves especially on being positive have looked for leadership to the exponents of physical science. Auguste Comte, for example, not only regarded men of science as the true modern priesthood, but actually disparaged moral effort on the part of the individual . . . . The net result of a merely scientific "progress" is to produce efficient megalomaniacs. Physical science, excellent in its proper place, is, when exalted out of this place, the ugliest and most maleficent idol before which man has as yet consented to prostrate himself . . . .

If one discovers frequently a pseudo-mystical element in the claims to leadership of the aesthetes, the supermen and the scientific intellectuals, this element is even more visible in those who would, in the name of democracy, dispense with leadership altogether. Thus Walt Whitman, as we have seen, would put no check on his "spontaneous me"; he would have every one else indulge his "idiocrasy" to the same degree, be a "genius," in short, in the full romantic sense of the term. A liberty thus anarchical is to lead to equality and fraternity. If one tells the democrat of this type that his programme is contrary to common sense and the facts of experience, he is wont to take refuge in mystical "vision." One needs in effect to be very mystical to suppose that men can come together by flying off each on his temperamental tangent. Whitman does not admit the need of the leader who looks up humbly to some standard and so becomes worthy to be looked up to in turn. The only leadership he contemplates apparently is that of the ideal democratic bard who flatters the people's pride and chants the divine average. He represents in an extreme form the substitution for vital control of expansive emotion under the name of love. Pride and self-assertion, when tempered by love, will not, he holds, endanger the principle of union. The Union, though "always swarming with blatherers, is yet," he says, "always sure and impregnable." The records of the past are not reassuring as to the maintenance of ethical union in a community that is swarming with "blatherers." At all events, the offset to the blatherers will be found, not in any divine average, but in the true leader—the "still strong man in a blatant land." We come here to another opposition that is one of first principles and is not therefore subject to mediation or compromise—the opposition, namely, between the doctrine of the saving remnant and that of the divine average. If one deals with human nature realistically one may find here and there a person who is worthy of respect and occasionally one who is worthy of reverence. Any one, on the other hand, who puts his faith in the divinity of the average is destined, if we are to trust the records of history, to pass through disillusion to a final despair. We are reaching the stage of disillusion in this country at the present moment. According to the author of *Main Street,* the average is not divine but trivial; according to the author of the *Spoon River Anthology,* it is positively hideous. It can scarcely be gainsaid that contemporary America offers an opening for satire. A great many people are gradually drifting into materialism and often cherishing the conceit at the same time that they are radiant idealists. But satire, to be worthwhile, must be constructive. The opposite of the trivial is the distinguished; and one can determine what is distinguished only with reference to standards. To see Main Street on a background of standards would be decidedly helpful; but standards are precisely what our so-called realists lack. They are themselves a part of the disease that they are attempting to define.

The democratic idealist is prone to make light of the whole question of standards and leadership because of his unbounded faith in the plain people. How far is this appeal to the plain people justified and how far is it merely demagogic? There is undoubted truth in the saying that there is somebody who knows more than anybody, and that is everybody. Only one must allow everybody sufficient time to sift the evidence and add that, even so, everybody does not know very much . . . . Even in this triumph of the sober judgment of the people over its passing impression, the role of the true leader should not be underestimated. Thus in the year 1795 the plain people of America were eager to give the fraternal accolade to the French Jacobins. The great and wise Washington opposed an alliance that would almost certainly have been disastrous, and as a result he had heaped upon him by journals like the *Aurora,* the forerunner of our modern "journals of opinion," epithets that, as he himself complained, would not have been deserved by a common pickpocket. In a comparatively short time Washington and his group were seen to be right, and those who seemed to be the spokesmen of the plain people were seen to be wrong. It is not clear that one can have much faith even in the sober second thought of a community that has no enlightened minority . . . . The democratic idealist does not, however, mean as a rule by an appeal to the plain people an appeal to its sober second thought. He means rather the immediate putting into effect of the will of a numerical majority . . . . Our American drift for a number of years has unquestionably been towards a democracy of this radical type, as is evident from the increasing vogue of the initiative, referendum, and recall (whether of judges or judicial decisions) as well as from popular primaries and the direct election of Senators. The feeling that the people should act directly on all measures has led to the appearance in certain States of ballots thirty feet long! Yet the notion that wisdom resides in a popular majority at any particular moment should be the most completely exploded of all fallacies . . . . But the plain people, it will be replied, has been educated and enlightened. The intelligence tests applied in connection with the selective draft indicate that the average mental age of our male voters is about fourteen. The intelligence testers are, to be sure, under some suspicion as to the quality of their own intelligence. A more convincing proof of the low mentality of our population is found, perhaps, in the fact that the Hearst publications have twenty-five million readers . . . .

"There is nothing," says Goethe, "more odious than the majority; for it consists of a few powerful leaders, a certain number of accommodating scoundrels and subservient weaklings, and a mass of men who trudge after them without in the least knowing their own minds." If there is any truth in this analysis the majority in a radical democracy often rules only in name. No movement, indeed, illustrates more clearly than the supposedly democratic movement the way in which the will of highly organized and resolute minorities may prevail over the will of the inert and unorganized mass. Even though the mass does not consent to "trudge" after the minority, it is at an increasing disadvantage in its attempts to resist it . . . .

It does not follow that the ethical State is impossible. Human nature, and this is its most encouraging trait, is sensitive to a right example. It is hard, indeed, to set bounds to the persuasiveness of a right example, provided only it be right enough. The ethical State is possible in which an important minority is ethically energetic and is thus becoming at once just and exemplary. Such a minority will also tend to solve the problem of union. A State that is controlled by men who have become just as the result of minding their own business in the Platonic sense will be a just State that will also mind its own business; it will be of service to other States, not by meddling in their affairs on either commercial or "idealistic" grounds, but by setting them a good example. A State of this kind may hope to find a basis of understanding with any other State that is also ethically controlled. The hope of cooperation with a State that has an unethical leadership is chimerical. The value of political thinking is therefore in direct ratio to its adequacy in dealing with the problem of leadership. The unit to which all things must finally be referred is not the State or humanity or any other abstraction, but the man of character.

2

The End of Democracy
RALPH A. CRAM

The title of this essay leaves something to be desired. The end of *a* democracy is certainly now in process of accomplishment, and so far as this particular democracy is concerned, as it has come to be today, both in

From *American Mercury*, 39 (September, 1936), pp. 23-31.

politics and in society, the words do well enough. Of this phenomenon it is true to say that it is at an end, at least so far as its energizing force is concerned. In a few countries its forms remain, voided of the original dynamic content, and these desiccations, mere shells or simulacra, give the illusion of reality and continuity.

Now the thesis I am prepared to defend is that there was once a High Democracy, not only in theory but in practice, and that this has now given place to a Low Democracy which is its antithesis. High Democracy was actually realized for a few centuries during the Middle Ages. It is known in contemporary histories as Monarchical Feudalism. In theory it was held by the Framers of the Constitution of the United States, though they thought of it as an Aristocratic Republic. After such fashion do what Jeremy Bentham called "impostor terms" and Roosevelt the First denominated "weasel words" seduce the fluid mind of a receptive public into grave error.

I apologize to the revered memory of Washington, Adams, Madison, Gerry, and all their fellows for attributing to them any intellectual commerce with democracy, for if they feared anything it was precisely this, whereby their prevision was highly justified. As Mr. Albert Jay Nock says: "One sometimes wonders how our Revolutionary forefathers would take it if they could hear some flatulent political thimble-rigger charge them with having founded 'the great and glorious democracy of the West'." Of course, as we know now, they never intended to do anything of the sort, but in spite of their elaborate precautions against the possibility of such a thing coming to pass through the malice of time and the propensity to evil of a reprobate human nature, their hopes were vain. Within a generation, decomposition of the body of their wisdom set in, to continue by process of mathematical progression until life had departed and a new and, so to speak, fungoid growth had insensibly taken its place.

This, the current type of democracy, founded on certain recently promulgated dogmas, none of them much more than a century and a half old, has little, if any, relationship to that ideal estate which in the past served as inspiration to the protagonists of the democracy of realization. It was based on a variety of doctrines that cannot be authenticated biologically, historically, or philosophically. Amongst these was that particularly disastrous dogma of "progressive" evolution whereby man was assumed to be engaged in an automatic and irresistible advance towards some "far-off, divine event," based on inherent perfectibility, with free, secular, universal, and compulsory education as the assured guaranty of this desirable result, and as its effective power. Bracketed with this was the amiable and humanitarian theory that all men are created free and equal.

Deriving from these pious aspirations, as of necessity, came the plausible scheme of representative, parliamentary government, founded on universal suffrage, with, as its own original contribution and essential quality, the Reconstruction Era principle that the electoral franchise is not a privilege (as it was prior to that Witches' Sabbath of corruption, infamy, and disgrace) but an inalienable right, inherent in man as man, and of equal validity with the incontestable right to life, liberty, and the pursuit of happiness. Finally, and in a way, the most curious (but imperative) of all, the dogma that the majority was practically sure to be more nearly right on all possible subjects than any minority, and that, anyway, the decision of the majority, right or wrong, wise or otherwise, must implicitly be accepted and obeyed.

This is the bastard form of an originally sane and fine idea. It has had to be abolished as a public nuisance in most of the countries of Europe.... Here in the United States we had, to start with, a great and preservative Fundamental Law that worked well until it became progressively vitiated by ill-considered Amendments, while some of the silliest features of the later parliamentary systems of the Continent were never taken over, though the suggestion has been made from time to time that we might well indulge in this wild adventure. It is true we have troubles enough of our own, but what remains intact, of the Constitution of 1787 has saved us thus far from the particular disasters that have brought the European democratic-parliamentary house of cards to destruction and established in its place communistic, military, or political dictatorships.

There are none too many citizens of these despotisms who would have the old system back. Whether they like the new autocracies or not, and probably the majority are not any too well pleased with what they have, they have had enough of parliamentary democracy and are vociferous in their denunciation of this, which has now become a sort of second and equally distasteful *Ancien Regime* .... In the greater part of Europe the daubed, disguised, defaced thing has already been thrown away. The same may happen here unless alteration is put in process. The wisdom of this course leaps to the mind.

The really vital and insistent question today is just such drastic alteration, in what it is to consist, and how it is to be accomplished. If we are to avoid that vain repetition of history which has been the way of the world since time out of mind (there are, admittedly, few historical precedents that would indicate such a possibility) and escape the Nemesis of their foolish ways that has at last caught up with the several states of Europe (not to mention the *ersatz* republics of South and Central America and China), these questions will have to be solved in short order. These are the vanishing volumes of the Sibylline Books. Only three are left, those earmarked for England, France, and America, and the price is steadily rising.

We have had no lack of warning during the last ten years. Indeed it is astonishing how many and how significant are the books that recently have appeared, all showing in varying words and from different points of view just where we are and how we got there. A century ago William Cobbett warned of what would happen if society kept on the way it had begun, and he did not nor could not have known the half of it; or the tenth. Others followed after him down to the time of Carlyle, Ruskin, and Morris, but the ethos of the nineteenth century was in full control, and no one for a moment believed a word of these discredited Cassandras. Now that all has happened that they predicted—and more—diagnosis has taken the place of prognosis. Spengler began it, I suppose, and following him have come Hilaire Belloc, G. K. Chesterton, R. H. Tawney, Ortega y Gasset, Nikolai Berdyaev, William Aylott Orton, W. G. Peck, Herbert Agar, Albert Jay Nock, Alexis Carrel, Christopher Dawson, and a score of others all following along the same line. And the two great Papal Encyclicals, *Rerum Novarum* and *Quadragesima Anno,* have their part here as well.

So far as the diagnostical works are concerned, most of them might not unjustly be called defeatist. For them . . . there seem but two alternatives, communism or dictatorship, once contemporary democracy is liquidated; a consummation they confidently and unanimously look on both as devoutly to be wished and as inescapable. For their convictions there is, it must be admitted, ample justification in conditions as they are and as they hurriedly progress, but to accept such disaster without at least a struggle, is, as I say, a defeatism that borders on Moslem fatalism. As Ortega y Gasset says, "A hurricane of farcicality, everywhere and in every form, is at present ranging over the lands of Europe," and it may be the nations that have not as yet had to make the terrible choice, may ultimately join the general debacle, with the second Dark Ages that the great Spanish philosopher envisages following after. It is neither easy nor pleasant to anticipate the same fate for the United States. With the great model of our original Constitution before us, and with the mental ingenuity of our inventors and discoverers turned to more really creative concerns than have been their prepossession during the past fifty years, we surely ought, by taking thought, to find a third alternative to communism and dictatorship.

II

The Great War was fought, we were told, to make the world safe for democracy, but we are beginning now to realize that it was the wrong sort of democracy. It was a thing not worth the saving. It was only a hundred years old anyway, but it had lived long enough to reveal its fallaciousness. Behind it stood another democracy of very different temper and it would seem to be the part of wisdom, first of all to go back to that and see if it might not serve as a basis to build upon.

The use of the word *democracy* is a little ambiguous. If what we have is that, then what we had before was not. A dictionary definition means nothing. The People never have governed and by their nature they never will. From town meeting to Congress, government—legislative, executive, and judicial—is determined, directed, and administered by small oligarchies of statesmen, professional politicians, money barons, industrialists, spell-binders, shysters, and gangsters—to cover the field from one end to the other—and its quality depends on the combination of these varied elements and the preponderance of one or the other. The people have very little to do with it, especially along constructive lines. They do not vote *for* a policy or candidate but *against* a candidate or policy. When mob psychology is aroused, they have a certain veto power that is effective through its very mass, and this, like all veto power, whether of a chief executive or a court, is as often used unwisely as wisely.

This is very far from being democracy, either in theory or practice, and if there were nothing more to it than the right to vote, representative, parliamentary government, rotation in office, free, secular, public education and social egalitarianism, and no standards of value, culture, or conduct determined and imposed from superior sources either human or divine, then the word could not be used in the sense in which I propose to use it. As a matter of fact, this is all no more than a pseudo-democracy, a sort of changeling foisted on a naive and unsuspecting public. Rightly it has no claim to the title. Is there, then, or has there been, a true democracy? If so, what are its distinguishing marks?

In the first place there are certain things true democracy definitely is not. It is not universal suffrage, the parliamentary system of government, direct legislation or those pet panaceas of democratic corruption and in-efficiency recommended to a very sick body politic in the time of Roosevelt the First, the initiative and referendum. The *forms* of the governmental machines are not implied by democratic ideology nor are they determined by its principles. There have been and are "democracies" that are tyrannical, oppressive, and destructive of legitimate human liberty; there have been and are "monarchies" that stand for and enforce the basic principles of the higher democracy.

Democracy is not the abolition of status, the elimination of grades or rank in the social organism, the establishing of one dead level of uniformity by pulling down from above and pushing up from below. Aristocracy and monarchy are not inconsistent with its ethos—but they must be of the right type. The contemporary aristocracy of wealth and the monarchies that followed the end of the Middle Ages and held pretty well down to the time of the Great War, are inconsistent with high democratic principle.

What is this "Higher Democracy" of which the current and dissolving type is little more than a caricature? As there has never been any authoritative and dogmatic revelation on this point, each individual must, I suppose, construct his own definition. What follows can only be the statement of a personal conviction, but I think it has some justification in history and in philosophy.

Democracy is that form of social organization which endeavors to assure to mankind Life, Liberty, and the Pursuit of Happiness.

This sounds axiomatic, indeed platitudinous, but it is worth repeating here simply because it has so completely been forgotten, that all democratic or pseudodemocratic communities have either completely lost, or are by way of losing, power on the part of the individual so to live his life as to make possible the achievement of these ends. In this respect the United States stands on a level with Italy, Germany, Mexico, and the U.S.S.R. As a matter of fact, our social, economic, and political estate is now, and has been for seventy years, the antithesis of a true democratic polity and state. Not only does it negate all the principles of the Higher Democracy, it has lost even the reality of its modern degenerate form. Let us see wherein some of these antitheses exist.

In a very suggestive book called *The Crisis of the Middle Classes,* Mr. Lewis Corey says, in estimating democracy, that "its form of expression and substantial reality was the liberty and equality of men owning their independent means of livelihood." This is pretty fundamental. What price money—capitalism, big business, mass production, and trustification? The anonymous author of *Our Lords and Masters* has put into very concise form what we already subconsciously knew but were laggard to realize—the actual nature, the cosmic sweep, the inclusive and dominating power of the controlling factors in current society. Exercising, as they do now, complete control of the life of the civilized portions of the planet, they made this first qualification of democracy impracticable. A century ago seventy percent of the American people lived in accordance with this first principle; they were free, independent, self-supporting, self-respecting citizens, owning their own land, practicing their own craft or trade; in a word, freemen. Today seventy percent of the populace are proletarians, whether they wear white collars or blue overalls. They have no means of support except the sale of their mental and manual services in a market daily becoming more and more congested and now close to the saturation point. They are unfree men. This is not democracy of any sort.

A stable democratic society must be based upon a populace, sixty percent of whom live on land which they own, or make their livelihoods from subsidiary craft and shop work, also individually or communally owned. Incidentally, such a social order offers the only visible cure for current unemployment. As William Green of the American Federation of Labor says, "While technological improvements in industry are steadily reducing the number of workers necessary to provide all the goods and services industry can market, the number of men and women who want work is steadily increasing." At one time it looked as though this very obvious solution of a critical social problem had suggested itself in Washington, but as soon as subsistence homesteads were tentatively put in process, the vested interests that so largely energize judicial opinion took alarm, and the Comptroller General found the scheme as unconstitutional as the Blue Eagle.

Very soon it will be necessary to decide whether we shall restore a truly democratic state of the original sort, or go on (there is no other alternative) to the corporative, totalitarian state or to that state socialism which is the negation of all democracy, whether original or derivative.

III

The original democratic idea has been transformed, distorted, and finally negatived by the measures adopted to implement it. The process was dual and reciprocal. The *zeitgeist* has for a century or more been busily at work inculcating what is known (and widely observed) as "democratic doctrine." This had a determining influence on the progressive changes necessarily taking place in the fundamental law and in the instruments and mechanism of the governmental organization, while each new modification of technical and operative methods intensified and exaggerated the "spirit of the age," whose workings were mysterious but actual and possibly irresistible. An example of this is the progressive amendment of the American Constitution where every change made since the promulgation of the Bill of Rights has been in answer to this—again so-called—democratic impulse. The original Constitution was conservative, constructive, anti-revolutionary, and anti-democratic, in the sense later manifested in the French Revolution. Once this epic event had occurred, the repercussions were universally widespread, and almost unconsciously it affected the whole course of later political development.

In the beginning, i.e., 1787, there was no clear conception of, or provision for, party government, partly because at that time political parties did not properly exist. Shortly thereafter they were in full swing, dividing the electorate on what became the standard bi-partisan, Conservative-Liberal lines. It was a foolish system, since it resulted in permanent warfare for office between the factions, a generally regular oscillation between two powers (except when war and the suppression of a conquered people and the party of their allegiance left the other party in power for a long period, incidentally with worse results than had followed the older system of rotation) which meant a complete lack of continuity in policy, domestic and foreign, and an unwholesome state of feverishness and uncertainty in society. The *reductio ad absurdum* of this plan, which finds its parallel only in *Alice in Wonderland,* is the parliamentary system of the Continent, where there were no plausible political parties, not even of the ins and outs, as in recent years in America, but anywhere from six to twelve personal and feudal followings. The result in point of conspiracy, corruption, and impotence through the shuffling of blocs in order that a government might achieve a brief lease of life, was on a par with *Of Thee I Sing* and would have been equally farcical and amusing if it had not had such tragic consequences . . . . This three-ringed circus of Continental parliamentary government was in itself enough to explain, if not to justify, the advent of Mussolini, Hitler, Pilsudski, and the daily dozen of other dictators from King Zog to Mustapha Kemal.

Now the parliamentary system based on political, partisan divisions is no essential part of sound democratic doctrine. It was a plausible device to implement a democratic doctrine that was rotting as it ripened. And it was a bad one . . . .

Social equality, i.e., a leveling of all human life and its component parts to the basic grade of those that are least distinguished in point of intelligence, character, and capacity for creative work, together with a similar leveling off of standards of value, is equally no part of sound democratic doctrine. Three things are essential: abolition of privilege; equality of opportunity; utilization of ability. What is the application of these principles to the Modern Age? . . .

. . . The first law in the Book of Man is inequality. Individuals vary in intelligence, character, capacity for doing one thing or another, and well or ill, far more than they do in their physical characteristics. From the Australian blackfellow, the writer of popular songs, or the publisher of a tabloid newspaper, to Akhnaton, Leonardo da Vinci, or Pope Leo XIII is a space that almost needs to be measured in astronomical terms. Any society that does not recognize this and attempts to liquidate this disparity can last but a short time and is doomed to quick dissolution after a sad and unsavory record. As a matter of fact, none has seriously made the attempt. The destruction of an aristocracy of Praetorian Guards of blood and breeding, of knighthood nobility, of great land-holders, of scholars and artists and poets, simply means that its place is immediately taken by something worse: party politicians and their subsidizers, multimillionaires, great industrialists, or the manipulators of securities on the stock exchange, and international money lenders. Where status is eliminated, caste takes its place and democracy is no longer attainable. There is only one equality that democracy demands, and that is equality before the courts of law.

Abolition of privilege, equality of opportunity, utilization of ability, are thus the three foundations of the democratic state. "Privilege" in this sense means power bought by money, control of natural resources or the means of production, or any other monopoly that is gained by force of any kind, not by merit of any kind. The present degenerate democratic society is shot through and through with this sort of privilege, just as the social system is dominated by an aristocracy of money lenders, tycoons of big business, cinema stars, and the publishers of amoral (and immoral) newspapers.

Democracy demands equality of opportunity. This means that the definite (but limited) potential inherent in every man must be given opportunity to develop to the full. Here is where the fact of fundamental human inequality comes into play. Free, secular, compulsory public school education may be the best way to ascertain just what this potential may be, as between one and another (the point is debatable), but beyond the beginnings it is worse than useless.

From one-half to two-thirds of the students now pushed through high schools, preparatory schools, technical schools, and colleges are not gifted with a potential that can be developed beyond a certain fairly low point, say that of the junior high school. Tempting them further is unfair, even cruel, to them and to those who can do better. The schools today are yearly turning out thousands of graduates who have been spoiled for doing the sort of thing they were by nature fitted to do. Either they crowd out those of real ability, working for lower pay and doing their job indifferently well, or else they join the cohorts of the white-collar unemployed. This is the bankruptcy of the idea of equality of opportunity.

Utilization of ability is closely tied up with this. Democracy should mean that every man would find and hold that place where his inherent and developed capacity can find its clearest field and where all that he is can best be used for the good of society, the community, and the larger synthesis of the race itself; incidentally, that he may participate, through self-expression and self-fulfillment, in that pursuit of happiness avowed by the Declaration of Independence as one of the rights of man. Under deformed and vitiated democracy, this desideratum becomes increasingly unattainable. The transvaluation of values and the progressive lowering of standards of value (not to say those of right and wrong) minimize these opportunities because the people (or those who control opportunity) are not interested.

Under our contemporary democratic government, employment, like kissing goes by favor. The doctrine that to the victors belong the spoils, initiated by General Jackson, that veritable Nemesis of true democracy, still obtains in full force, in fact if not by avowal, and in spite of civil service reform and similar well-meant but ineffectual panaceas. Today professors and teachers fight for their scholastic lives against bigotry and political tyranny in high places; potential statesmen must become party politicians or must hire themselves out to money to get a hearing; Hollywood seduces the actor, the writer, the artist into selling his soul if he would gain recognition, fame, and a competence; the Hearstified press reduces to the lower depths the literary and moral standards of men who would follow the high profession of letters; the radio and broadcasting lay their heavy, deleterious hand on all forms of the creative instinct. Religion is becoming ballyhoo, and philosophy the pragmatic doctrine of whatever will work and whatever the People are willing to take. This is not democracy in any rational sense.

IV

The new democracy is cancelling the freedom that was to have been guaranteed us by the old. We may perhaps be able to recover some of this through the material means of new laws, revision of the implements of government, or other technical action. Whatever we might accomplish would in the end prove both hollow and ephemeral, unless it were energized by a corresponding reorientation of the individual parts of the community . . . .

As a result of the rushing and cumulative events that have driven him onward for the last three hundred years, man, searching avidly for freedom both of body and spirit, has lost the reality of both. Losing this he has paid too high a price for bodily comfort, money values, and technological triumphs. Without spiritual liberty he becomes enslaved to the plausible subterfuges of the low, but materially successful, grades of the mass-man, accepting his reversed standards of value and so in time becoming not only a participant in his degenerative actions, but unconscious even of his own enslavement.

My memory goes clearly back to that Presidential campaign when Tilden, the Democratic candidate, was counted out, and Hayes, who had lost the election, was made President by the Republican cabal. I think it safe to say that since that time public opinion, standards of value, and overt activities have scarcely ever reached a lower level than now. I offer as substantial evidence three of the many recent examples that force themselves on our attention. The Hauptmann case, Huey Long's Louisiana, and the Veterans' Bonus.

If these instances of public intelligence, mob-psychology, and mass action, with their other unnumbered panaceas, are indeed indicative, as they appear to be, of the downfall of the American Idea as this was envisaged by the Founders of the Republic, then are we justified in expecting any wide support for material changes in the social framework or that of the political organism? I answer yes, but only if our people can regain their spiritual liberty. If this is accomplished, anything is possible; if we fail of this, then we must take our place with the disintegrating states of Europe.

Part Two

Scientism and Human Management

Part Two

Scientism and Human Management

A. Eugenics

One outgrowth of the popularization of Charles Darwin's theory of evolution was an enthusiastic dedication to a scientific reordering of genetic structure. Its most positive contributions were advances in improved plant and animal varieties, the systematic breeding practices which boosted American agricultural productivity at the beginning of the twentieth century. Inevitably, however, a sizable group of laymen and a few overzealous scientists banded together to urge the "purification" of human stock through selective breeding methods similar to those which appeared so effective in the livestock industry and horticulture.[1] Eugenics, as this pseudo-scientific movement was called, claimed to seek the perfection of the species by the manipulation of man's elemental instincts.[2]

This cult appealed not only to men for whom science supplanted religion, but it also had a magnetic attraction for Americans seeking some single principle that would explain the rapid, confusing, often demoralizing changes of their world. Eugenics offered an all-encompassing set of social solutions to those already confirmed in nativist bigotry; those who were fearful about modern socio-economic complexities; those convinced that the political corruption they witnessed on every hand was directly traceable to the millions of Southern and Eastern European aliens who swarmed into urban America after 1870; and those enamored of the myth of Anglo-Saxon superiority and afraid for the future of that "race."[3] Eugenists viewed all the aspects of an open, pluralistic society with chagrin. Unregulated immigration, free choice in mating, democracy, and universal suffrage were to be opposed adamantly. The raising up of a "great strain" in American society which could be depended on for "original enterprise and moral worth" would require tight federal restrictions of immigration, education of the public to scientific mating, government control of courtship and marriage, and the segregation and sterilization of "defective strains."[4] The nature of such proposals and their source in an assumed standard of biological or racial superiority represented a political dogma which was elitist and authoritarian.[5] As one eugenics spokesman noted, believers in the scientific breeding of human beings inevitably were believers in aristocracy: "they are forced by their studies to recognize that men are not equal, are not even born equal."[6] Their fondest hope was "that for the good of the race the best shall prevail, that we shall be led and governed by them."[7] The American insistence on indiscriminate ethnic mixture and democracy was an invitation to instability and national suicide; dimly perceiving their own inferiority, the masses would use popular government to eradicate the racial elite.[8]

The shrill message of Madison Grant (1865-1937) in *The Passing of the Great Race* was a final call to a waning aristocracy to reassert its natural superiority by checking the flow of aliens into the United States, self-consciously increasing the birth rate of the Nordic strain (a proposal earnestly recommended by Theodore Roosevelt in his work, *Race Suicide*), and remolding the institutional structure so as to end mass participation in government. Grant was an almost archetypal eugenist: a dilettante lawyer and conservative Manhattan socialite whose reputation as gentleman-sportsman led him to assume the chairmanship of New York's Zoological Society, and whose acquaintance with men of science encouraged him to clothe his biases in pretentious scientific language.[9] Grant's book found considerable public favor. Although it was the work of a "Park Avenue naturalist," and packed with contradictions and absurdities, *The Passing of the Great Race* went through three editions, sold more than 15,000 copies in the United States, was translated into three foreign languages, and proved of much use to nativist congressmen who relied on it as source material during debates on immigration restriction in the early 1920's.[10]

A sprinkling of politicians and other public figures, and writers in popular magazines like Alleyne Ireland, allowed the alleged facts produced by the eugenists to frighten them into advocacy of immigration quota legislation and measures at the state level for the sterilization of persons deemed unfit. A few went so far as to question the durability of American democracy. Charles Davenport, an academician fanatically dedicated to the eugenics cause and sincerely convinced that only a hurried breeding of an elite could save America, would "lift his eyes reverently and, with his hands upraised as though in supplication, quiver emotionally as he breathed, 'Protoplasm. We want more protoplasm.' "[11] Such rash demands and hysterical claims were symptomatic of the true nature of the movement. As the Nazis were to prove so terribly, the crusade for selective human breeding was rooted in a diseased viewpoint, a composite of prejudice and resentments, not in scientific proof.[12] And the uniformity eugenists sought was not only scientifically undesirable, but fundamentally and dangerously antidemocratic.[13]

NOTES

1. Mark H. Haller, *Eugenics: Hereditarian Attitudes in American Thought* (New Brunswick: Rutgers University Press, 1963), p. 20.

2. Donald K. Pickens, "American Eugenists: Conservative Naturalists as Progressives" (unpublished Ph.D. dissertation, University of Texas, 1964), *passim.*

3. Haller, *Eugenics,* pp. 54, 57.

4. Wilhelmine E. Key, *Heredity and Social Fitness: A Study of Differential Mating in a Pennsylvania Family* (Washington, D. C.: Carnegie Institution, 1920), pp. 100-102.

5. Haller, *Eugenics,* p. 93.

6. George Adami, "The True Aristocracy," *Eugenics Review,* 14 (1922), p. 174.

7. *Ibid.;* also, Haller, *Eugenics,* p. 94.

8. Albert E. Wiggam, *The New Decalogue of Science* (Indianapolis: Bobbs-Merrill Company, Inc., 1923), p. 187; Lothrop Stoddard, *The Revolt Against Civilization: The Menace of the Under Man* (New York: Charles Scribner's Sons, 1922), *passim;* William McDougall, *Is America Safe for Democracy?* (New York: Charles Scribner's Sons, 1921), *passim;* Charles C. Alexander, "Prophet of American Racism: Madison Grant and the Nordic Myth," *Phylon,* XXIII (Spring, 1962), p. 79.

9. Haller, *Eugenics,* pp. 149-150; Alexander, "Prophet of American Racism," p. 73.

10. Alexander, "Prophet of American Racism," pp. 73, 77-78; Haller, *Eugenics,* p. 151.

11. Quoted in Margaret Sanger, *Margaret Sanger, An Autobiography* (New York: W. W. Norton & Company, 1938), p. 374.

12. Edward Shils, "Daydreams and Nightmares: Reflections on the Criticism of Mass Culture," *Sewanee Review,* LXV (October-December, 1957), p. 596.

13. Peter B. Medawar, "Science and the Sanctity of Life," *Encounter,* 27 (December, 1966), pp. 101, 103.

3

The Passing of the Great Race
MADISON GRANT

In the democratic forms of government the operation of universal suffrage tends toward the selection of the average man for public office rather than the man qualified by birth, education and integrity. How this scheme of administration will ultimately work out remains to be seen but from a radical point of view it will inevitably increase the preponderance of the lower types and cause a corresponding loss of efficiency in the community as a whole.

The tendency in a democracy is toward a standardization of type and a diminution of the influence of genius. A majority must of necessity be inferior to a picked minority and it always resents specializations in which it cannot share. In the French Revolution the majority, calling itself "the people," deliberately endeavored to destroy the higher type and something of the same sort was in a measure done after the American Revolution by the expulsion of the Loyalists and the confiscation of their lands, with a resultant loss to the growing nation of good race strains, which were in the next century replaced by immigrants of far lower type.

In America we have nearly succeeded in destroying the privilege of birth; that is, the intellectual and moral advantage a man of good stock brings into the world with him. We are now engaged in destroying the privilege of wealth; that is, the reward of successful intelligence and industry and in some quarters there is developing a tendency to attack the privilege of intellect and to deprive a man of the advantage gained from an early and thorough classical education. Simplified spelling is a step in this direction. Ignorance of English grammar or classic learning must not, forsooth, be held up as a reproach to the political or social aspirant.

Mankind emerged from savagery and barbarism under the leadership of selected individuals whose personal prowess, capacity or wisdom gave them the right to lead and the power to compel obedience. Such leaders have always been a minute fraction of the whole, but as long as the tradition of their predominance persisted they were able to use the brute strength of the unthinking herd as part of their own force and were able to direct at will the

From Madison Grant, *The Passing of the Great Race,* Charles Scribner's Sons, New York, 1921. Reprinted by permission of D. G. Brinton Thompson.

blind dynamic impulse of the slaves, peasants or lower classes. Such a despot had an enormous power at his disposal which, if he were benevolent or even intelligent, could be used and most frequently was used for the general uplift of the race. Even those rulers who must abused this power put down with merciless rigor the antisocial elements, such as pirates, brigands or anarchists, which impair the progress of a community, as disease or wounds cripple an individual.

True aristocracy or a true republic is government by the wisest and best, always a small minority in any population. Human society is like a serpent dragging its long body on the ground, but with the head always thrust a little in advance and a little elevated above the earth. The serpent's tail, in human society represented by the antisocial forces, was in the past dragged by sheer strengh along the path of progress. Such has been the organization of mankind from the beginning, and such it still is in older communities than ours. What progress humanity can make under the control of universal suffrage, or the rule of the average, may find a further analogy in the habits of certain snakes which wiggle sideways and disregard the head with its brains and eyes. Such serpents, however, are not noted for their ability to make rapid progress.

A true republic, the function of which is administration in the interests of the whole community—in contrast to a pure democracy, which in last analysis is the rule of the demos or a majority in its own interests—should be, and often is, the medium of selection for the technical task of government of those best qualified by antecedents, character and education, in short, of experts.

To use another simile, in an aristocratic as distinguished from a plutocratic or democratic organization the intellectual and talented classes form the point of the lance while the massive shaft represents the body of the population and adds by its bulk and weight to the penetrative impact of the tip. In a democratic system this concentrated force is dispersed throughout the mass. It supplies, to be sure, a certain amount of leaven but in the long run the force and genius of the small minority is dissipated, and its efficiency lost. *Vox populi,* so far from being *Vox Dei,* thus becomes an unending wail for rights and never a chant of duty.

Where a conquering race is imposed on another race the institution of slavery often arises to compel the servient race to work and to introduce it forcibly to a higher form of civilization. As soon as men can be induced to labor to supply their own needs slavery becomes wasteful and tends to vanish. From a material point of view slaves are often more fortunate than freemen when treated with reasonable humanity and when their elemental wants of food, clothing and shelter are supplied.

The Indians around the fur posts in northern Canada were formerly the virtual bond slaves of the Hudson Bay Company, each Indian and his squaw and papoose being adequately supplied with simple food and equipment. He was protected as well against the white man's rum as the red man's scalping parties and in return gave the Company all his peltries—the whole product of his year's work. From an Indian's point of view this was nearly an ideal condition but was to all intents serfdom or slavery. When through the opening up of the country the continuance of such an archaic system became an impossibility, the Indian sold his furs to the highest bidder, received a large price in cash and then wasted the proceeds in trinkets instead of blankets and in rum instead of flour, with the result that he is now gloriously free but is on the highroad to becoming a diseased outcast. In this case of the Hudson Bay Indian the advantages of the upward step from serfdom to freedom are not altogether clear. A very similar condition of vassalage existed until recently among the peons of Mexico, but without the compensation of the control of an intelligent and provident ruling class.

In the same way serfdom in mediaeval Europe apparently was a device through which the landowners repressed the nomadic instinct in their tenantry which became marked when the fertility of the land declined after the dissolution of the Roman Empire. Years are required to bring land to its highest productivity and agriculture cannot be successfully practised even in well-watered and fertile districts by farmers who continually drift from one locality to another. The serf or villein was, therefore, tied by law to the land and could not leave except with his master's consent. As soon as the nomadic instinct was eliminated serfdom vanished. One has but to read the severe laws against vagrancy in England just before the Reformation to realize how widespread and serious was this nomadic instinct. Here in America we have not yet forgotten the wandering instincts of our Western pioneers, which in that case proved beneficial to every one except the migrants.

While democracy is fatal to progress when two races of unequal value live side by side, an aristocracy may be equally injurious whenever, in order to purchase a few generations of ease and luxury, slaves or immigrants are imported to do the heavy work. It was a form of aristocracy that brought slaves to the American colonies and the West Indies and if there had been an aristocratic form of governmental control in California, Chinese coolies and Japanese laborers would now form the controlling element, so far as numbers are concerned, on the Pacific coast.

It was the upper classes who encouraged the introduction of immigrant labor to work American factories and mines and it is the native American gentleman who builds a palace on the country side and who introduces as servants all manner of foreigners into purely American districts. The farming and artisan classes of America did not take alarm until it was too late and they are now seriously threatened with extermination in many parts of the country. In Rome, also, it was the plebeian who first went under in the competition with slaves but the patrician followed in his turn a few generations later.

The West Indian sugar planters flourished in the eighteenth century and produced some strong men; to-day from the same causes they have vanished from the scene.

During the last century the New England manufacturer imported the Irish and French Canadians and the resultant fall in the New England birthrate at once became ominous. The refusal of the native American to work with his hands when he can hire or import serfs to do manual labor for him is the prelude to his extinction and the immigrant laborers are now breeding out their masters and killing by filth and by crowding as effectively as by the sword.

Thus the American sold his birthright in a continent to solve a labor problem. Instead of retaining political control and making citizenship an honorable and valued privilege, he intrusted the government of his country and the maintenance of his ideals to races who have never yet succeeded in governing themselves, much less any one else.

Associated with this advance of democracy and the transfer of power from the higher to the lower races, from the intellectual to the plebeian class, we find the spread of socialism and the recrudescence of obsolete religious forms. Although these phenomena appear to be contradictory, they are in reality closely related since both represent reactions from the intense individualism which a century ago was eminently characteristic of Americans.

4

Democracy and the Accepted Facts of Heredity

ALLEYNE IRELAND

It would be necessary to go back to the period of the French Revolution and of the American War of Independence to find a public discussion of political principles as voluminous as that which has poured from the printing-presses of the world during the past four years.

From *Journal of Heredity*, IX (December, 1918), pp. 339-342.

Of this vast literature I cannot profess to have read more than a small proportion; but what has fallen under my eye discloses the extremely interesting fact that, after more than two thousand years of controversy about political forms, opinion at the beginning of the twentieth century appears to be unanimous in accepting democracy based upon universal suffrage as the best system of government. Not the least curious phase of this unanimity is that it should have been reached at a time when democracy was engaged in a struggle in which its very existence was for a long time under the gravest threat, and from which it finally emerged triumphant only because it completely abandoned, for the duration of the war, every principle upon which democracy rests.

During the course of the discussions which are now taking place at Versailles every aspect of political practice is certain to be taken up by the delegates, and conventional political theory will, no doubt, receive the homage of oratory. The moment, then, is not inopportune to advance a certain consideration about politics which has hitherto received very scant attention—the bearing of biological laws upon political principles.

It is not without great diffidence that I embark upon this undertaking, for I am not a biologist. A simple explanation will, however, make my position clear. For twenty-five years I have been a student of government; and my studies have taken me to a score of countries, and have made me familiar with a dozen governmental systems, ranging between the extremes of the autocratic and of the democratic forms.

The broadest generalisation which my observation justifies—the one subject to the fewest exceptions—is that the best governed countries were those in which the mass of the people had the least control over the administration of public affairs. By "best governed" I mean best provided with internal peace, with justice, with honest and competent officials, with protection for life, property, with freedom of individual action, with arrangements for promoting the general welfare.

To have reached, after very long and very careful investigation, a conclusion so violently opposed to popular opinion and to the teaching of the schools, was sufficiently disturbing to lead me to a reconsideration of the whole subject for the purpose of discovering, if possible, why almost everything I had observed about democratic governments discredited almost everything I had read in their praise. To this task I devoted a great part of my time during 1916 and 1917. I proceed to summarize the results, leaving for a future article, should the matter prove to be of sufficient public interest, a fuller discussion of certain phases which are here but lightly touched upon.

On the level plain of routine, where most of us pass our lives, intelligent men are agreed that in material affairs human progress is best served by expert knowledge and firm leadership, held by the few and by them employed to direct the energy of the mass. The recognition of this fact is, indeed, the regulating principle of commerce, of industry, and of agriculture. In the field of conduct the same principle is accepted—the rare man of high morality as the guide and inspiration for the common run of men. The priest does not poll his flock as to the sinfulness of murder, nor the captain his crew as to the vessel's course, nor the architect his workmen as to the span of the arch, nor the farmer his hands as to the rotation of the crops.

Yet the moment we enter the field of politics we are asked to reverse the whole process of reasoning which has been our guide in the familiar round of duty, and to apply to the most complicated, the most technical, the most pressing problem ever presented to man's genius—the problem of modern government—a method no one has ever applied to his simple, personal affairs; the control of the expert by the inexpert.

Take a simple case. If I, a student of government, attempt to advise two axmen as to the felling of a tree, the humor of the situation strikes them at once. But if they, the axmen, differ with me as to the comparative merits of a tax levy and a bond issue, of an appointive and an elective judiciary, of specific and ad valorem customs duties, no one's sense of humor intervenes to prevent the axmen making their view prevail at the next election.

The assumption in the former case is that their judgment is better than mine, in the latter that mine is better than theirs. But, whereas, in the former case their rightness and not their number is properly accepted as the determining cause of action, in the latter the issue is held to be properly decided by *their* number and not by *my* rightness.

The explanation of this phenomenon is, in fact, simple. The principles upon which we act in our non-political capacities have been gradually evolved through a process of trial and error, and they represent a qualitative foundation for authority. The determining principles of modern political action were on the contrary, evolved in the heat of revolutions, and represent a quantitative foundation for authority. They were given their currency by rhetoric and not by reason; and they were surrounded, through the violence attending their birth, with a sanctity which has imparted to all criticism of their eternal truth the odium of sacrilege.

From these causes, and from our blind acceptance of a religious doctrine—the natural rights of man—as a practical political principle, we have fallen into a rhapsodical posture toward the democratic form of government. That this posture reflects the influence of an ultra-rational sanction is suggested by the circumstance that when, after a century or two of democratic control, democracy finds its public affairs besmirched by corruption and bedevilled by incompetence, the cry ascends to heaven "Give us *more* democracy, and all will be well!"

This is precisely the reaction of the drug-fiend. The worse his symptoms become, the louder does he call for a larger allowance of his drug. We have, in a word, brought ourselves to regard democracy as a magic elixir which, if we take enough of it, will transmute the base metal of human frailty into a glittering amalgam of virtue, wisdom, and gentleness.

So general opinion has taken up a position behind two points of defense, one that mental and moral habits acquired during the lifetime of the parents can be transmitted to offspring, the other that the law of heredity applies only to physical traits. That these theories are mutually destructive has not in any way affected their popularity amongst those who do not know that each of them is false.

Those who assume the task of reconciling the facts of democratic control with its theory adopt an expedient which places the whole issue beyond the reach of reason. They lay down the rule that democracy must not be judged by its yesterday or by its today, but by its tomorrow; and that so fast as tomorrows become yesterdays even so fast must all adverse evidence be discarded as worthless. Just below the ever-receding horizon of time there lies, almost in sight of those who accept this rule, the pleasant land where education and dietetics shall have made the majority of mankind into political units from which there can be built up a government of benevolence, righteousness, and efficiency.

The Biological Factor in Politics

My strong dissent from this view of politics rests mainly upon four broad grounds:

1. That acquired characteristics are not inheritable.
2. That within the field of man's mental and moral traits there operate immutable laws analogous to those, which are almost universally accepted by biologists, for physical inheritance.
3. That assortative mating operates unremittingly to depress one end of the moral and intellectual scale and to elevate the other.
4. That the individual and not the mass is the main source of human advancement.

Now these statements are either true or false. Of the first three biologists alone are competent to express an authoritative judgment. In my mouth they are no more than opinions. Subject, however, to what biologists may determine to be their value, it is clear that, if they are true, the whole argument for democratic government falls to the ground, or, more precisely the argument that efficiency in government arises from, or can be made to depend upon its democratic quality.

The non-inheritance of acquired traits deals a fatal blow to the common belief that education can give the offspring of educated parents a better natural endowment than the offspring of uneducated parents. Our misconception of the function which education performs has, indeed, become embedded in the English language, for we employ the word "education" in the sense of training or instruction, whereas its fundamental meaning is "bringing out." This distinction goes to the very root of the matter. Education *can* bring out that which is in a man; it *cannot* put into a man that which is not there. It can impart facts to ignorance (ad-ducate, if there were such a word); but it cannot make a dullard bright or a fool sagacious. It is, of course, highly desirable that each generation should be, as it were, dipped by the schools into the ocean of fact, even though, for most of us, the point of saturation is very quickly reached.

Government, however, does not derive its efficiency from a mere knowledge of facts, but from their intelligent interpretation; and the reason why education cannot have a cumulative effect upon government is that intelligence cannot be taught and that knowledge cannot be inherited.

Few persons, I imagine, will refuse their assent to the statement that any political system, however perfect its mechanism, must be rendered wholly ineffective if its administration is entrusted to men of low intelligence. But it is a matter of common observation that intelligence is a quality native to some minds and foreign to others; that is to say, it is born in the brain and cannot be imparted to it from without. Those who have it possess something which cannot be bestowed or withheld by the authority of a monarch or by the vote of an assembly. Perhaps the most acute observation which has been made about the Germans is that they know everything and understand nothing.

What is true of intelligence is true also of the other mental qualities; and it is of the utmost importance to the present enquiry that we should know whether these qualities, which cannot be produced by education, are transmitted by inheritance. So far as this question relates to genius it has been the subject of a number of researches, of which Francis Galton's "Hereditary Genius" is a familiar example. But so far as it relates to all the mental qualities—good and bad, strong and weak—I know of but one careful and extensive investigation, that contained in Dr. Frederick Adams Woods's "Mental and Moral Heredity in Royalty."

From an elaborate study of the royal families of Europe during four centuries, Dr. Woods reaches the conclusion that mental and moral differences are almost entirely due to the influence of heredity, and that they are but slightly affected by environment. Dr. Woods's investigation is, so far as I am aware, the first in which the influences of heredity and of environment in man have been separated and measured. Of great interest from the political and social standpoint is the correlation between mental and moral qualities, which Dr. Woods's figures revealed. Averages show that persons strong in mental qualities are usually strong in moral qualities as well.

Importance of Leadership

To these facts about the hereditary quality of mental and moral traits another must be added if a full appreciation of their force is to be reached. Throughout all human society there is a strong tendency for like to mate with like—the rich with the rich, the successful with the successful, the poor with the poor, the intelligent with the intelligent. This tendency exerts a powerful cumulative influence, which is constantly widening the gulf which separates mediocrity from talent; and the lapse of time is, therefore, making, talented families more talented, and forcing others further and further below the line of mediocrity. It appears, then, that mankind is not breeding towards an average, but towards two extremes.

I pass finally to what history teaches us of the importance of greatness in the individual. The question resolves itself actually into a choice between a qualitative and a quantitative theory of causation in human achievement.

To whatever phase of human development we turn, history fails to furnish a single instance in which an accomplished step in human progress can be referred, ultimately, to any cause other than the quality of greatness in the individual. It is this quality which has given the world all that has ennobled man's character, elevated his culture, and extended his mastery over the material elements of life. It is to the genius of a few hundred individuals among the thousands of millions who have lived, that we owe all the inspiration of religion, philosophy, music, art, and literature; all the benefactions of science, discovery, and invention.

We appear to be at the threshold of an era in which the last shred of authority is to be stripped from wisdom and talent, in which the destiny of the world is finally to be committed to the blind God of Numbers. If biology can enforce a teaching by which this catastrophe may be averted, the interest of humanity demands that the effort should be made before the hour of its possibilities has vanished.

B. Psychology and the "Mass Mind"

The eugenists' insistence on the incapacity of common men for self-rule was lent unexpected support when, at the close of World War I, the results of mental tests given American soldiers were made public. The testing program had been supervised by a committee of the American Psychological Association and was meant to aid in weeding out incompetents, choosing officer candidates, and making assignments to duty. By the end of January, 1919,[1] 1,726,000 men had been tested. When viewed as a sampling, the results appeared to show that nearly half of the American population was feeble-minded! Worried laymen like the free-lance writer Cornelia J. Cannon and a host of delighted apologists for elitism seized on the results as evidence that the popular wisdom on which democracy depended was ephemeral. Representative government required an alert, educable citizenry, wrote Edwin Conklin, yet "nearly one-half of the whole population will never develop mentally beyond the state represented by a normal twelve-year-old child."[2] Edward M. East, a Harvard University professor, concluded: "Suffrage is exercised by every individual above the grade of imbecile who has accomplished 21 years of mundane existence. Thus our whole governmental system is out of harmony with genetic common sense."[3]

The noted American psychologist Henry H. Goddard urged that the army tests' results proved the necessity for a nationwide testing program which would fit every American into the social niche to which his aptitude entitled him.[4] More cautious observers viewed this stampede toward anti-democratic conclusions with suspicion. J. E. Wallace Wallis, also a trained psychologist, pointed out that the procedures for measuring human intelligence were still in a primitive stage and that the tests administered in the United States Army confused a lack of formal knowledge with a lack of native intelligence. Such results did not prove the people's incapacity for self-government, but merely illustrated how misleading the tests really were.[5] Closely reasoned critiques written by Wallis and others were not sensationalist, however, and were confined to the pages of technical journals, while peddlers of the more superficial interpretation broadcast their opinions in popular magazines. The disillusion that wrapped itself about public attitudes at war's end lent credence to a cynical discounting of one more article in the democratic creed. Furthermore, this first experience with global war had made another contribution to doubts about popular wisdom by showing how effectively psychological theories could be applied to the problem of mobilizing American public opinion.[6]

Federal regulation of news dissemination was placed in the hands of a Committee on Public Information headed by George Creel (1875-1953), a crusading journalist and long-time Wilson supporter. Creel's boundless energy and his total faith in the President enabled him, in the two years of the Committee's existence, to organize and direct an enormous propaganda apparatus.[7] The Committee on Public Information had 250 paid workers and claimed the voluntary labors of 5000 artists and writers, and 20,000 public speakers.[8] Creel's busy agency tapped virtually every source of public awareness.[9] "Campaigning," according to one member of the Committee, "to make ideals and principles take hold upon characters and prevail in public," this experiment in news management was credited with effectively galvanizing patriotic fervor.[10]

After the war, a former member of the Committee, Edward L. Bernays (1891-), capitalized on the experience by establishing a public relations firm. If a nation could be persuaded to support an unprecedented military involvement, certainly the same techniques could be employed to sell goods and services. When political workers like Emily Blair called for help, Bernays was equally optimistic about the successful utilization of behaviorist concepts in partisan campaigns.[11] Doubtless Bernays' enthusiasm, innovations, and writings—*Crystallizing Public Opinion* (1923), *Propaganda* (1928), *Biography of an Idea: Memoirs of Public Relations Counsel Edward L. Bernays* (1965)—contributed significantly to the growth and pervasive influence of the American advertising industry.[12] The politicos' invitation to the supersalesmen was accepted readily, and contemporary Americans are all too familiar with the extent to which current political campaigning depends on Madison Avenue. Critics of the persuaders' methods charge that the average voter's exposure to the cleverly manipulated mass media could result in the transformation of majority approval into a commodity. Unprincipled experts, coached by a "value-free," behaviorist political science, could use today's technology to form opinion almost magically.[13] "A free society," one worried social scientist has suggested, "can also be seen as an excellent breeding ground for gullibility, along with such consequences as ignorance, panic, and hysteria."[14]

Probably the politician's need to reach the greatest possible number of potential supporters and the availability of mass media have made the public relations man a permanent fixture in American politics.[15] Probably, also, there will be temptations to permit admen to choose the issues or distort the facts.[16] Yet those who believe that voters can be packaged, priced, and carried away in a shopping cart betray a signal distrust of human rationality, as well as a naive faith in the actual effectiveness of advertising.[17] The persuaders, and their most fearful critics, assume that there *is* a "mass society" which is easy prey for a supposedly magical conversion; yet experienced public relations counsel admit quietly that, very often, the most shrewdly devised propaganda effort fails because of the public's stubborn rationality and its suspicion of advertisers' motives.[18]

The theoretic assumptions of modern propaganda have changed little since the day of the Creel Committee, resting on the behaviorists' assurances that the human mind is malleable, that human beings, like sheep (as B. F. Skinner so aptly suggests in *Walden Two*), can be conditioned to a passive acceptance of virtually anything. Accused of holding antidemocratic beliefs by such intellectual opponents as Joseph Wood Krutch, Skinner's reply has been a frank confirmation. According to Skinner, democratic processes represent a fumbling approach toward reality; freedom is randomness. Science, he promises, can substitute methodical truth and controlled purpose. Skinner's utopia bears a striking resemblance to Huxley's *Brave New World.*[19]

Behaviorism's penchant for reducing man's nature to the measurable and malleable has been matched by the pretensions of a Freudian cult dedicated to the assumption that since the sublime cannot be quantified, it must not exist—that human motives and goals are never what they seem to be—since man is an irrational organism distinguishable from other animals only by his facility for clothing elemental drives in the camouflage of reason. Freudianism, with a persistent hedonism as its touchstone, strikes democratic theory in two crucial ways: (1) by seeing human existence as a quest for ways of expressing antisocial urges instead of a search for meaning, it denies the existence of reasonable man; (2) by portraying all institutions as barriers to the natural expression of elemental urges, it casts doubt on the possible representativeness of *any* social or political structure.[20]

In an undoubtedly sincere effort to salvage a few human values in the contemporary world by synthesizing Freudian psychology and Marxist economics, Erich Fromm (1900-) has concluded that even American democracy has had mortally corrosive effects on the human condition.[21] The peculiar combination of self-government and capitalism, Fromm insists, only intimidates man and makes him ripe for authoritarianism.[22] The human being is a "need mechanism," historically conditioned by his economic environment; his ideas and ideals are simply rationalized expressions of drives and desires.[23] True freedom Fromm defines as freedom from insecurity: an involvement in action, creativity, a sense of productivity, an absence of inhibitions, tensions, and distractions.[24] In the United States, however, capitalism forces the individual to go it alone, and what is heralded as economic liberty is actually a sense of personal isolation, bafflement, anxiety, and insecurity.[25]

Fromm's concept of freedom and his set of solutions (made specific in *The Sane Society*) are profoundly if unwittingly antidemocratic. He first reduces man's limitless, unpredictable choices to a craving for busy-work. Truth, he argues, is measurable feeling, and justice is traceable to wish fulfillment. An open society, with its toleration of political debate, is pathological because it promotes subjectivity.[26] Having redefined freedom as placidity, Fromm finds the need for a cure so pressing that he must kick over the traces of constitutionalism. He would eradicate alienation by reducing America's massive institutional structure to cell groups of about 500 persons. He would eliminate the tensions produced by political differences by creating a "politically independent" corporation which would unravel the complex issues and then pass along the "facts" to the cells for digestion.

The neutral corporation, composed, of course, of persons chosen for their "outstanding achievements and moral integrity," would make all orderly and rational and tension-free—on the lines, it might be noted, of a mausoleum.[27]

NOTES

1. Mark H. Haller, *Eugenics: Hereditarian Attitudes in American Thought* (New Brunswick: Rutgers University Press, 1963), p. 113.

2. Edwin G. Conklin, "Some Biological Aspects of Immigration," *Scribner's Magazine,* LXIX (March, 1921), p. 354.

3. Edward M. East, *Heredity and Human Affairs* (New York: Charles Scribner's Sons, 1929), p. 300.

4. Henry H. Goddard, *Psychology of the Normal and Subnormal* (New York: Dodd, Mead & Company, 1924), p. 238.

5. J. E. W. Wallis, "The Concept of the Feeble-Minded, Especially the Moron," *Training School Bulletin,* XVII (May, 1920), p. 50.

6. See, for example, James R. Mock and Cedric Larson, *Words that Won the War* (Princeton: Princeton University Press, 1939), *passim;* and H. C. Peterson, *Propaganda for War* (Norman: University of Oklahoma Press, 1939), pp. 12-15 and *passim.*

7. Bernard Rubin, "Propaganda and Ideological Conflicts, 1917-1945; the Need for Psychological Peacefare," *Contemporary Review,* 200 (December, 1961), p. 633; *The National Cyclopedia of American Biography* (New York: James T. White & Company, 1956), XLI, pp. 575-576.

8. Rubin, "Propaganda," p. 634.

9. Mark Sullivan, *Our Times* (New York: Charles Scribner's Sons, 1933), Vol. 5, pp. 423-456; *Preliminary Statement to the Press of the United States* (Washington, D. C.: Committee on Public Information, 1917), p. 6.

10. Stuart P. Sherman, *American and Allied Ideals* (Washington, D. C.: Committee on Public Information, *n.d.*), p. 4; Rubin, "Propaganda," p. 635.

11. *Who's Who in the East* (Chicago: Marquis—Who's Who, 1968), Vol. 11, pp. 95-96.

12. *Ibid.*

13. Howard B. White, "The Processed Voter and the New Political Science," *Social Research,* 28 (July, 1961), pp. 127-150.

14. K. R. Minogue, "How to Make Trends and Influence People," *American Scholar,* 30 (Summer, 1961), p. 323.

15. Joseph J. Selden, "Selling Presidents Like Soap," *American Mercury,* 83 (September, 1956), pp. 5-10.

16. White, "The Processed Voter," p. 150.

17. The late Senator Robert F. Kennedy, accused by opponents of "buying" votes through the use of costly television commercials, noted correctly that the high cost of advertising set by the media, not an individual's wealth, was the real danger.

18. Raymond A. Bauer and Alice H. Bauer, "America, Mass Society, and Mass Media," *Journal of Social Issues,* XVI, No. 3 (1960), pp. 3-66; Horace Busby, "Propaganda? Or Public Information?" *Public Management,* 45 (March, 1963), pp. 58-61.

19. Skinner appears unaware of the fact that science creates new problems as well as new opportunities. "The power of science magnifies man's ability," writes Walter Orr

Roberts, "to achieve utopia or to destroy all that is civilized, or free, or beautiful." Roberts, "Science, A Wellspring of our Discontent," *American Scholar,* 36 (Spring, 1967), pp. 250-251.

20. *Cf.* Ernest Becker, "Social Science and Psychiatry: the Coming Challenge," *Antioch Review,* 23 (Fall, 1963), pp. 359-360; and Sigmund Freud, *Civilization and its Discontents* (New York: J. Cape and H. Smith, 1930), *passim.*

21. Erich Fromm, *Escape from Freedom* (New York: Holt, Rinehart, & Winston, 1941), *passim;* A. J. Titarenko, "Erich Fromm in the Chains of Illusion," *Science and Society,* XXIX (Summer, 1965), pp. 319-329; Thomas I. Cook, "Democratic Psychology and a Democratic World Order," *World Politics,* I (July, 1949), pp. 553-564.

22. Henry S. Kariel, "The Normative Pattern of Erich Fromm's Escape from Freedom," *Journal of Politics,* 19 (November, 1957), p. 640.

23. Kariel, "Normative Pattern," pp. 642-643.

24. *Ibid.,* p. 651.

25. *Ibid.,* pp. 645-646.

26. *Ibid.,* p. 653.

27. Erich Fromm, *The Sane Society* (New York: Rinehart, 1955), pp. 327, 340-343.

5

American Misgivings

CORNELIA J. CANNON

O such themes—equalities! O divine average! – Walt Whitman

I

The World War brought us many strange revelations, perhaps none more unexpected than the discovery that intrinsic values inhere in the supposedly purely ornamental aspects of our intellectual life. Before the spring of 1917, our meteorologists had been for years pursuing their innocent vocation, unnoted and unsung. They had sent up their kites from obscure little hills by day and by night; they had charted the layers of air-currents above our indifferent heads; they had made pictures of clouds and studies of storm motions, with an ardor that seemed to require no appreciation from us. We had tolerated them on the theory that curiosity is in itself a valuable asset, and that, having once given this particular aspect of it a professional status, we must philosophically accept the lean with the fat.

From *Atlantic,* 129 (February, 1922), pp. 145-157.

When we had joined the Allies, these quaint enthusiasts were found to be the only persons in the world who knew enough to advise our aviators and to protect them from the terrors of the celestial deep. From previously unheeded laboratories the meteorologists were proudly brought forth into the light of day. They were asked to serve on important committees, and to spend much of their time imparting to thousands of eager students the knowledge they had acquired through years of patient study. Prophets are seldom so honored in their own country.

Another group of searchers for the truth, the psychologists, had likewise borne their years of indifference from the multitude, and of active opposition from the ignorant. They had spent such money as was available from vested funds, and such leisure as university duties allowed them, to pursue the study of mankind. Their particular penchant was the mind of man; its qualities, its capabilities, its methods of functioning. They had gone up and down the scale of creation in their search for light. Every type of reaction to the universe of which the brain-substance seemed capable was tabulated and analyzed. These activities were tolerated, though the knowing shrugged their shoulders at such fatuous endeavors.

Then upon America fell the task of selecting and preparing, within the short space of a few weeks or, at most, months, millions of men for a great diversity of duties requiring varied and different abilities. It was instantly clear that the selection could be done neither by rule of thumb nor by any haphazard game of counting out, however rapid and easily administered such a method might be. Those who knew something of the delicate art of choosing a man for a job must come to the help of a nation facing a desperate emergency under conditions of the greatest stress.

As it happened, we were better able than any other of the allied nations to undertake this responsibility, for the methods of measuring human abilities, initiated by Cattell in America and Binet in France, had been carried to a higher degree of perfection in this country, and tested out on a far greater scale, than in any other country in the world. The intelligence-rating in our army was the fruit of 'preparedness' on the part of the American psychologists. In the first weeks of the war they threw themselves into the work of preparing tests to be given on a gigantic scale; and as soon as the drafted men were in the cantonments, and the assistance psychology could render was recognized by those in authority, their work of making the tests and grading the enlisted men was begun. During the anxious and strenuous months of 1917 and 1918, when the army was being built up for its fateful activities in France, the psychologists were rapidly putting in the hands of the army officers data concerning the mental alertness of the enlisted men, to be used as an aid in the assignment of each individual to the task to which he was best suited.

The tests did their important service during the days of war, but they have left in our hands, for the days of peace, data the value of which is just beginning to be realized.

II

The army intelligence tests were given to 1,726,966 of our officers and men, in the years 1917 and 1918. The tests were of two types: the Alpha examination for those who could read and write English readily; and the Beta examination for the illiterate, the non-English-speaking, and for those who could read and write English, but without facility. The first, which comprised a series of eight markedly different tests, although it required almost no writing on the part of the subject, did demand ability in using written and oral instruction. The second type was, in effect, the first translated into pictorial form, in which written and oral instructions were replaced by pantomime and demonstration. Individual examinations were given to those making a very low score on one or both of the standard examinations.

The object of the tests was to sift out the mental defectives not qualified for military service; to classify soldiers according to their mental capacity for proper assignment in the army; to discover men of superior ability, for report to their officers; and to select men with marked special skill. The tests were carefully devised and given; in the early stages of critical study of the data, each record was checked, so far as possible, by comparison with the actual performance of the individual tested, and by the practical judgment of his officers on his ability. The results have been carefully analyzed, so that we have in the totals a significant psychological picture of the young manhood of the country.

What is the kind of intelligence these tests were devised to grade? Our newspapers and magazines have been flooded lately by popular so-called intelligence tests—a mixture of catch-questions, inquiries about facts not worth knowing, and upheavings of the dust-bins of general information. They are, of course, utterly valueless as a measure of mental ability as well as of discrimination in the accumulation of details. The army intelligence tests were distinctly not of this type. They were, in the first place, not tests of verbal or literary proficiency; for as high a grade could be attained by the non-English-speaking individual as by one readily conversant with the language. They did not measure educational acquirement or general information; for the illiterate was at no disadvantage with the most erudite university graduate. Nor were they tests of rapidity of mental processes; for though the time was strictly limited, control-tests given with double time showed only a slight improvement in the records of the lower grades of mind. This was doubtless due to the fact that the tests were not primarily tests of memory, in which associations could be slowly summoned to mind, but tests of intelligence, which was once for all capable or incapable of recognizing the situations which the questions presented. Nor was there discrepancy due to the two types of examination; for those who took high rank in the Alpha examination took equally high rank in the Beta, and those who took a low rating in the Alpha did the same in the other.

The intelligence the examinations were primarily designed to test was capacity to see things in relation, ability to grasp situations as a whole, and power to reason. These are innate qualities, independent of circumstance, yet characterizing the individual's every reaction to his environment. The men were grouped, according to their standing in the tests, in five grades, from A to E. A and B represented superior intelligence, the two being recommended for officer rank; the C group was average intelligence, varying from fair non-commissioned-officer type to average soldier; and D and E indicated inferior to very inferior intelligence, in some cases fit for certain kinds of low-grade service, in others only for dismissal from the army. Men of the superior grades were found in all ranks, officers and privates, the educated and the uneducated, but the individuals stood out markedly from their fellows.

In terms of mental age, a classification used by the psychologists, based on studies of the capacities of schoolchildren of different ages, the range of the drafted men was from eighteen years or over, the superior grade, down to a mental age of below nine years, the inferior grade. In civil life a moron, or high-grade feeble-minded person, has been defined as any adult with a mental age of from seven to twelve years. If this definition can be interpreted as meaning any adult below the mental age of thirteen, almost half of the white draft, 47.3 per cent, would have been classed as morons. It is clear that a very much larger proportion of low-grade intelligence must exist in our population than has been heretofore suspected. The totals from all the tests give the following percentages of the different levels of mental ability found in our white drafted army: superior men, 12 per cent; average men, 66 per cent; and inferior men, 22 per cent. Probably this is, roughly, the average of the community as a whole; for the men of superior ability, kept out of the draft for work in essential industries, and officers not included in the total, were offset by the feeble-minded and the defective rejected by the draft boards and never sent to the cantonments.

There are several reasons why the results of these examinations possess particular authority and significance. In the first place, they worked. When the grading was used with care and discrimination, a man's actual performance corresponded closely to the probabilities forecast by the examination record. The officers found it a rapid method of ranking men according to ability to do the tasks required in army service, so that fewer men wasted time attempting work beyond their capacity or burning their hearts out at inferior duties. The army authorities have recognized the value of the tests as an adjunct of the service, and the examinations continue in use in the permanent military organization.

The tests were applied on so huge a scale, and with so complete an elimination of personal slant on the part of the examiners, that the data are of unprecedented and enormous value—almost in a class by themselves. Even making every allowance for errors in individual tests, the numbers are so great as to give assurance that incidental errors balance one another. We can therefore feel justified in using, for the wiser organization of our democracy, the new insight into the mental make-up of our people which the tests have brought. We must ask ourselves how far these revelations of our intellectual quality as a nation affect our judgment of the value or futility of the different governmental expedients—representation, the initiative, referendum, and recall, direct election of senators, education for citizenship, restriction of immigration and naturalization—with which we have been experimenting; and from what mistaken course in the use of these devices of our national life they may rescue us. . . .

III

From the point of view of our national problem, the developing of democratic institutions and forms of government, what are the proportions of citizens of the varied mental abilities which promise to bring, most certainly and speedily, the desired end of universal justice and happiness? Would democracy flourish best in a community made up entirely of D men, or in one made up entirely of A men? Is true democracy attainable only when natural equality is coexistent with political equality? The assumption in any discussion based on questions of this character is that intelligence is of positive value, a yardstick by which human worth is to be measured. Is this a just estimate of the importance of intelligence in community life, or would its absence create only a momentary inconvenience? . . .

In the future, the inferior type is certain to be far more of a perplexity; for we cannot expect a less complex civilization until the race is born again. But what are the present prospects of reducing the 22 per cent of inferior intelligences already in our population?

IV

The army intelligence tests have been analyzed on the basis of country of origin of the foreign-born. Some data of quite appalling significance are assembled. The white draft, as a whole, had 22 per cent of inferior men: those of the draft who were born in Poland had 70 per cent; in Italy, 63, in Russia, 60. Of all the foreign-born, 46 per cent were of this very low grade of intelligence, with an almost negligible number of superior individuals.

We could argue that from these inferior strains might emerge, in some future age, a race of superior capacity; for from some such undeveloped types must have evolved the best strains of our day. But our problem as Americans is immediate. We cannot make our decisions in terms of geological eras when we discuss the referendum, universal suffrage, the segregation of the unfit, and the reduction of tubercular infection throughout the country. We must have a population to which these words convey some meaning, if we are to share alike in the privileges and responsibilities of democracy. In the light of recent revelations as to the country of origin of those now pressing for entrance into the United States, these statistics are like the handwriting on the wall. Our melting-pot may fuse these elements with the others, but the resulting metal does not promise to be one to stand heavy strains.

We cannot draw comfort from the thought that residence in this country will alter the mental characteristics of the immigrant and transmute the lead into fine gold. An analysis of the draft on the basis of length of stay in this country does not bear out any such assumption. The tables show a very slight difference in favor of those who had been here longer; but the difference is so slight as to lead the examiners to suggest that it may be an artifact of the method of examination itself.

There is no doubt that to throw our gates open to these groups is to add to our racial stocks the poorest that Europe has to give. The eastern European comes to us with a slant toward revolution, a hatred of whatever power there may be, engendered by centuries of finding that every power was inimical. His admission to a country engaged in the hazardous task of working out a self-governing community might seem somewhat of a risk. Given a high grade of intelligence, however, the danger is negligible; for education can train in the ideals of democracy, and each national group would have opportunity and ability to make characteristic contributions to a solution of the complexities of democratic society.

But what chance of this is there with the inferior grade of intelligence? Such individuals form the material of unrest, the stuff of which mobs are made, the tools of demagogues; for they are peculiarly liable to the emotional uncontrol which has been found to characterize so many of the criminals who come before our courts. They are persons who not only do not think, but are unable to think; who cannot help in the solution of our problems, but, instead, become a drag on the progress of civilization. In a crude society they have a place, may even serve a use. In a society so complex as that which we are developing, they are a menace which may compass our destruction.

We might well eliminate the D and E intelligences which are not home-grown by stiffening the exclusion laws and more adequately backing our medical-port officers in their efforts to keep down our intake of defectives. If our legislative intelligence is not sharp enough to realize that we might keep out many of the persons of average ability, to our ultimate advantage, there can certainly be no two opinions about the exclusion of the inferior mind. It is not only the individual whom we exclude, but that ever-widening circle of his descendents, whose blood may be destined to mingle with and deteriorate the best we have. Theoretically the inferior-minded are ineligible for admission to our country. How liberally this provision is interpreted, and how ineffective is the exclusion practised, may be surmised from the proportions of this type found among the foreign-born in the draft.

A democracy is the most difficult form of government to perfect, because it demands of each citizen so much understanding and cooperation. Its achievement halts because of the imperfection of its component members. However much the forms of democracy may be clung to, when the majority of the citizens of a country are of a low grade of intelligence, an oligarchy is inevitable. Contrast the so-called democracy of Mexico with the so-called monarchies of England and Holland, whose nationals in our army ranked in intelligence above those of any other nation in the draft, and far above the average for America as a whole. An enthusiast for education might see in this disparity evidence that the sole impediment to the coming in of a true democracy is illiteracy. Let all the potential citizens learn to read and write, and the difficulties will vanish. But the differences in the liberties of men in these contrasted countries lie deeper than any difference in the dissemination of education; they run back to the gray substance in the brain-cases of the people themselves.

If the building-up of democratic institutions in a population composed in large part of inferior men presents difficulties, what would be the case in a world of superior men? Would the citizens of such a country be high-strung, nervous, exacting, unwilling to do, and perhaps incapable of doing, heavy physical labor—the flower of civilization without the roots and leaves?

Australia and New Zealand have a population more homogeneous, on a higher level economically, and, judging from similar communities in our own country—for example, Oregon, Washington, and Montana, whose cities were tested in the draft—of a higher general level of intelligence than is found, perhaps, anywhere else in the world; and yet their pleasant lands are not free from problems. Their very homogeneity and equality develop sharp jealousies and antagonisms between labor and capital, which threaten to destroy them both. Stagnation seizes many of their industries, and internal dissension dries up the sources of their wealth. In the life of the family in New Zealand, the labor of the woman who has a home to manage is so unrelieved, the aid that the community brings to the reduction of her burden so slight, that late marriages and small families are becoming the rule and not the exception. A country in which the men will not adjust themselves to doing the exacting tasks of a developing civilization, and the women will not bear children, is a country which is doomed. Can it ever hold the "Islands of the Blessed" in the South Seas, against the pressure of a fecund race of fierce industry and diversified talents, such as the Japanese, for instance?

We may well doubt whether a civilization composed wholly of inferior, or wholly of superior men and women would be a complete success. The subject cannot, unfortunately, be put to experimental proof, because the laboratory would have to be the world, and men are not so tractable as guinea-pigs. There is nothing left for us save to observe the proportions of mind of the different classes in that democracy which seems to serve best the interests of all its citizens, and take those proportions as the working basis for a balanced community. Given our own country's present distribution of mental abilities,—12 per cent of the best type and 22 per cent of the poorest, the average lying between,—what adaptation of governmental organization would be helpful in bringing about the most successful functioning of the groups?

V

What do we mean when we say that a country is not ready for self-government? Do we mean that the citizens are illiterate, that they have not studied history, or been taught how to cast a ballot? or do we mean that they have not yet evolved sufficient intelligence to grapple with the problems incident to the administration of a democracy? In the first interpretation, we could name a date for the coming in of freedom. Fifteen years of schooling and a little practice in running the machinery of government would make a nation ready to manage its own affairs. In the second interpretation, we might feel that generations must elapse, and even then nothing entitled to the name of self-government would characterize the type of political organization which such people might devise.

What are the qualities essential in human beings for the running of a democracy? The difficulties of administration are inherently great. So many men, so many minds; such conflicts of wills and wants; such need for endless patience and tolerance to make compatible the inevitable incompatibility of political equality and natural inequality! To work out these never-ending problems of the adjustments of man to man demands mental abilities of a high order, inventiveness, inexhaustible ingenuity. So far as we can judge, it promises best in communities where there is homogeneity of language and of ideals, and at least a fair average of intelligence. What prospect of success is there here in America, with the average of intelligence of the citizens already so much lower than we could have expected, and with an increasing influx of potential citizens who are destined to bring the average still lower?

The ideal of our constitution-builders was that of a representative government. There has been of late years a wave, perhaps past its crest, of desire for more direct government through the initiative, the referendum, and the recall. In theory, these forms promise the purest and surest democracy, a method of making the voice of the people heard and the will of the people immediately effective. In fact, they have everywhere disappointed the high hopes of those who advocated their adoption as an advance in the art of freedom. They have not worked for progress. It is difficult to say why, though indifference, inborn conservatism, ignorance of the issue, and reluctance on the part of the voter to make the effort to understand the issue, have all been given as explanations for their failure. The recall has made self-respecting men unwilling to take positions from which any disgruntled faction could recall them, and in which their effectiveness would be limited by the constant need of conciliating the malcontents.

The trade-union movement, itself an experiment in democracy, has had to give up the high hope with which it hailed the expedients of the initiative and the referendum, and admit the non-fulfillment of their original promise of good.

Is it not possible that the failure of these devices of democracy is due, not to any imperfection inherent in the devices themselves, but to a fundamental inferiority in the average intelligence of the voters, which makes them unable to use the methods wisely? How can we expect a man with a mental age of less than ten years to deal intelligently with the complicated questions submitted to the voters in a referendum? Has not the impossible been demanded of a nation, nearly half of whose population is under the mental age of thirteen? How can such men and women determine the relative values of the sales tax and the surtax, or display a discriminating preference for a tariff on lemons over a tariff on wheat?

Our forefathers, who were a canny lot of men, in spite of the handicap of being behind our times, organized a representative government because they felt that there was one thing that every man could do intelligently—select leaders to represent him. Man shares with many lower forms of animal life a desire to follow leaders. The elk, the buffalo, the wild geese, the sheep, the creatures that hunt or feed in flocks or herds, follow leaders who are, so far as we can judge, the most intelligent, the best equipped, and the speediest in reaction-time of all the group. If we could develop as sound a sense of the type of leader we need as seems to come intuitively to the lower animals, our worst difficulties might be overcome. Can we be trained to recognize and choose the best to lead us? Can we learn not to weary, as did the Athenians of old, of hearing Aristides called "the Just," and refrain from selecting a good mixer in his stead?

The psychologists have not as yet offered us tests to detect in the individual an ability to recognize wisdom in others. We do see in children, however, an almost eerie understanding of the character and capacities of parents and teachers. Their failure to use the same unerring instinct in adult life may be due to the fact that the opportunities to observe those to whom they must look for guidance in later years are not so great as in childhood. Perhaps the problem of the future is to bring about more frequent and intimate contacts between the potential leaders of our democracy and their sovereigns, the voters. We must teach our children to look for the qualities that characterize the able, and to reject the cheap attractions of the demagogue. They must see and hear in our schools the persons of ability and character in the community.

Our tendency in this country is to deplore our selection of leaders, to throw up our hands in despair at the choices of the electorate, and make no effort to create new standards of choice. In so far as we can, we must imitate in the large cities the safeguard of first-hand information as to the qualities and abilities of those to whom we plan to entrust our common interests, which was possible in the early days of the Republic. It may be that the final test of our civilization and the assurance of the continuation of our democracy will be our capacity to recognize and follow the true leaders of our race.

If we can train our electorate to choose honest men of the superior type to represent them, we can count on protection from our worst dangers. The very basis of representative government is the opportunity for knowledge of the many-sided problems of government possible to the representative, but impossible to the individual voter. From the conflicts of minds and ideals in representative groups, truth, and finally wisdom, may emerge.

The A and B man may appear from any social group in the community; the only point the C or D man need consider is, that it is to the interest of all to be represented by those possessing the highest abilities. He is choosing, not a master, but a servant. He must learn that his best servant is not the politician who gives him a turkey on Thanksgiving, but the representative who insists on clean streets and the prompt collection of garbage. The average man can learn this in time; the inferior man may not be able to grasp a situation presenting so many complications. Indeed, we may have to admit that the lower-grade man is material unusable in a democracy, and to eliminate him from the electorate, as we have the criminal, the insane, the idiot, and the alien.

The direct election of senators was hailed as a great step forward. As a matter of fact, the senators so chosen show no distinct rise in quality. The men sent to the Senate by the older method had their defects, and the system its danger; but the innovation is at least of problematic value. We try one type of city charter; then in desperation, we try another; but, in the end, we are about where we were at the beginning—inefficiency appearing where we should have efficiency, and dishonesty where honesty is the prime requisite. Is it possible that we might be brought to recognize political offices as technical jobs, requiring a technical training which could be determined by examination? Then, if we still wished to exercise our prerogative of choice, we could elect, from a list submitted by the examiners, the officers of our preference.

We have shown an eagerness to naturalize the newcomers to our shores as promptly as possible, and an inclination to make the way easy and discrimination difficult. Is this the part of true wisdom? Should not the goal of membership in the great Republic be attainable only through special effort and distinct merit? How much do we augment our collective wisdom by adding inferior minds to it? Has not the time come to withhold the privilege and responsibility of citizenship from the majority of the newer immigrants, whose quality shows so marked a falling-off from that of the immigrants of fifty years ago, and whose intelligence is so far below that of the ordinary American, and bestow it only upon carefully selected members of the group? . . .

VI

The average man belongs to that group which gives significance to the history of the race. He conserves the achievements of the past, keeps our machinery of the everyday life going, does the work that the superior man will not and the inferior man cannot do, and by his steadiness, his patience, and his control, keeps the world from tearing itself to pieces. But he cannot better his fate without the help of the men of superior ability. To them he must look for leadership, for an understanding of the way out of the dark and tragic stages in our evolving civilization. They are the men who invent our machinery, make possible the telephone, the wireless, the electric light, the steamship, the airplane; who wipe out disease, write the great literature of the world, organize our industries and our methods of distribution, make the laws, write the constitutions, guide the revolts for freedom, destroy superstitions, read the mystery of the rocks, study the motions of the stars, interpret the evolution of man. They are the members of our race who have led us up from barbarism and keep us from sinking back into it. There is nothing of the wisdom of the ages which can be offered to them, no opportunity for advancing them, which does not bring rich dividends of added prosperity and happiness to the rest of us.

One happy finding of the army tests was the very large proportion of the A and B men who had had the advantages of higher education. This does not extenuate the deprivation of the hundreds who had not—our country is so much the poorer for that—but it does show how difficult it is to keep real ability from coming into its own.

Our civilization halts, and our unsolved problems pile up in the lean generations; then the powers that watch over us smile upon us, and fill our cradles with wonder-children, as in 1809, that *annus mirabilis,* and the world leaps forward again. The highest wisdom demands that we cherish those in our midst who show even a flickering of the divine flame, and guard against the dying-down of the sacred fire because of our preoccupation with matters of less importance. In a democracy, our major hope, as well as our major responsibility, must always lie in the discovery and development of those among us who are endowed with the capacity to inspire us, and the ability to lead us to a fuller life.

6

The Activities of the Committee on Public Information

COMMITTEE ON PUBLIC INFORMATION

As will be seen by the accompanying report, the Committee on Public Information has grown to be a world organization. Not only does it touch every part of the great machinery that coordinates the forces of America for victory, but it carries the meanings and purposes of America to all peoples, making the fight for public opinion in every country.

Selected excerpts from *War Information Series,* No. 17 (February, 1918).

Besides the daily war news, which it issues to the whole press of the country, it supplies some 30,000 newspapers with feature articles, a weekly news service, and governmental publicity material of all sorts.

It has prepared and printed for distribution to all parts of the world 18,000,000 copies of 15 different pamphlets in seven languages.

It conducts speaking campaigns in every State of the Union, arranges meetings, books speakers, conducts war conferences, and organizes tours; and in the Four Minute Men alone it commands the volunteer services of 15,000 public speakers.

It has wireless and cable news service that is being extended to every capital in Europe, Scandinavia, the Orient, South and Central America, and Mexico, and a feature-article service of similar proportions.

It sends to foreign countries motion-picture exhibits showing America's social, industrial, and war progress.

It has mobilized the advertising forces of the country—press, periodical, car, and outdoor—for a patriotic campaign that will give $30,000,000 worth of free space to the national service. It designs posters, window cards, and similar material of pictorial publicity for the use of various Government departments and patriotic societies.

It prepares moving-picture films showing our war progress and exhibits them to hundreds of thousands of people daily.

It issues an official daily newspaper for the Government, with a circulation of 90,000 copies a day.

With the aid of a volunteer staff of several hundred translators, it keeps in direct touch with the foreign-language press, supplying selected articles designed to combat ignorance and disaffection.

It has organized, and now directs, a round dozen of societies and leagues designed to appeal to certain classes and particular foreign-language groups, each body carrying a specific message to its section of America's adopted peoples.

It acts as a bureau of information for all persons who seek its direction in volunteer war work, in acquiring knowledge of any administrative activities, or in approaching business dealings with the Government.

It supervises the voluntary censorship of the newspaper and periodical press.

It establishes rules and regulations for the cable censorship with respect to press dispatches.

It prepares and distributes, advises upon, and censors photographs and moving pictures to the number of more than 700 a day.

It has only 250 paid employees, but it directs and coordinates the patriotic work of 5,000 volunteer writers and artists and 20,000 public speakers.

To carry on its multifarious activities in the United States, it has spent from its beginning in April, 1917, down to December 31, 1917, $119,821.96 for salaries and $325,713.20 for all its other expenses.

This remarkable showing has been made possible by the generous co-operation of patriotic groups and individuals, the sacrifice of volunteer workers, and the devotion of others in accepting service at half the salary received in private employment.

It is not an economy, however, that can be or should be maintained. I can assure you that the country, as a whole, is behind the war, but in every section there is a vast amount of ignorance and misunderstanding that may possibly fester and inflame. Forces of dissension and disloyalty are steadily at work, and particularly is this true among the foreign population. We shall not discharge our full duty to the national defense until we have reached every community in the United States by written or spoken word or motion picture; until every individual, native, naturalized, or alien, has it seared into his consciousness that this war is a war of self-defense, and that it has got to be master of his every thought and action.

Our greatest need, however, is in other lands. England and France attach prime importance to educational and informative campaigns, and Germany, I am credibly informed, spent $3,000,000 a month in Russia alone. For years the United States has been known to the rest of the world through dribbles of information supplied by foreign news agencies, and as the result there is not a country that has any exact or comprehensive idea of American life, activity, or ideals. This ignorance has lent itself with peculiar effect to the lies of the enemy, and there is no work more important than this fight for better understanding and a more intelligent public opinion.

Much has been done, but it can only be regarded as experimental. Machinery has been created and tested, and we are now able to commence 100 per cent operation in all confidence. It is for this that I ask sanction. There is no detail in connection with these activities that we shall be ashamed to reveal. No paper will be subsidized, no official bought, and no corruption employed.

From a thousand sources we hear of the wonders of German propaganda, but my original determination has never altered. Always do I try to find out what the Germans are doing, and then I *don't do it*. Even if the very loftiness of our war aims did not command honesty at every point, I have the conviction that corrupt methods work their own destruction.

Russia is a case in point. For years, first secretly and at last quite openly, Germany has poisoned the people with lies, yet within the short space of a few months our own open publicity campaign was able to work a fundamental change in public sentiment. We do not argue or exhort or censure, but confine all activities to a plain, straightforward presentation of *our* aims, *our* purposes, and *our* ideals. We have nothing to fear from the truth; it can be made our principal weapon.

May I ask that you permit me to have copies of this report printed and sent to the press? A policy that is absolutely open will preclude confidential arrangements, to be sure, but it is best to forego a certain percentage of effort rather than that the whole should be weakened and impaired by suspicions and distrusts. . . .

Despite general opinion, censorship plays but a small part in the work of the committee.

The desires of the Government with respect to the concealment from the enemy of military policies, plans, and movements are set forth in certain specific requests. No law stands behind them. Their observance rests entirely upon honor and patriotism. There are violations, as a matter of course, and papers holding to the unwritten agreement have suffered injury from papers less careful and less honest, but, on the whole, the press has responded in the same spirit of unselfish service that animates the firing line.

The continuing weak spot is due to a persistent misunderstanding in the matter of regulation. When a violation occurs, such papers as have observed the agreement straightway demand that rebuke be administered or penalty inflicted. Yet on the printed card that carries the desires of the Government there appears this significant paragraph.

These requests go to the press without larger authority than the necessities of the war-making branches. Their enforcement is a matter for the press itself.

The bargain is the bargain of the press, and it must of necessity provide its own discipline. As it is realized, however, that the requests of the Government are concerned with human lives and national hopes, as it is driven home that the passing satisfaction of a news item may endanger a transport or a troop train, the voluntary censorship grows in strength and certainty. . . .

The committee, at the time of its appointment, had as its chief purpose the coordination and control of the daily news of military operations given out by the Army and Navy. The work is now being done by the Division of News. It is the sole medium for the issuance of official war information, and now acts not only for the Army and Navy but for the Department of Justice, the Council of National Defense, the War Industries Board, the War Trade Boards, and the Alien Property Custodian. It has its sworn representatives in the war-making branches of the Government, trained newspaper men, whose duty it is to open up operations to the inspection of the people as far as military prudence will permit. The committee believes that public support is a matter of public understanding, and it is the duty of the division to take deadwood out of the channels of information, permitting a freer, more continuous, flow. This is not the simplest thing in the world. On one hand is the press, impatient of reticence and suspicious of concealments, and on the other hand we have generals and admirals reared in a school of iron silence. Both, however, are in process of education. The press is commencing to realize our honesty of purpose, and the military experts are growing to have an increasing faith in the power of absolute frankness. The Army and Navy, through this Division of News, have pledged themselves to give to the people instant and honest announcement of all casualties, all accidents, all disasters. We do not have to conceal reverses because we do not have to fear for the courage of America.

In the progress of this work the division has formed several independent departments whose business it is to supply specialized needs of various sorts. About 14,000 country newspapers are being furnished a weekly service of condensed war news of two or three columns in length. About 2,000 papers in the smaller cities will soon be receiving a similar service. The matter is sent largely in plate form, the newspapers bearing the expense of plate and ready print.

The News Division is organized to render its service day and night. There are 17 paid employees. It has spent $25,422.74 for salaries and $2,125.52 for all other expenses. . . .

The Division of Civic and Educational Cooperation prepares pamphlets upon the war for world-wide circulation. It commands the voluntary services of more than 3,000 writers, chiefly college professors, historians, and publicists. It has now issued 15 different pamphlets setting forth America's side of the controversy that led to the war, explaining this country's objects and methods in prosecuting the war, and exposing the enemy's misrepresentations, aggressions, and malpractices. Up to December 31, 1917, the following pamphlets had been printed:

Pamphlet	Number of copies
Red, White, and Blue Series *How the War Came to America*	
English	4,533,250
German	237,500
Bohemian	70,750
Polish	80,000

Pamphlet	Number of copies
Italian	97,800
Spanish	14,500
Swedish	30,000
National Service Handbook	148,360
Battle Line of Democracy	9,980
The President's Flag-Day Address	5,927,000
Conquest and Kultur	100,000
German War Practices, Part I	100,000

War Information Series	
War Message and Facts Behind It	1,658,250
The Nation in Arms	1,052,500
Government of Germany	1,053,000
The Great War: From Spectator to Participant	1,098,000
A War of Self-Defense	715,600
American Loyalty by American Citizens of German Descent	278,000
American Loyalty (German translation of above)	337,500
American Interest in Popular Government Abroad	489,000
Home Reading Course for Citizen Soldiers	251,000
First Session of War Congress	271,000
Total	18,533,890

This total does not take account of hundreds of thousands of copies printed and distributed by corporations and individuals at their own cost. And the number, while seemingly large, may not be considered as other than a preliminary distribution. The United States must be covered, and foreign countries have just commenced to be touched. From now on our deliveries will average 100,000 a day.

The following pamphlets are now in press:

German Treatment of Conquered Territory: Part II of *German War Practices.*

The German War Code: Contrasted with the war manuals of the United States, Great Britain, and France.

German Militarism and its German Critics: Covering the Rosa Luxemburg trial and the Zabern incident.

Why Labor Supports the War. By John R. Commons.

War Cyclopedia: A handbook for ready reference on the Great War.

The following are some of the publications which are in course of preparation:

Neutral Europe and the U-Boat.
The President's Reply to the Pope: German, Spanish, and Portuguese translations.
Thinking It Through: By Prof. Charles Beard.
Pan-Germanism and America: Spanish and Portuguese translations of section 14 of *Conquest and Kultur.*
War Organizations: A description of the powers, purposes, and controlling personnel of special war organizations.
The War for Peace: Expressions of pacifists on the issues of the war. Edited by Arthur D. Call, editor of the Advocate of Peace.
German Intrigues as a System. By S. S. McClure, E. E. Sperry, Wallace Notestein, Samuel Hopkins Adams.
Syllabus for the Study of the War: For schools, colleges, and clubs.
American and Allied Ideals.
Why America Fights Germany.

The division has had the assistance of 40 or 50 college men, all giving their services as unpaid volunteers, with the exception of about 10, whose expenses were paid during the period of a few weeks each in which they stayed in Washington. Besides these, cooperation has been given by the National Board of Historical Service, through which body literature has been distributed for study in schools and colleges.

The Historical Board, at the instance of the division, is also stimulating the study of the war by teachers, pupils, and communities by means of a series of prizes for essays by teachers; arranging the publication of some 40 articles dealing with the teaching of history in the four main fields, with special reference to the war; and preparing to give in each cantonment a series of six lectures on the historical and geographical background of the war.

Six great associations of universities and colleges, through their officers, are cooperating to distribute to their faculties and students the publications of the division. The work is taking on such large proportions that it has been placed in the special charge of Dean Olin Templin of the University of Kansas, the complete idea being to mobilize the country's great institutions of learning.

Through the Bureau of Education and the State superintendents, teachers of public schools are receiving the division's publications together with directions as to how they may be obtained for use in the classes. The Boy Scouts are being used as a distributing agency, and a plan is nearing completion that will make every rural free-delivery carrier a distributor.

Through these agencies millions of pupils and homes will be reached. Summer sessions, teachers' institutes, and similar gatherings were used in the summer of 1917 to bring before those in attendance both the division's literature and the national cause by lectures and addresses.

Other organizations assisting in effective distribution are the Department of Agriculture, the American Federation of Labor, the Department of State, the Chamber of Commerce of the United States, the Young Men's Christian Association National War Council, the American Library Association, the State defense councils, Members of both Houses of Congress, and the political parties. Besides the usual newspaper notices given when pamphlets have been released, the last two, Conquest and Kultur and German War Practices as well as the Flag Day Speech (with annotations) and the War Message (with annotations) have been published serially in many papers throughout the country. . . .

[The Division of Syndicate Features] collects and issues informative and educational war articles. Some 50 American authors and as many college presidents and professors have volunteered for the work without pay. The division has been releasing a series of weekly articles by Samuel Hopkins Adams, Ellis Parker Butler, Booth Tarkington, Meredith Nicholson, Harvey O'Higgins, Herbert Quick, John Spargo, William English Walling, Mary Roberts Rinehart, Wallace Irwin, Richard Washburn Child, Samuel Merwin, Rowland G. Usher, Ralph D. Paine, Martha Bensley Bruere, Edward Mott Wooley, John Reed Scott, Prof. John Erskine, Prof. Eugene Davenport, Crittenden Marriott, James H. Collins, James M. Beck, Virginia Frazer Boyle, and many others. Some 75 important articles have been put out in the two months that the division has been at work, and this service has been given to more than 2,000 Saturday and Sunday papers in every part of the country. . . .

The Division of Foreign Language Newspapers, working with 289 volunteer translators, follows closely every newspaper not printed in English, and serves the needs of the Department of Justice and the Post Office Department. Its more positive function, however, is concerned with the translation of pamphlets into the various languages and the preparation of editorial and news matter for publication in the foreign-language press of the United States. Particular attention is paid to the enemy-language press, and thousands of columns of patriotic matter have been printed as a result of its activities. The division also reads the papers received from Germany and Switzerland and supplies digests and verbatim translations to the Division of News and the Division of Syndicate Features. . . . [An] Official Bulletin is issued to assure the full and legal publication of all official announcements of Government heads in the course of governmental business. A free list was established by Executive order. It includes every Member of the House of Representatives and the United States Senate, the Supreme Court, the heads of all Government departments, the judiciary of the country, the mayor of every city, the governor of every State, all chambers of commerce and boards of trade, all colleges and universities, all libraries, every officer in the United States Army and every officer in the United States Navy, every post office in the United States, every daily newspaper, all large magazines, all Washington newspaper correspondents, the State councils of defense, art, literary and scientific bodies, and other bodies and committees, connected directly or indirectly with the Government of the United States. . . .

The division of Women's War Work was established November 1, 1917, to encourage the war activities of the women of America and to act as a clearing house for information concerning their service. It collects news and writes articles about the work of American women in the war and issues this matter not only by wire but in a weekly feature service to 9,000 newspapers. It has prepared and distributed 75 such articles during the month of November. It maintains contact with 32 war boards and women's organizations in Washington and assists them in their publicity. It keeps a reference department of war work for the use of women. It reports public meetings, obtains interviews, and collates news of war activities among the women here and abroad for purposes of education and direction. . . .

[The Division of Four Minute Men] . . . manages over 15,000 volunteer speakers who address moving-picture audiences during intermissions. There are State Chairmen in every State of the Union and Territorial chairmen in Alaska and Hawaii. Under the State chairmen there are more than 3,000 local chairman directing the campaigns in their districts. The office expenses of State and local organizations are paid either by State councils of defense or by subscriptions of private citizens. The State and Territorial chairmen receive Government salaries of $1 a month. There is also a national advisory Council of five members in various parts of the country who serve at a salary of $1 a month each. . . .

The subjects are assigned by the director in Washington, who mails to the local chairmen bulletins of instructions with budgets of material containing the facts necessary for the preparation of an effective speech. More than 100,000 have been distributed. Secretary of War Baker and Maj. Gen. Biddle, Acting Chief of Staff, have asked that the bulletins be sent to camp commanders as an aid to the officers in their talks to the men.

The Four Minute Men of the average town are the leading patriotic citizens of the community. They reach the "all-American" audiences of the popular movies. Their speakers are continually supervised and reported upon in order to insure their efficiency in presenting their subjects and interesting their audiences. . . .

The Division of Public Speaking was formed to coordinate the efforts of a dozen or more national speakers' bureaus by establishing a sort of central clearing house for speaking campaigns, so that duplication of effort and overlapping of territory might be avoided. . . .

The division has three chief activities. It fills requests for speakers and has approximately 300 noted volunteers on its lists. It routes throughout the country speakers of national and international reputation. And most important of all, it conducts State conferences to organize State campaigns, to determine local platform needs, and to cooperate with all State agencies in finding audiences and educating them in war-time problems. . . .

The great aim of these campaigns is to reach the citizens of the smaller communities, particularly the farmer and the laborer, so as to bring home the meaning of the war to the whole country, to educate even the most isolated communities in their patriotic duties, and to unite them in war-time work. . . .

The Division of Pictures issues permits for the taking of photographs of Government activities, decides what pictures may be published under the voluntary censorship, and distributes official photographs, drawings, pictorial records, motion pictures, War and Navy Department films and war films taken under the jurisdiction of foreign governments.

The division has arranged with representatives of the French Government for the exclusive issue of the French official war pictures. A like arrangement for the British official war photographs is now being made.

The division is aiding the distribution of still pictures by making them available to post-card manufacturers, calendar manufacturers, and art-goods manufacturers, and by selling them to schools, colleges, societies, and individuals at a nominal price. Sets of stereopticon slides are being prepared for the use of ministers, patriotic societies, lecturers, etc., and these sets will be put out with but a small charge to cover cost and breakages.

The distribution of official motion pictures is made by the American Red Cross to whom the profits accrue.

The established motion-picture weeklies, however, are entitled to buy a certain amount of official film each week. The photographic syndicate industry has formed a board of representatives to deal with the Division of Pictures. A board of editors of the art sections of the New York papers has been formed for the same purpose. The division has also formed a committee of editors of the motion-picture weeklies, so that this great machinery of publicity is virtually at the committee's call.

It is a tribute to the patriotism of the photographic and motion-picture industries that this division, without a law of any kind behind it, enforces a censorship more effective than any in force in any other belligerent country. *No request has ever been ignored. . . .*

[The Division of Films] . . . was organized to make and distribute moving pictures to inform the American people about the purposes and progress of the Government's war activities. At first, the division had its own staff of operators to take its photographs. Later arrangements were made to have this work done by the photographic division of the Army Signal Corps.

Distribution is carried on through the councils of defense in the various States; wherever the councils of defense are unable to take on the extra work of the distribution it is done by various patriotic committees or societies in the different communities. The films are shown at public meetings of all sorts to half a million people a week.

There are two kinds of service: First, the weekly service that distributes one new subject a week of educational or propaganda value; second, the feature service, whose pictures, comprising an evening's entertainment, are wholly of a propagandist character. . . .

Dr. George Pierce Baker is in charge of the scenario department. It is located at Harvard University, which institution has turned over all its facilities and has given Dr. Baker leave of absence on pay. Radcliffe College, with which institution Dr. Baker is also associated, has extended a similar courtesy to the division. . . .

[The Committee] has mobilized the artists of the Nation for war service, and supplies every department of Government with posters, window cards, car cards, placards, and every other form of art appeal. These free gifts of famous men and women run high into the thousands already. . . .

The Division of Advertising has just been formed to give the various departments of the Government an organized advertising service made up of the volunteer help of all the national advertising agencies in the country. Among the organizations already enrolled for patriotic service under the direction of the division are the Associated Advertising Clubs of the World, the Association of National Advertisers, the Associated Business Papers, the Periodical Publishers' Association, the National Advertising Advisory Board, the American Association of Advertising Agencies, the Agricultural Publishers' Association, the Bureau of of Advertising of the American Newspaper Publishers' Association, and several leaders in the field of poster, paint, and car-card advertising. These organizations now form a single patriotic organization for the purpose of rendering advertising service to the Government in all departments of its war work. . . .

It has never been the idea that all effort should be centered in Washington, but rather has the committee attempted to stimulate group activity and independent energy. Many organizations have been brought into being for certain specific purposes, and while possessed of absolute independence in every respect, nevertheless maintain a constant and intimate contact with the committee. Among these may be mentioned such bodies as the American Alliance of Labor and Democracy, the League for National Unity, the Friends of German Democracy, and various smaller organizations bearing upon specific problems connected with our foreign population. The plan is being extended rapidly, and it is only a matter of weeks before every race group in the United States will have its own war campaign organization, each with its own literature, news service, and speakers, to drive home the great truths of Americanism.

7

Another Job for the Supersalesman

EMILY NEWELL BLAIR

During the last national campaign I received a telegram urging me to go posthaste to a certain town to join a United States Senator and do a week's campaign tour with him, preceding him on each program with a thirty-minute talk to the women. "Listen now," as campaign orators say, to the results of that tour: During five days the Senator and I had traveled 885 miles each, which, at three and six tenths cents a mile, was an expenditure of $63.72. Our other expenses had amounted to $50 more. Entertainment provided by local committees must have cost them $130. We had given up five days each, to the value, at our regular earning rate, of at least $520, the total cost of the trip being $763.72. We had worn out our patience and our bodies. And we had spoken to 1,105 people, most of whom were already committed to our candidates and cause. It is possible—but not probable—that fifty of our listeners changed their votes. If so, these votes cost approxi-

From *The Independent*, 120 (March 10, 1928), pp. 222-224.

mately $15.27 each. At that rate a majority of 50,000 would cost $763,500, and a bare majority of 5,000 would be $76,350.

What would a company executive say to a sales manager who sent a high-priced speaker to describe his product to less than 1,200 people at a cost of $15.27 for each possible buyer? And, after all, a political campaign is just that—a selling campaign. It is a drive for votes just as an Ivory Soap advertising campaign is a drive for sales. What is amazing is that the very men who make their millions out of cleverly devised drives for soap and bonds and cars will turn right around and give large contributions to be expended for vote-getting in an utterly inefficient and antiquated fashion.

As a matter of fact, the present styles in campaigning were designed in the days of Andrew Jackson, and very little change has been made since in the pattern. The change is in its availability. It is as little in line with the present mode in publicity as a calash bonnet with the popular *cloche*. Take political meetings, for instance. They were designed when people were interested in politics; when people believed that their future, their everything, depended on them, and they cared for them as people do care who believe this. So a campaign manager's demand for his product was already created; all he had to do was to sell his particular article. Today, the campaign manager must first sell politics, interest the public in his product, create a desire in the men and women of the electorate to vote.

In those days, the political meeting had little competition when it came to entertainment. It beat a revival or an evening at the corner grocery. The audience did not give up an evening with John McCormack or Mary Garden or Will Rogers over the radio or even an illustrated weekly in order to attend. They did not have to pass a picture show on the way to the meeting. And they liked talk. It was their form of recreation. Books were scarce, talk abundant; their ears were in practice. And people respond to what they are accustomed to. Today the daily reading of books, periodicals, library books, and the attendance on picture shows have made our eyes the route to our brains.

There was another reason why meetings were once good psychology: they served to increase enthusiasm. When listeners were already partisan, it was easy for a speaker to rouse their emotion. A national election in those far-off days was what a national baseball series is today. Everyone took a side, bet money on it, and cared about the result. Everyone had opinions, nay, even convictions, and was ready to do violence to his neighbor for them. A partisan came gladly to a meeting where he would hear his opinions reiterated and those of his opponents lambasted. A public debate was as thrilling as bear baiting or a chicken fight. Today it is only the old codger on the front row with his hand to his ear who roars out, "Hurray!"

People are satiated with speeches and crowds. The war sounded the death knell of the public meeting as an enthusiasm stirrer. Even when our patriotism was at white heat, we had to limit our speeches to four minutes and depend on the readymade meeting. And what salesman today strives to sell goods by the ear route? He has posters and exhibits and electric signs and full-page advertisements and moving-picture slides. If, in addition, he had to create his demand, would he send a speaker across the country to talk about it? If he did he would have him descend from an airplane and turn on a moving-picture machine. Thus, at least, curiosity would be aroused in the men and women he was seeking to impress, and the important breaking down of "sales resistance" on the part of the indifferent voter would have been accomplished.

If I would scrap the political meeting as not satisfying present trade conditions what, then, would I put in its place? For something must be substituted. First of all, I would discard the old-type political manager and engage a high-salaried, successful sales manager to "sell" my candidate. The first thing such a sales manager would do would be to survey his territory and decide where he had the best chance of selling his product. He would find out the habits of his desired customers so as to discover how he might most easily and quickly bring his candidate and cause to their notice. He would study their tastes so that he might choose how best to present his product to their favor. He would treat his problem just as a problem in the marketing of tooth paste would be handled.

Nor would he do this by office theorizing. He would send experts or go himself over this territory to learn these things. He would then plan his campaign: no guessing about it, no sending speakers hither and yon with no idea of how much he would get for a dollar. He would carefully weigh one method of presenting a candidate against another, deciding for the method which would reach the most voters per dollar of expense. He would, for instance, realize that the expense of reaching large numbers in congested cities was less per vote than reaching them in small towns, so he would plan to focus the campaign in that city which normally returned a majority for his party. He would then concentrate on how to put his candidate before them in the best guise. He would, of course, arrange for newspaper advertising. By this, I do not mean a small announcement on the last Sunday before the election. Early in the campaign he would buy space and fill it daily or weekly. Under his candidate's picture would appear a few short, terse, telling statements, either clever, witty, or epigrammatic. If the candidate could not write them, he would buy them from some not-yet-arrived Will Rogers or some expert on tooth-paste advertisement writing. If Alice Roosevelt and Mrs. Borah and Queen Marie can sell a face cream, an actor, a baseball player, a bank president ought to sell a Senator, and even an opera singer or a movie star might help. He might raise an electric sign—not of a name, but of an overflowing beer mug or a hand across the sea or a full dinner pail or an empty sugar bowl. He might hang his posters, not showing names and carrying long statements, but those drawn by a Gibson or a Flagg showing mountains of taxes being excavated by "our candidate" in the guise of Economy or a manufacturer heaping taxes upon the mountain called Tariff.

He might produce a movie film built around a real plot and at least one star, setting his candidate in the midst of some drawing-room of Wild West scene, inserting a fight and a dance (not by the candidate), offering it with a vaudeville to the local committee with a request that they buy out the house and make it pay for itself. It would cost no more money than they now spend for the opera house and the band when the speaker comes to town and assuredly they would get more for their money.

Of course, he would not neglect free advertising. In addition to the paid advertising he would "make" news, do stunts that the newspapers would have to report. Nor need the stunts necessarily be undignified. What is a White House breakfast for the actors but a stunt, a pilgrimage of women to a front porch to hear a statement on bills of interest to women, a demonstration of Presidential dexterity with a rake, or a back-platform tour? Some of them would border on the ridiculous. It might tax the campaign manager's ingenuity to make the front page with dignity, but an expert could do it.

Oh, yes, there are ways to get candidates and causes into the newspapers, and not only get them in but get them read. And such accounts are not read by the city voter only. Every stunt reported in the city newspapers advertises cause and candidate to its country readers, also. But the good sales manager will not stop with city stunts. He will stimulate local stunts to be reported in local papers. Nor will he need to insist on them: the same spirit of imitation that carries the newest shade in hosiery to the remotest village, that makes the same book a best seller in every city and town, that makes the D.A.R. and the Rotary Club national in scope and gives a fall festival to every hamlet will lead the towns to initiate a stunt of their own and report it in their own papers.

Speakers? Oh, yes, this campaign manager will have speakers. But he will have them documented. And he will know just where a certain kind of speaker must go for a certain reason. He will have his "give-'em-hell" speakers for enthusiasm, his distinguished Senators for the places where the Associated Press can report them. He will have his women speakers to talk to groups of women as only women can talk to each other. He will have few meetings because he will know that a public meeting is the most difficult thing to work up. And he will insist that those he does permit be worked up, planned for, arranged, planted.

Some day a genius of a salesman may devise a new kind of public meeting. He may be able to start debating teams between rural towns or speaking Marathons or oratorical tournaments, but to do it he will need to employ some appeal to human nature as clever and irresistible as was the Rotarians' use of exclusiveness or the lodges' seductive glamour of secrecy and exotic finery.

In the meantime, he may depend on ready-made meetings where he can find them or on the old-fashioned street-corner meeting which is still so successful in New York City. He may even return to the day of the patent-medicine man with an automobile instead of a wagon, with a radio or Victrola instead of a banjo, and a candidate instead of a medicine.

Long ere this many a reader has exclaimed that the cost of such campaigning would make it prohibitive. Yet I wonder if many soap manufacturers, tooth-paste makers, or automobile factories make an appropriation for their annual advertising of more than $4,270,469.01, the expenditures reported for the Presidential campaign of 1924 by the Republican National Committee. I wonder if a great many do not spend less than the $903,908.21 reported by the Democratic National Committee for the same campaign. If there were added to these amounts the sums raised and expended by forty-eight State committees and 3,000 county committees, by organizations of supporters, such as manufacturers' associations and labor groups and committees of independent voters, by individual workers paying their own expenses, by candidates and their families and friends, would not this goodly total, if appropriated and expended with discrimination and thrift and an eye to results, finance the most indefatigable and gifted sales manager?

Think of the money now wasted that never brings in any return. Take the one item of literature. Hundreds of thousands of dollars are spent for it. Hours are spent in preparing it. Its distribution must be left to local people, and the day after the campaign usually finds it stored in some lawyer's office closet. But ever since the day of the pamphlet it has been "customary" to issue campaign literature, and political customs must be observed whether they accomplish anything or not. So each campaign someone in headquarters "gets an idea" and the idea is printed and distributed. The begetter of the idea may be a sophisticated college professor, though it is designed for the bootblack's union. There is no committee of expert publicists to pass upon it, no business manager to check up on the number of votes it buys.

If campaign managers would only realize that the readers at whom they aim have access to the daily press and the five-cent magazines, that their campaign literature comes in competition with the output of the highest paid and most popular word slingers in the English language! Is it likely that the work of some penny-a-liner out of a job will meet this competition?

Some campaign literature is, of course, necessary—sales letters from the manager to his local workers, confidential information as to the method and tactics, and a data book which the local salesmen should crib. For the rest, there are always the advertising pages, any one of which is well worth $2,000 worth of literature. Advertisers are not limited to any one form of advertisement display. A sales manager could buy from a popular and clever writer the same kind of article contained in the body of the magazine and run it on the advertising pages. If it were as good and convincing as those articles it would have as many readers and be as effective. As many people read Will Rogers in a tobacco advertisement as on a front page. Cost? Of course. It would cost anywhere from $5,000 to $10,000, according to the circulation of the magazine and the reputation of the writer. But wouldn't five of these articles win as many votes as $50,000 worth of pamphlets? Of course the articles would need to be related to a central scheme, would need to fit in with a policy. But a sales manager has a policy. He has an objective, and his ability to frame a publicity policy that shall lead to that objective is the measure of his success.

Does campaigning by advertising seem ridiculous? Observe how the associations newly designed and organized to affect public opinion get results. Do they go back to the outgrown system of public meetings? How does the chamber of commerce go to work? How the Associated Industries? How the labor unions? How, even, the new parties? Do they follow a pattern cut by the politicians of 1840 to meet voters of that day? Why, then, should the parties of today hang on to those old methods as the English do to the beefeaters of the Tower of London? Will they always do so or will we some day have another Andrew Jackson daring enough and forceful enough to adopt current publicity methods to win a current campaign? Campaigning by advertising after all is merely that: employing present-day methods of reaching and influencing people, as the politicians of 1840 applied the current methods of influencing people of that day.

8

Putting Politics on the Market
EDWARD L. BERNAYS

Politics was the first big business in America. Therefore, there is a good deal of irony in the fact that business has learned everything politics has had to teach it, but politics has failed to learn very much from business methods in mass distribution of ideas and products. Emily Newell Blair's excellent article, "Another Job for the Supersalesman," in *The Independent* for March 10 will undoubtedly give much food for thought to the many political leaders who are preparing for the forthcoming political campaigns. Mrs. Blair spoke of the wasteful and archaic methods still in vogue in political campaigning. It is just as incomprehensible to me as to Mrs. Blair that astute politicians do not make use of the elaborate and successful business methods that industry has built up to achieve its own ends. Politicians who know political strategy and who can develop campaign issues, who can devise strong planks for platforms and envisage broad policies cannot be given the responsibility of selling ideas to a public of more than 100,000,000.

The politician understands the public. He knows what the public wants and what the public will accept. But the politician is not necessarily a general sales manager, a public relations counsel, or a man who knows how to secure a mass distribution of ideas. His wasteful methods of presentation are evidence of the extent to which this inefficiency is carried.

The successful business man today apes the politician. He has adopted the glitter and the ballyhoo of the campaign. He has set up all the side shows. He has annual dinners that are a compendium of speeches, flags, bombast, stateliness, pseudodemocracy slightly tinged with paternalism. On occasion he doles out honors to employees, much as the republic of classic times rewarded its worthy citizens. But these are merely the side shows, the drums of big business, by which it stimulates an image of public service, and of honorary service. This is but one of the methods by which business stimulates loyal enthusiasms on the part of directors, workers, stockholders, and the consumer public. It is one of the methods by which big business performs its function of making and selling products to the public. The real work and campaign of business consists of intensive study of the public, the

From *The Independent*, 120 (May 19, 1928), pp. 470-472.

manufacture of products based on this study, and exhaustive use of every means of reaching the public.

The political campaign today is all side shows, all honors, all bombast, glitter, and speeches. These are for the most part unrelated to the main business of studying the public scientifically, of supplying the public with party, candidate, platform, and performance, and selling the public these ideas and products. Obviously, it is not true that every political leader is incapable of combining every feature of leadership. In business there are certain brilliant industrial leaders who are financiers, factory directors, engineers, and sales managers, and public relations counsel all rolled into one.

Big business is conducted on the principle that it must prepare its policies carefully and that, in selling an idea to the large buying public of America, it must proceed according to broad plans. The political strategist must do likewise. The entire campaign should be worked out according to broad basic plans. Platforms, planks, pledges budgets, activities, and personalities must be as carefully studied, apportioned, and used as they are when a business desires to get what it wants from the public. The first step in a political campaign is to determine on the objectives, and to express them exceedingly well in the current form—that is, as a platform. In devising the platform the leader should be sure that it is an honest platform. Campaign pledges and promises should not be lightly considered by the public, and they ought to carry something of the guarantee principle and money-back policy that an honorable business institution carries with the sale of its goods.

To aid in the preparation of the platform there should be made as scientifically as possible an analysis of the public and of the needs of the public, in order to determine just what the platform should contain. A survey of public desires, demands, and needs would come to the aid of the political strategist whose business it is to make a proposed plan of the activities of the party and its elected officials during their terms of office. A business that wants to sell a product to the public surveys and analyzes its market before it takes a single step either to make or to sell the product. If one section of the community is absolutely sold to the idea of this product, no money is wasted in reselling it. If, on the other hand, another section of the public is irrevocably committed to another product, no money is wasted on a lost cause. Very often the analysis is the cause of basic changes and improvements in the product itself, as well as an index of how it is to be presented. So carefully is this analysis of markets and sales made that when a company makes out its sales budget for the year it subdivides the circulation of the various magazines and newspapers it uses and calculates with a fair degree of accuracy how many times a section of that population is subjected to the appeal of the company.

The expenses of a political campaign should be budgeted. A large business today knows exactly how much money it is going to spend on advertising and sales promotion during the next year or period of years. It knows that a certain percentage of its gross receipts will be given over to advertising, a certain percentage to circularization and sales promotion—such as house organs and dealer aids—and a certain percentage to the supervisors and special salesmen who travel around the country to infuse extra stimulus in the local sales campaigns. So it should be with a political campaign.

The first question which should be decided is the amount of money to be raised for the campaign. This decision can be reached by a careful analysis of campaign costs. There is enough precedent in business procedure to enable experts to work this out accurately. Then the second question of importance is the manner in which money should be raised. It is obvious that politics would gain much in prestige if the money-raising campaign were conducted candidly and publicly, just as the war campaign funds were raised. Charity drives might be made excellent models for political-fund drives. The elimination of the "little-black-bag" element in politics would raise the entire prestige of politics in America, and the public interest would be infinitely greater if the actual participation occurred earlier and more constructively in the campaign. The third step is to decide how the money is to be spent. This should be done according to the most careful and exact budgeting, wherein every step in the campaign is given its proportionate importance, and the funds allotted accordingly. Advertising in newspapers and periodicals, by posters and street banners, the exploitation of personalities in motion pictures, in speeches, lectures, and meetings, and spectacular events, and all forms of propaganda should be considered proportionately according to the budget and always should be coordinated with the whole plan. Certain expenditures may be warranted if they represent a small proportion of the budget and may be totally unwarranted if they make up too large a proportion.

In the same way the emotions by which the public is appealed to may be made part of the broad plan of the campaign. Unrelated emotions become maudlin and sentimental too easily, are often costly, and too often waste effort because the idea is not part of the conscious and coherent whole. Big business has realized that it must touch as many and as basic emotions as possible. The politician, however, has exploited the emotions swayed by words almost exclusively. This tendency no longer convinces.

To appeal to the emotions of the public in a political campaign is sound; in fact, it is an indispensable part of the campaign. But the emotional content must, first, coincide in every way with the broad basic plans of the campaign and all its minor details; second, it must be adapted to the many groups of the public at which it is to be aimed; and third, it must conform to the media of the distribution of ideas. The emotions that have heretofore been used in political campaigning hark back for the most part to the Patrick Henry era. The emotions of oratory have been worn down through long years of overuse. Parades, mass meetings, and the like are successful when the public has a frenzied emotional interest in the event to start with. The candidate who holds babies on his lap while he has his photograph taken is doing a wise thing emotionally, if this act epitomizes a plank in his platform. The public activities of a business or industry are synchronized with their general platforms of policies. But the haphazard staging of emotional events without regard to their value as part of the whole campaign is wasted effort. In the same way it would be wasted effort for the vendor of hockey skates to advertise a picture of a church surrounded by spring foliage. It is true that the church appeals to our religious impulses and that everybody loves the spring, but these impulses do not help to prove the value of hockey skates.

Another curious anachronism in politics today is the emphasis that has been placed on personality. An entire party, a platform, an international policy are sold to the public, or are not sold, on the basis of an intangible "personality." A charming candidate is considered the alchemy that alone can transmute a prosy platform into the gold of votes. The party and its aims are actually far more important than the personality—a mystic product, it would seem—of the candidate. Ideally the candidate will carry out the party's program adequately, and therefore the program is the product which should be emphasized in the campaign plan. Even Henry Ford, most picturesque personality in American business today, is known through his product and not his product through him.

To be sure, there must be a certain amount of personality salesmanship in a political campaign at the present day, since that is a form of competitive marketing that no party can afford to forego. But that too must be subjected to the most rigid scrutiny to determine the effectiveness of every move in the light of the entire program. The politician today who relies heavily on his personal friendships in order to get his message across is relying on a very uncertain weapon. The day of back-slapping and first-name politics is gone. And this because there are so many people in the country that one must use other means for getting one's personality across and for selling the idea that the politician is seeking to help, befriend, or paternalize the public. One can't know a hundred million people personally. One can know several thousand, but that takes a long time and is a difficult procedure. Political friendship today must be syndicated just as the comic strip and the motion picture are syndicated. Can anyone imagine King C. Gillete going on the stump for safety-razor blades, relying solely on his oratorical ability to sell a million packages a year?

It is essential for the campaign manager to educate emotions in terms of groups. The public is not made up merely of Democrats and Republicans. People today are largely uninterested in politics as such, and their interest in the issues of the campaign must be secured by coordinating these with other interests. The public is made up of overlapping groups—economic, social, religious, educational, cultural, racial, collegiate, local, sports, and hundreds of others. The importance of the group formation of society was recognized during the war when the official interest in each group and the adherence of the members of the group were enlisted to carry on the thousands of activities that were necessary to the war.

When President Coolidge invited an actor to breakfast, he did so because he realized that not only were actors a group, but that audiences—the large group of people who like amusements, who like people who amuse them, and who like people who can be amused—ought to be aligned with him.

Publishers know how to appeal to the groups, as is shown in the departmentalizing of the average daily newspaper. Realizing that the public is, in fact, many publics, and that the vote of the public means circulation and advertising profits, the newspapers appeal on one page to the sporting public, on another to the musical public, on others to the financial, to the trade, to the political, to the internationally minded, to the industrial publics. The political campaign having defined its broad objects and its basic plans, having defined the group appeal which it must use and the groups which it must reach, must now define the various channels through which it can appeal to the public as a whole.

The mediums through which a political campaign may be brought home to the public are numerous and fairly well defined. Events and activities must be created in order to put ideas into circulation through channels which are as varied as the means of human communication. Every object which presents pictures or words which the public can see, everything that presents intelligible sounds, can be utilized in one way or another. At present, the political campaign relies heavily on the banquet hall, the mass meeting, the lecture platform, and the stump generally as a means for furthering its ideas. But this localization of a message is only a small part of what may actually be done. Actually there are infinitely more varied events that can be created to dramatize the campaign and to make people talk of it with one another. Exhibitions, contests, institutes of politics, the coopera- tion of educational institutions, the dramatic cooperation of many groups which hitherto have not been drawn into active politics, and many others may be made the vehicle for presenting ideas to the public.

But whatever is done must be synchronized accurately with all other forms of appeal to the public. Many events can be planned, events which must dramatize the ideas for which the candidate or the party or the plat- form stands. Activities must be coordinated, the platform itself must be so presented that every plank of it may be as understandable, as graphic, as concise as the slogan of a soap manufacturer or a motor company. News reaches the public visually—through printed words in books, magazines, letters, posters, circulars, banners, and newspapers, and through photo- graphs and motion pictures; as well as through the ear—in lectures, speeches, band music, campaign songs, and by radio. All these means must be em- ployed by the political party if its campaign is to succeed. One method of appeal is merely one method of appeal, and in this age wherein a thousand movements and ideas are competing for public attention, all the available eggs must not be risked in a single basket. Diversified appeal is an essential.

Politics needs to acquire the technique of big business to do away with inefficiency in campaigning. When this is achieved, it is possible that poli- tical supply and demand can be brought closer together. Scientific methods and sales charts will supersede the guesses and the betting that form so large a part of the campaigning today. Charts and diagrams with neat little pins stuck in them, while they are not necessarily aesthetic in themselves, will take the place of mud-bespattered campaign photographs. Epithets will not be heard over the roar of facts, and the honorable citizen can step into the political arena without fearing the abuse or the exaggerated praise which are equally unsavory to a temperate and principled man.

9

Freedom and the Control of Men
B. F. SKINNER

The second half of the twentieth century may be remembered for its solution of a curious problem. Although Western democracy created the conditions responsible for the rise of modern science, it is now evident that it may never fully profit from that achievement. The so-called "democratic philosophy" of human behavior to which it also gave rise is increasingly in conflict with the application of the methods of science to human affairs. Unless this conflict is somehow resolved, the ultimate goals of democracy may be long deferred.

I

Just as biographers and critics look for external influences to account for the traits and achievements of the men they study, so science ultimately explains behavior in terms of "causes" or conditions which lie beyond the individual himself. As more and more causal relations are demonstrated, a practical corollary becomes difficult to resist: it should be possible to *produce* behavior according to plan simply by arranging the proper conditions. Now, among the specifications which might reasonably be submitted to a behavioral technology are these: Let men be happy, informed, skillful, well-behaved and productive.

This immediate practical implication of a science of behavior has a familiar ring, for it recalls the doctrine of human perfectibility of eighteenth- and nineteenth-century humanism. A science of man shares the optimism of that philosophy and supplies striking support for the working faith that men can build a better world and, through it, better men. The support comes just in time, for there has been little optimism of late among those who speak from the traditional point of view. Democracy has become "realistic," and it is only with some embarrassment that one admits today to perfectionistic or utopian thinking.

The earlier temper is worth considering, however. History records many foolish and unworkable schemes for human betterment, but almost all the great changes in our culture which we now regard as worthwhile can be traced to perfectionistic philosophies. Governmental, religious, educational,

---

Selected passages from *American Scholar*, 25 (Winter, 1955-1956).

economic and social reforms follow a common pattern. Someone believes that a change in a cultural practice—for example, in the roles of evidence in a court of law, in the characterization of man's relation to God, in the way children are taught to read and write, in permitted rates of interest, or in minimal housing standards—will improve the condition of men: by promoting justice, permitting men to seek salvation more effectively, increasing the literacy of a people, checking an inflationary trend, or improving public health and family relations, respectively. The underlying hypothesis is always the same: that a different physical or cultural environment will make a different and better man.

The scientific study of behavior not only justifies the general pattern of such proposals; it promises new and better hypotheses. The earliest cultural practices must have originated in sheer accidents. Those which strengthened the group survived with the group in a sort of natural selection. As soon as men began to propose and carry out changes in practice for the sake of possible consequences, the evolutionary process must have accelerated. The simple practice of making changes must have had survival value. A further acceleration is now to be expected. As laws of behavior are more precisely stated, the changes in the environment required to bring about a given effect may be more clearly specified. Conditions which have been neglected because their effects were slight or unlooked for may be shown to be relevant. New conditions may actually be created, as in the discovery and synthesis of drugs which affect behavior.

This is no time, then, to abandon notions of progress, improvement or, indeed, human perfectibility. The simple fact is that man is able, and now as never before, to lift himself by his own bootstraps. In achieving control of the world of which he is a part, he may learn at last to control himself.

II

Timeworn objections to the planned improvement of cultural practices are already losing much of their force. Marcus Aurelius was probably right in advising his readers to be content with a haphazard amelioration of mankind. "Never hope to realize Plato's republic," he sighed, ". . . for who can change the opinions of men? And without a change of sentiments what can you make but reluctant slaves and hypocrites?" He was thinking, no doubt, of contemporary patterns of control based upon punishment or the threat of punishment which, as he correctly observed, breed only reluctant slaves of those who submit and hypocrites of those who discover modes of evasion. But we need not share his pessimism, for the opinions of men can be changed. The techniques of indoctrination which were being devised by the early Christian Church at the very time Marcus Aurelius was writing are relevant, as are some of the techniques of psychotherapy and of advertising and public relations. Other methods suggested by recent scientific analyses leave little doubt of the matter.

The study of human behavior also answers the cynical complaint that there is a plain "cussedness" in man which will always thwart efforts to improve him. We are often told that men do not want to be changed, even for the better. Try to help them, and they will outwit you and remain happily wretched. . . . But that such perversity is a fundamental reaction of the human organism to controlling conditions is sheer nonsense.

So is the objection that we have no way of knowing what changes to make even though we have the necessary techniques. That is one of the great hoaxes of the century—a sort of booby trap left behind in the retreat before the advancing front of science. . . .

Designing a new cultural pattern is in many ways like designing an experiment. In drawing up a new constitution, outlining a new educational program, modifying a religious doctrine, or setting up a new fiscal policy, many statements must be quite tentative. We cannot be sure that the practices we specify will have the consequences we predict, or that the consequences will reward our efforts. This is in the nature of such proposals. They are not value judgments—they are guesses. To confuse and delay the improvement of cultural practices by quibbling about the word *improve* is itself not a useful practice. Let us agree, to start with, that health is better than illness, wisdom better than ignorance, love better than hate, and productive energy better than neurotic sloth.

Another familiar objection is the "political problem." Though we know what changes to make and how to make them, we still need to control certain relevant conditions, but these have long since fallen into the hands of selfish men who are not going to relinquish them for such purposes. Possibly we shall be permitted to develop areas which at the moment seem unimportant, but at the first signs of success the strong men will move in. This, it is said, has happened to Christianity, democracy and communism. There will always be men who are fundamentally selfish and evil, and in the long run innocent goodness cannot have its way. The only evidence here is historical, and it may be misleading. Because of the way in which physical science developed, history could until very recently have "proved" that the unleashing of the energy of the atom was quite unlikely, if not impossible. Similarly, because of the order in which processes in human behavior have become available for purposes of control, history may seem to prove that power will probably be appropriated for selfish purposes. The first techniques to be discovered fell almost always to strong, selfish men. History led Lord Acton to believe that power corrupts, but he had probably never encountered absolute power, certainly not in all its forms, and had no way of predicting its effect.

An optimistic historian could defend a different conclusion. The principle that if there are not enough men of good will in the world the first step is to create more seems to be gaining recognition. The Marshall Plan (as originally conceived), Point Four, the offer of atomic materials to power-starved countries—these may or may not be wholly new in the history of international relations, but they suggest an increasing awareness of the power of governmental good will. They are proposals to make certain changes in the environments of men for the sake of consequences which should be rewarding for all concerned. They do not exemplify a disin-terested generosity, but an interest which is the interest of everyone. We have not yet seen Plato's philosopher-king, and may not want to, but the gap between real and utopian government is closing.

III

But we are not yet in the clear, for a new and unexpected obstacle has arisen. With a world of their own making almost within reach, men of good will have been seized with distaste for their achievement. They have uneasily rejected opportunities to apply the techniques and findings of science in the service of men, and as the import of effective cultural design has come to be understood, many of them have voiced an outright refusal to have any part in it. Science has been challenged before when it has encroached upon institutions already engaged in the control of human behavior; but what are we to make of benevolent men, with no special interests of their own to defend, who nevertheless turn against the very means of reaching long-dreamed-of goals?

What is being rejected, of course, is the scientific conception of man and his place in nature. So long as the findings and methods of science are applied to human affairs only in a sort of remedial patchwork, we may continue to hold any view of human nature we like. But as the use of science increases, we are forced to accept the theoretical structure with which science represents its facts. The difficulty is that this structure is clearly at odds with the traditional democratic conception of man. Every discovery of an event which has a part in shaping a man's behavior seems to leave so much the less to be credited to the man himself; and as such explanations become more and more comprehensive, the contribution which may be claimed by the individual himself appears to approach zero. Man's vaunted creative powers, his original accomplishments in art, science and morals, his capacity to choose and our right to hold him responsible for the consequences of his choice—none of these is conspicuous in this new self-portrait. Man, we once believed, was free to express himself in art, music and literature, to inquire into nature, to seek salvation in his own way. He could initiate action and make spontaneous and capricious changes of course. Under the most extreme duress some sort of choice remained to him. He could resist any effort to control him, though it might cost him his life. But science insists that action is initiated by forces impinging upon the individual, and that caprice is only another name for behavior for which we have not yet found a cause.

In attempting to reconcile these views it is important to note that the traditional democratic conception was not designed as a description in the scientific sense but as a philosophy to be used in setting up and maintaining a governmental process. It arose under historical circumstances and served political purposes apart from which it cannot be properly understood. In rallying men against tyranny it was necessary that the individual be strengthened, that he be taught that he had rights and could govern himself. To give the common man a new conception of his worth, his dignity, and his power to save himself, both here and hereafter, was often the only resource of the revolutionist. When democratic principles were put into practice, the same doctrines were used as a working formula. This is exemplified by the notion of personal responsibility in Anglo-American law. All governments make certain forms of punishment contingent upon certain kinds of acts. In democratic countries these contingencies are expressed by the notion of responsible choice. But the notion may have no meaning under governmental practices formulated in other ways and would certainly have no place in systems which did not use punishment.

The democratic philosophy of human nature is determined by certain political exigencies and techniques, not by the goals of democracy. But exigencies and techniques change; and a conception which is not supported for its accuracy as a likeness—is not, indeed, rooted in fact at all—may be expected to change too. No matter how effective we judge current democratic practices to be, how highly we value them or how long we expect them to survive, they are almost certainly not the *final* form of government. The philosophy of human nature which has been useful in implementing them is also almost certainly not the last word. The ultimate achievement of democracy may be long deferred unless we emphasize the real aims rather than the verbal devices of democratic thinking. A philosophy which has been appropriate to one set of political exigencies will defeat its purpose if, under other circumstances, it prevents us from applying to human affairs the science of man which probably nothing but democracy itself could have produced.

IV

Perhaps the most crucial part of our democratic philosophy to be reconsidered is our attitude toward freedom—or its reciprocal, the control of human behavior. We do not oppose all forms of control because it is "human nature" to do so. The reaction is not characteristic of all men under all conditions of life. It is an attitude which has been carefully engineered, in large part by what we call the "literature" of democracy. With respect to some methods of control (for example, the threat of force), very little engineering is needed, for the techniques or their immediate consequences are objectionable. Society has suppressed these methods by branding them "wrong," "illegal" or "sinful." But to encourage these attitudes toward objectionable forms of control, it has been necessary to disguise the real nature of certain indispensable techniques, the commonest examples of which are education, moral discourse, and persuasion. The actual procedures appear harmless enough. They consist of supplying information, presenting opportunities for action, pointing out logical relationships, appealing to reason or "enlightened understanding," and so on. Through a masterful piece of misrepresentation, the illusion is fostered that these procedures do not involve the control of behavior; at most, they are simply ways of "getting someone to change his mind." But analysis not only reveals the presence of well-defined behavioral processes, it demonstrates a kind of control no less inexorable, though in some ways more acceptable, than the bully's threat of force.

Let us suppose that someone in whom we are interested is acting unwisely—he is careless in the way he deals with his friends, he drives too fast, or he holds his golf club the wrong way. We could probably help him by issuing a series of commands: don't nag, don't drive over sixty, don't hold your club that way. Much less objectionable would be "an appeal to reason." We could show him how people are affected by his treatment of them, how accident rates rise sharply at higher speeds, how a particular grip on the club alters the way the ball is struck and corrects a slice. In doing so we resort to verbal mediating devices which emphasize and support certain "contingencies of reinforcement"—that is, certain relations between behavior and its consequences—which strengthen the behavior we wish to set up. The same consequences would possibly set up the behavior without our help, and they eventually take control no matter which form of help we give. The appeal to reason has certain advantages over the authoritative command. A threat of punishment, no matter how subtle, generates emotional reactions and tendencies to escape or revolt. Perhaps the controllee merely "feels resentment" at being made to act in a given way, but even that is to be avoided. When we "appeal to reason," he "feels freer to do as he pleases." The fact is that we have exerted *less* control than in using a threat; since other conditions may contribute to the result, the effect may be delayed or, possibly in a given instance, lacking. But if we have worked a change in his behavior at all, it is because we have altered relevant environmental conditions, and the processes we have set in motion are just as real and just as inexorable, if not as comprehensive, as in the most authoritative coercion.

"Arranging an opportunity for action" is another example of disguised control. The power of the negative form has already been exposed in the analysis of censorship. Restriction of opportunity is recognized as far from harmless. As Ralph Barton Perry said in an article which appeared in the Spring, 1953, *Pacific Spectator,* "Whoever determines what alternatives shall be made known to man controls what that man shall choose *from.* He is deprived of freedom in proportion as he is denied access to *any* ideas, or is confined to any range of ideas short of the totality of relevant possibilities." But there is a positive side as well. When we present a relevant state of affairs, we increase the likelihood that a given form of behavior will be emitted. To the extent that the probability of action has changed, we have made a definite contribution. The teacher of history controls a student's behavior (or, if the reader prefers, "deprives him of freedom") just as much in *presenting* historical facts as in suppressing them. Other conditions will no doubt affect the student, but the contribution made to his behavior by the presentation of material is fixed and, within its range, irresistible.

The methods of education, moral discourse, and persuasion are acceptable not because they recognize the freedom of the individual or his right to dissent, but because they make only *partial* contributions to the control of his behavior. The freedom they recognize is freedom from a more coercive form of control. The dissent which they tolerate is the possible effect of other determiners of action. Since these sanctioned methods are frequently ineffective, we have been able to convince ourselves that they do not represent control at all. When they show too much strength to permit disguise, we give them other names and suppress them as energetically as we suppress the use of force. Education grown too powerful is rejected as propaganda or "brain-washing," while really effective persuasion is decried as "undue influence," "demogoguery," "seduction," and so on.

If we are not to rely solely upon accident for the innovations which give rise to cultural evolution, we must accept the fact that some kind of control of human behavior is inevitable. We cannot use good sense in human affairs unless someone engages in the design and construction of environmental conditions which affect the behavior of men. Environmental changes have always been the condition for the improvement of cultural patterns, and we can hardly use the more effective methods of science without making changes on a grander scale. We are all controlled by the world in which we live, and part of that world has been and will be constructed by men. The question is this: Are we to be controlled by accident, by tyrants, or by ourselves in effective cultural design?

The danger of the misuse of power is possibly greater than ever. It is not allayed by disguising the facts. We cannot make wise decisions if we continue to pretend that human behavior is not controlled, or if we refuse to engage in control when valuable results might be forthcoming. Such measures weaken only ourselves, leaving the strength of science to others. The first step in a defense against tyranny is the fullest possible exposure of controlling techniques. A second step has already been taken successfully in restricting the use of physical force. Slowly, and as yet imperfectly, we have worked out an ethical and governmental design in which the strong man is not allowed to use the power deriving from his strength to control his fellow men. He is restrained by a superior force created for that purpose—the ethical pressure of the group, or more explicit religious and governmental measures. We tend to distrust superior forces, as we currently hesitate to relinquish sovereignty in order to set up an international police force. But it is only through such counter-control that we have achieved what we call peace—a condition in which men are not permitted to control each other through force. In other words, control itself must be controlled.

Science has turned up dangerous processes and materials before. To use the facts and techniques of a science of man to the fullest extent without making some monstrous mistake will be difficult and obviously perilous. It is no time for self-deception, emotional indulgence, or the assumption of attitudes which are no longer useful. Man is facing a difficult test. He must keep his head now, or he must start again—a long way back . . .

V

. . . We may be sure that many steps in the scientific design of cultural patterns will produce unforeseen consequences. But there is only one way to find out. And the test must be made, for if we cannot advance in the design of cultural patterns with absolute certainty, neither can we rest completely confident of the superiority of the status quo. . . .

VII

The two great dangers in modern democratic thinking are illustrated in a paper by former Secretary of State Dean Acheson. "For a long time now," writes Mr. Acheson, "we have gone along with some well-tested principles of conduct: That it was better to tell the truth than falsehoods;... that duties were older than and as fundamental as rights; that, as Justice Holmes put it, the mode by which the inevitable came to pass was effort; that to perpetrate a harm was wrong no matter how many joined in it . . . and so on . . . .Our institutions are founded on the assumption that most people follow these principles most of the time because they want to, and the institutions work pretty well when this assumption is true. More recently, however, bright people have been fooling with the machinery in the human head and they have discovered quite a low . . . Hitler introduced new refinements [as the result of which] a whole people [were] utterly confused and corrupted. Unhappily neither the possession of this knowledge nor the desire to use it was confined to Hitler. . . . Others dip from this same devil's cauldron."

The first dangerous notion in this passage is that most people follow democratic principles of conduct "because they want to." This does not account for democracy or any other form of government if we have not explained why people *want* to behave in given ways. Although it is tempting to assume that it is human nature to believe in democratic principles, we must not overlook the "cultural engineering" which produced and continues to maintain democratic practices. If we neglect the conditions which produce democratic *behavior*, it is useless to try to maintain a democratic *form* of government. And we cannot expect to export a democratic form of government successfully if we do not also provide for the cultural practices which will sustain it. Our forebears did not discover the essential nature of man; they evolved a pattern of behavior which worked remarkably well under the circumstances. The "set of principles" expressed in that pattern is not the only true set or necessarily the best. Mr. Acheson has presumably listed the most unassailable items; some of them are probably beyond question, but others—concerning duty and effort—may need revision as the world changes.

The second—and greater—threat to the democracy which Mr. Acheson is defending is his assumption that knowledge is necessarily on the side of evil. All the admirable things he mentions are attributed to the innate goodness of man, all the detestable to "fooling with the machinery in the human head." This is reminiscent of the position, taken by other institutions engaged in the control of men, that certain forms of knowledge are in themselves evil. But how out of place in a democratic philosophy! Have we come this far only to conclude that well-intentioned people cannot study the behavior of men without becoming tyrants or that informed men cannot show good will? Let us for once have strength and good will on the same side.

VIII

Far from being a threat to the tradition of Western democracy, the growth of a science of man is a consistent and probably inevitable part of it. In turning to the external conditions which shape and maintain the behavior of men, while questioning the reality of inner qualities and faculties to which human achievements were once attributed, we turn from the ill-defined and remote to the observable and manipulable. . . .

10

Escape from Freedom

ERICH FROMM

Freedom—a Psychological Problem?

Modern European and American history is centered around the effort to gain freedom from the political, economic, and spiritual shackles that have bound men. The battles for freedom were fought by the oppressed, those who wanted new liberties, against those who had privileges to defend. While a class was fighting for its own liberation from domination, it believed itself to be fighting for human freedom as such and thus was able to appeal to an ideal, to the longing for freedom rooted in all who are oppressed. In the long and virtually continuous battle for freedom, however, classes that were fighting against oppression at one stage sided with the enemies of freedom when victory was won and new privileges were to be defended.

Despite many reverses, freedom has won battles. Many died in those battles in the conviction that to die in the struggle against oppression was better than to live without freedom. Such a death was the utmost assertion of their individuality. History seemed to be proving that it was possible for man to govern himself, to make decisions for himself, and to think and feel as he saw fit. The full expression of man's potentialities seemed to be the goal toward which social development was rapidly approaching. The principles of economic liberalism, political democracy, religious autonomy, and individualism in personal life, gave expression to the longing for freedom,

From Erich Fromm, *Escape from Freedom* (Chapter 1), 1941. Reprinted by permission of Holt, Rinehart and Winston, Inc., and Routledge & Keegan Ltd.

and at the same time seemed to bring mankind nearer to its realization. One tie after another was severed. Man had overthrown the domination of nature and made himself her master; he had overthrown the domination of the Church and the domination of the absolutist state. The *abolition of external domination* seemed to be not only a necessary but also a sufficient condition to attain the cherished goal: freedom of the individual.

The World War was regarded by many as the final struggle and its conclusion the ultimate victory for freedom. Existing democracies appeared strengthened, and new ones replaced old monarchies. But only a few years elapsed before new systems emerged which denied everything that men believed they had won in centuries of struggle. For the essence of these new systems, which effectively took command of man's entire social and personal life, was the submission of all but a handful of men to an authority over which they had no control.

At first many found comfort in the thought that the victory of the authoritarian system was due to the madness of a few individuals and that their madness would lead to their downfall in due time. Others smugly believed that the Italian people, or the Germans, were lacking in a sufficiently long period of training in democracy, and that therefore one could wait complacently until they had reached the political maturity of the Western democracies. Another common illusion, perhaps the most dangerous of all, was that men like Hitler had gained power over the vast apparatus of the state through nothing but cunning and trickery, that they and their satellites ruled merely by sheer force; that the whole population was only the will-less object of betrayal and terror.

In the years that have elapsed since, the fallacy of these arguments has become apparent. We have been compelled to recognize that millions in Germany were as eager to surrender their freedom as their fathers were to fight for it; that instead of wanting freedom, they sought for ways of escape from it; that other millions were indifferent and did not believe the defense of freedom to be worth fighting and dying for. We also recognize that the crisis of democracy is not a peculiarly Italian or German problem, but one confronting every modern state. Nor does it matter which symbols the enemies of human freedom choose: freedom is not less endangered if attacked in the name of anti-Fascism or in that of outright Fascism.* This truth has been so forcefully formulated by John Dewey that I express the

---

*I use the term Fascism or authoritarianism to denote a dictatorial system of the type of the German or Italian one. If I mean the German system in particular, I shall call it Nazism.

thought in his words:

The serious threat to our democracy," he says, "is not the existence of foreign totalitarian states. It is the existence within our own personal attitudes and within our own institutions of conditions which have given a victory to external authority, discipline, uniformity and dependence upon The Leader in foreign countries. The battlefield is also accordingly here—within ourselves and our institutions.*

If we want to fight Fascism we must understand it. Wishful thinking will not help us. And reciting optimistic formulae will prove to be as inadequate and useless as the ritual of an Indian rain dance.

In addition to the problem of the economic and social conditions which have given rise to Fascism, there is a human problem which needs to be understood. It is the purpose of this book to analyze those dynamic factors in the character structure of modern man, which made him want to give up freedom in Fascist countries and which so widely prevail in millions of our own people.

These are the outstanding questions that arise when we look at the human aspect of freedom, the longing for submission, and the lust for power: What is freedom as a human experience? Is the desire for freedom something inherent in human nature? Is it an identical experience regardless of what the degree of individualism reached in a particular society? Is freedom only the absence of external pressure or is it also the *presence* of something—and if so, of what? What are the social and economic factors in society that make for the striving for freedom? Can freedom become a burden, too heavy for man to bear, something he tries to escape from? Why then is it that freedom is for many a cherished goal and for others a threat?

Is there not also, perhaps, besides an innate desire for freedom, an instinctive wish for submission? If there is not, how can we account for the attraction which submission to a leader has for so many today? Is submission always to an overt authority, or is there also submission to internalized authorities, such as duty or conscience, to inner compulsions or to anonymous authorities like public opinion? Is there a hidden satisfaction in submitting, and what is its essence?

What is it that creates in men an insatiable lust for power? Is it the strength of their vital energy—or is it a fundamental weakness and inability to experience life spontaneously and lovingly? What are the psychological conditions that make for the strength of these strivings? What are the social conditions upon which such psychological conditions in turn are based? . . .

---

*John Dewey, *Freedom and Culture*, G. P. Putnam's Sons, New York, 1939.

. . . in our own society we are faced with the same phenomenon that is fertile soil for the rise of Fascism anywhere: the insignificance and power-lessness of the individual.

This statement challenges the conventional belief that by freeing the individual from all external restraints modern democracy has achieved true individualism. We are proud that we are not subject to any external author-ity, that we are free to express our thoughts and feelings, and we take it for granted that this freedom almost automatically guarantees our individuality. The *right to express our thoughts,* however, *means something only if we are able to have thoughts of our own;* freedom from external authority is a lasting gain only if the inner psychological conditions are such that we are able to establish our own individuality. Have we achieved that aim, or are we at least approaching it? This book deals with the human factor; its task, therefore, is to analyze this very question critically. In doing so we take up threads that were dropped in earlier chapters. In discussing the two aspects of freedom for modern man, we have pointed out the economic conditions that make for increasing isolation and powerlessness of the individual in our era; in discussing the psychological results we have shown that this power-lessness leads either to the kind of escape that we find in the authoritarian character, or else to a compulsive conforming in the process of which the isolated individual becomes an automaton, loses his self, and yet at the same time consciously conceives of himself as free and subject only to himself . . . .

The particular difficulty in recognizing to what extent our wishes—and our thoughts and feelings as well—are not really our own but put into us from the outside, is closely linked up with the problem of authority and freedom. In the course of modern history the authority of the Church has been replaced by that of the State, that of the State by that of conscience, and in our era, the latter has been replaced by the anonymous authority of common sense and public opinion as instruments of conformity. Because we have freed ourselves of the older overt forms of authority, we do not see that we have become automatons who live under the illusion of being self-willing individuals. This illusion helps the individual to remain unaware of his insecurity, but this is all the help such an illusion can give. Basically the self of the individual is weakened, so that he feels powerless and extremely insecure. He lives in a world to which he has lost genuine relatedness and in which everybody and everything has become instrumentalized, where he has become a part of the machine that his hands have built. He thinks, feels, and wills what he believes he is supposed to think, feel, and will; in this very process he loses his self upon which all genuine security of a free individual must be built.

The loss of the self has increased the necessity to conform, for it results in a profound doubt of one's own identity. If I am nothing but what I believe I am supposed to be—who am "I"? We have seen how the doubt about one's own self started with the breakdown of the medieval order in which the individual had had an unquestionable place in a fixed order. The identity of the individual has been a major problem of modern philosophy since Descartes. Today we take for granted that we are we. Yet the doubt about ourselves still exists, or has even grown. In his plays Pirandello has given expression to this feeling of modern man. He starts with the question: Who am I? What proof have I for my own identity other than the continuation of my physical self? His answer is not like Descartes'—the affirmation of the individual self—but its denial: I have no identity, there is no self excepting the one which is the reflex of what others expect me to be: I am "as you desire me."

This loss of identity then makes it still more imperative to conform; it means that one can be sure of oneself only if one lives up to the expectations of others. If we do not live up to this picture we not only risk disapproval and increased isolation, but we risk losing the identity of our personality, which means jeopardizing sanity.

By conforming with the expectations of others, by not being different, these doubts about one's own identity are silenced and a certain security is gained. However, the price paid is high. Giving up spontaneity and individuality results in a thwarting of life. Psychologically the automaton, while being alive biologically, is dead emotionally and mentally. While he goes through the motions of living, his life runs through his hands like sand. Behind a front of satisfaction and optimism modern man is deeply unhappy; as a matter of fact, he is on the verge of desperation. He desperately clings to the notion of individuality; he wants to be "different," and he has no greater recommendation of anything than that "it is different." We are informed of the individual name of the railroad clerk we buy our tickets from; handbags, playing cards, and portable radios are "personalized," by having the initials of the owner put on them. All this indicates the hunger for "difference" and yet these are almost the last vestiges of individuality that are left. Modern man is starved for life. But since, being an automaton, he cannot experience life in the sense of spontaneous activity he takes as surrogate any kind of excitement and thrill: the thrill of drinking, of sports, of vicariously living the excitements of fictitious persons on the screen.

What then is the meaning of freedom for modern man?

He has become free from the external bonds that would prevent him from doing and thinking as he sees fit. He would be free to act according to his own will, if he knew what he wanted, thought, and felt. But he does not know. He conforms to anonymous authorities and adopts a self which is not his. The more he does this, the more powerless he feels, the more he is forced to conform. In spite of a veneer of optimism and initiative, modern man is overcome by a profound feeling of powerlessness which makes him gaze toward approaching catastrophes as though he were paralyzed.

Looked at superficially, people appear to function well enough in economic and social life; yet it would be dangerous to overlook the deep-seated unhappiness behind that comforting veneer. If life loses its meaning because it is not lived, man becomes desperate. People do not die quietly from physical starvation; they do not die quietly from psychic starvation either. If we look only at the economic needs as far as the "normal" person is concerned, if we do not see the unconscious sufferings of the average automatized person, then we fail to see the danger that threatens our culture from its human basis: the readiness to accept any ideology and any leader, if only he promises excitement and offers a political structure and symbols which allegedly give meaning and order to an individual's life. The despair of the human automaton is fertile soil for the political purposes of Fascism.

Freedom and Spontaneity

So far this book has dealt with one aspect of freedom: the powerlessness and insecurity of the isolated individual in modern society who has become free from all bonds that once gave meaning and security to life. We have seen that the individual cannot bear this isolation; as an isolated being he is utterly helpless in comparison with the world outside and therefore deeply afraid of it; and because of his isolation, the unity of the world has broken down for him and he has lost any point of orientation. He is therefore overcome by doubts concerning himself, the meaning of life, and eventually any principle according to which he can direct his actions. Both helplessness and doubt paralyze life, and in order to live man tries to escape from freedom, negative freedom. He is driven into new bondage. This bondage is different from the primary bonds, from which, though dominated by authorities or the social group, he was not entirely separated. The escape does not restore his lost security, but only helps him to forget his self as a separate entity. He finds new and fragile security at the expense of sacrificing the integrity of his individual self. He chooses to lose his self since he cannot bear to be alone. Thus freedom—as freedom from—leads into new bondage.

Does our analysis lend itself to the conclusion that there is an inevitable circle that leads from freedom into new dependence? Does freedom from all primary ties make the individual so alone and isolated that inevitably he must escape into new bondage? Are *independence* and freedom identical with *isolation* and fear? Or is there a state of positive freedom in which the individual exists as an independent self and yet is not isolated but united with the world, with other men, and nature?

We believe that there is a positive answer, that the process of growing freedom does not constitute a vicious circle, and that man can be free and yet not alone, critical and yet not filled with doubts, independent and yet an integral part of mankind. This freedom man can attain by the realization of his self, by being himself. What is realization of the self? Idealistic philosophers have believed that self-realization can be achieved by intellectual insight alone. They have insisted upon splitting human personality, so that man's nature may be suppressed and guarded by his reason. The result of this split, however, has been that not only the emotional life of man but also his intellectual faculties have been crippled. Reason, by becoming a guard set to watch its prisoner, nature, has become a prisoner itself; and thus both sides of human personality, reason and emotion, were crippled. We believe that the realization of the self is accomplished not only by an act of thinking but also by the realization of man's total personality, by the active expression of his emotional and intellectual potentialities. These potentialities are present in everybody; they become real only to the extent to which they are expressed. In other words, *positive freedom consists in the spontaneous activity of the total, integrated personality*. . . .

. . . It has been the thesis of this book that freedom has a twofold meaning for modern man: that he has been freed from traditional authorities and has become an "individual," but that at the same time he has become isolated, powerless, and an instrument of purposes outside of himself, alienated from himself and others; furthermore, that this state undermines his self, weakens and frightens him, and makes him ready for submission to new kinds of bondage. Positive freedom on the other hand is identical with the full realization of the individual's potentialities, together with his ability to live actively and spontaneously. . . .

What are the general conditions for that? The irrational and planless character of society must be replaced by a planned economy that represents the planned and concerted effort of society as such. Society must master the social problem as rationally as it has mastered nature. . . .

Genetics and psychology were not the only "scientific" sources for anti-democratic trends. The impressive technological and scientific advances of the nineteenth and twentieth centuries encouraged some to believe that scientific method could be applied directly to government, reducing the slow-moving and complicated policy to a smooth-running mechanism. The technicians who had initiated and directed the industrial revolution might engineer a perfect social system. A grounding in the Marxist doctrine that economics conditions politics, and an awareness of the increasing importance of automation in modern industry led a former Trotskyite communist, Professor James Burnham of New York University, to posit a novel theory of socio-economic evolution.[1] According to Burnham, the growing economic role of a manager class in industrially mature societies would precipitate a conflict between these experts, on whom technology depended, and the old entrepreneurial class which had held almost unchallenged power in the earlier phases of development. The outcome of this power struggle was inevitable; grasping the reigns of industrial regulation, the managers would wrest political control from the capitalists. With the predictable demise of capitalism would come the death of middle-class democracy, through which the financial interest had ruled. Such a result was not to be mourned. Perceiving in Franklin Roosevelt's "brain trust" the initial flowering of his determinist pattern in America, Burnham predicted that soon political decisions would be made by a managerial elite.[2]

A group of men, initially inspired by Thorstein Veblen, which included engineering professors and practising engineers, along with a sprinkling of economists, chemists, and biologists, agreed with Burnham that history was about to take a new turn and that automation was the key to an understanding of the future.[3] Since 1920, these men had interested themselves in statistical studies of energy and resources, power consumption, production and employment, and the anatomy of American corporate control.[4] At the dawning of the Great Depression, leadership was assumed by Howard Scott, "a free-lance engineer and peripatetic social philosopher."[5] Lent public attention because of the deepening despair and economic disorder that marked the early 1930's, Scott's movement—Technocracy, Incorporated—presented its program for socio-economic reconstruction under the auspices of Columbia University's Industrial Engineering Department.[6] The scientific jargon with which the technocrats argued their case and the apparent integrity of the sponsoring institution helped technocracy attain temporary respectability among some business leaders and professionals.[7]

The technocrats attributed the depression to a final breakdown of capitalism's price structure and predicted "imminent and progressive instability . . . with corresponding social disorder."[8] They claimed to represent a genuine public call for the supplanting of political decision-makers by "technologists."[9] Technocracy, according to an official statement, stood "ready with a plan to salvage American civilization, if and when democracy as now functioning can no longer cope with the inherent disruptive forces."[10] This plan foresaw creation of a hierarchic dictatorship, similar in organization to a corporation, in which all citizens would participate. Money and trade would disappear; each person would receive a specific work assignment. "All citizens are to be given tickets entitling them to an equal share of the total product. The values of products . . . are to be stated in ergs of energy, and each citizen is to have his dividend expressed in ergs."[11]

The technocrats made very clear their view of democracy. They saw but two alternatives: democratic chaos or their form of managed society.[12] As Howard Scott explained to a convention of the National Education Association, "Political equality, religious freedom, and civil rights were all right when our forefathers adopted the Constitution of this country, but they adopted that Constitution in the days of ox-carts, spades, and other obsolete equipment. Today we have reached a point where it is not necessary . . . ."[13] Posing in the mantle of scientific objectivity, technocracy, like Burnham's "inevitable" managerial revolution, represented a "statistical mysticism, a resounding rumble-bumble of irrelevant engineering jargon."[14] Proponents of human management conjured up a mechanistic vision which refused "to recognize in its calculus the fundamental creative force of the individual human spirit," an essentially antidemocratic scientism which resembled "the hard, hideous ideology of Marx . . . in its indifference to all human values."[15]

NOTES

1. Lewis Corey, "James Burnham Rides Again," *Antioch Review,* Volume VII (June, 1947), p. 315; *Who's Who in America* (Chicago: Marquis-Who's Who, 1967), Vol. 34, p. 302.

2. Corey, "James Burnham Rides Again," p. 316; and James Burnham, "Rhetoric and Peace," *Partisan Review,* Vol. XVII (November-December, 1950), pp. 861-871.

3. "Personal and Otherwise," *Harper's Magazine,* Vol. 166 (January, 1933), p. 257; Louis Filler, *A Dictionary of American Social Reform* (New York: Philosophical Library, 1963), pp. 756-757; and Virgil Jordan, "Technocracy—Tempest on a Slide Rule," *Scribner's Magazine,* Vol. 93 (February, 1933), p. 66.

4. Jordan, "Technocracy," p. 66.

5. *Ibid.*

6. *Ibid.,* pp. 65-66.

7. David C. Coyle, "An Uncyclic Crisis and Capitalism for Culture," *American Scholar,* Vol. II (January, 1933), pp. 20-21.

8. "Technocracy, Inc., to Editors of the New Republic," *New Republic,* Vol. 75 (May 17, 1933), p. 20; also, see Howard Scott, "Technology Smashes the Price System," *Harpers Magazine,* Vol. 166 (January, 1933), pp. 129-142.

9. "Technocracy to New Republic," p. 20.

10. *Ibid.*

11. Coyle, "Uncyclic Crisis," p. 20

12. *Ibid.*, pp. 13-23; "Technocracy," *The New Statesman and Nation*, Vol. 5 (January 21, 1933), pp. 64-65.

13. Howard Scott, "The Imminence of Social Change; the Impact of Technology on a Price System of Production," *National Education Association Addresses and Proceedings*, Vol. 71 (1933), p. 564.

14. Jordan, "Technocracy," p. 66.

15. *Ibid.*, pp. 69, 66.

11

The Theory of the Managerial Revolution
JAMES BURNHAM

We are now in the midst of a major social transition (revolution), during which, as in other major transitions, the chief economic and political institutions in society, the dominant ideologies, and the class relations are being sharply and rapidly altered. This transition is *from* the structure of society which we call capitalist—that is, a structure characterized economically by "private enterprise," the owner-"wage worker" relation, production for individual profit, regulation of production as a whole by "the market" rather than by deliberate human control, and so on; characterized politically by the existence of numerous sovereign national states, strong in their own political sphere but *limited* as to their intervention into other spheres of life, especially the economic sphere, and by typical parliamentary institutions; characterized in terms of class relations through the position of private capitalists as the ruling class; and characterized ideologically by the prominence of individualist and "natural rights" notions in widespread social beliefs.

The transition, which it is well to emphasize is already in mid-course, is *to* a type of society that I call "managerial." The economic structure of managerial society is to be based upon state ownership of the chief means of

From Partisan Review, VIII (May-June, 1941), pp. 188-197. ©1941 by Partisan Review. Reprinted by permission of the author and publisher.

production, in contrast to the predominantly private ownership of the means of production in capitalist society. The new economy will be an exploiting (class) economy; but, instead of exploitation's taking place directly, as in capitalism, through ownership vested in individuals, it takes place indirectly, through control of the state by the new ruling class, the state in turn owning and controlling the means of production.* Through the new economic structure, as we already see from the examples of Russia and Germany, mass unemployment can be done away with, capital funds released from idleness, foreign trade carried on (by, for example, barter methods at what would be an intolerable loss for capitalism, exploitation of backward territories and peoples resumed and stepped up, and the *capitalist* type of economic crisis eliminated. What is in question here is not whether we approve of the means whereby these ends are achieved (we might, from a moral standpoint, prefer unemployment to state labor camps), but merely the observation that they are achieved. They are achieved, moreover, not through the cleverness of individual leaders, but through new institutional arrangements which remove the private profit requirements that have brought a dying capitalism to mass unemployment, idle funds and dried-up trade. There is thus every reason to believe that the achievements are not episodic, but a consequence of the newly rising structure of society.

Within any society, primary social power is in general held by those persons who have the chief measure of control over the instruments of production. Nevertheless, in the political order, power or "sovereignty" cannot simply float in the air; it must be concretized or "localized" in some definite human institution which is recognized and accepted by the given society as the body from which laws, decrees, and rules properly issue. There is a natural enough tendency for each major structure of society to develop its own typical sort of institution to serve this function of the localization of sovereignty. All historians recognize the great symptomatic importance of what might be described as the "shift in the localization of sovereignty" which occurs as a phase of every social transition (revolution). As the old order decays, sovereignty departs from the institution where it has been localized, and comes to rest in a new type of institution which, though it exists as a rule within the old order, is there secondary in influence and in reality representative of the new order that is on its way up.

---

*Some of the possible mechanisms of this new mode of exploitation, as they have been developed in Russia, are clearly shown in Freda Utley's very interesting recent book, *The Dream We Lost.* Trotsky, committed to the view that Russia is a "workers' state," was forced to hold that Russia's rulers got their heavy share of the national income through fraud and graft, that Russia has a "fraud economy"—since, by definition, there could not be "exploitation" in a workers' (socialized) state. Miss Utley's analysis shows how superficial was this opinion to which Trotsky was driven by his unshakable faith in the "either capitalism or socialism" assumption.

Under capitalism, political sovereignty has been most typically "localized" in parliaments (or some similar sort of institution, by whatever name it may have been called). Parliaments have been the "law-makers" of capitalism. During the generation since the first world war, sovereignty has been quickly shifting away from parliaments, and in most nations today parliamentary sovereignty has ended. In the new, managerial society, we can already see that sovereignty is to be localized where it has been in fact coming to rest, in the administrative commissions, boards, bureaus, of the new *unlimited* state.

In place of the dominant ideologies of capitalism, focusing around the concepts and slogans of "natural rights," "free enterprise," "private initiative," "life, liberty and the pursuit of happiness," and other offspring of "individualism," the ideologies of managerial society will focus around such concepts and slogans as the collectivity ("state," "race," "proletariat," "people"), "human rights *vs.* property rights," "discipline," "order," "sacrifice," and so on. As examples of early variants of managerial ideologies may be cited Leninism-Stalinism (Bolshevism), fascism-Nazism, and, at a still more primitive level, New Dealism.

The managerial social structure will mean the reduction to impotence, and finally the disappearance, or virtual disappearance, or the class of capitalists (to say that capitalist institutions will disappear is at the same time to say that capitalists will disappear). Within the new structure, the new ruling class—that is, those who have the principal control over the instruments of production and who get the principal differential rewards from the products of those instruments (for such persons are what we mean by the ruling class in any society)—will be the managers together with their bureaucratic colleagues in the strictly political movement. Under the institutions of managerial society, with the unlimited state at once the sovereign political and the controlling economic apparatus, these two latter groups (managers and bureaucrats) will be on the whole fused.

By "managers" I mean those who for the most part are already actually managing production nowadays, whether within the narrowing sphere of private enterprise or the expanding arena of state enterprise: the production executives, administrative engineers, supervisory technicians, plant coordinators, government bureau heads and commissioners and administrators. Under modern technological conditions, these managers (or administrators) are seldom identical as persons (as they usually used to be) with the capitalists, are not themselves capitalists; and in any event there is no necessary connection of any kind between the managerial and the capitalist *functions* in the total economic process.

To employ for a moment the metaphorical language of the class struggle: Just as once the early capitalists built up their power "within the womb of feudal society," but found that their power could not be consolidated and extended without smashing the foundations of feudalism; so the managers have built up their power within the womb of capitalism—more and more *de facto* power coming into their hands as the capitalists proper, pushed by technological, social and moral changes, withdraw from production to finance to economic idleness. For more than six hundred years, from the fourteenth century until the first world war, the curve of capitalist social domination rose without interruption. The end of every decade found a greater percentage of the total economy subject to capitalist rule and capitalist social relations than the beginning. During the course of the first world war, the curve turned catastrophically downward. The Russian Revolution snatched at one stroke a sixth of the world's surface and a twelfth of its population away from the capitalists and capitalism. The Nazis, it turns out, though more slowly are bringing about the same result in an even more decisive section of world economy. And in all nations, rapid structural changes are reducing everywhere both the area of the economy subject to capitalist relations as well as the degree of control exercised by the capitalists. The continuous economic process is abruptly accentuated, but not altered in direction, by political explosions.

The managers cannot consolidate their power without smashing the foundations of capitalism. Whether the managers themselves realize it or not, their problem can be solved only by doing away with "private enterprise" and parliamentarism,* and replacing them by state economy and government by boards and bureaus. In the process, the managers do not, of course, do the actual fighting or construct the appropriate ideologies, any more than did the early capitalists. The masses do the fighting and intellectuals construct the ideologies. The result is what counts, and the result is already apparent: a society in which the class of managers, together with a group of political allies with whom the managers largely fuse in the apparatus of the new unlimited state, are the ruling class.

The achievement and consolidation of the managerial revolution faces a triple problem: (1) the reduction to impotence of capitalist institutions (and thus of the capitalists) at home, and in the end also abroad; (2) the curbing

---

*I am unable, in this article, to discuss the difficult and humanly most important problem of the relations among the managerial institutional structure, democracy, and totalitarianism. This much seems clear: Rapid advance toward the managerial structure has so far been accompanied by totalitarian politics. Nevertheless, totalitarianism is no more identical with the managerial structure than is democracy with the capitalist social structure; totalitarianism is merely one political form for the managerial structure. It is certainly at least possible that managerial society, when consolidated, will develop its own kind of democracy—though not, it would seem, a parliamentary democracy, and certainly not capitalist democracy; it is even *possible* that the transition to managerial society should be accomplished democratically.

of the masses in such a manner that the masses accept the new order of managerial society; (3) competition among various sections of the managers for dominant positions in the new world order. The second step, it should be remarked, though it requires at certain intervals the use of force, above all demands a change of ideological and institutional allegiance. The masses must be led to accept one or another variant of the managerial institutions and the ideologies built upon the basis of managerial concepts and slogans; they must, we might say, come to see the (social) world in managerial terms. When that happens, the general structure of managerial society is reasonably assured; conflicts remain possible and likely, but they take place within the framework of managerial society, do not endanger its foundations, do not threaten to move toward the restoration of the capitalist structure or toward the overthrow of all forms of class structure—that is, toward socialism.

There is no pre-arranged temporal order in which these three parts of the managerial problem must be solved. Many different patterns or combinations are possible, and several are already being witnessed. Local social, political, cultural circumstances and even the specific influence of local leaders and organized political groups may rightly be expected to affect the pattern which we discover in any given instance. For example:

The Russian Revolution we must understand not as a socialist but as a managerial revolution. As soon as we make this shift, the general course of Russian events becomes intelligible. Instead of being forced to spend all our time "explaining" why Russia has "deviated" from the socialist course, has failed to develop as expected, has constantly done the opposite of what theory demanded, we are able to show through the theory of the managerial revolution how Russia has developed consistently along the lines to be deduced from theory, granted the specific circumstances of the Russian position. The triple managerial problem in Russia worked out as follows: First, in a rapid and drastic fashion, the capitalist institutions and the capitalists at home were reduced to impotence; and, after an armed defense, a temporary truce was reached with capitalist institutions and capitalists abroad. Then (though this second step began during the solution of the first step), more gradually, the masses were curbed in such a manner as to lead them to accept the new exploiting order. The curbing of the masses began long before the death of Lenin (Lenin's and Trotsky's leadership in the smashing of the power of the Factory Committees and of the autonomy and rights of the trade unions and local soviets were decisive early moves, for instance); Stalin's definitive victory and the Moscow Trials merely symbolized the completion of the second part of the triple managerial problem. The Nazi-Soviet Pact and the inability of Britain to move against Russia during the Finnish war showed that capitalism from abroad was no longer capable of overturning the new order. The third part of the managerial problem remains: the competition with other sections of the managers for first fruits in the managerial world system. In this competition, the Russian weaknesses indicate that Russia will not be able to endure, that it will crack apart, and fall toward east and west.

Russia has today advanced furthest, from a structural or institutional point of view, toward the managerial goal, the rest of the world, however, plainly moves in the same general direction, though the specific route being followed need not be the same as the Russian. In Germany, for example, the pattern for the solution of the triple managerial problem is different, though the problem and the outcome are the same. The order of the first two stages in Germany is on the whole the reverse of what we found in the case of Russia. In Germany, the curbing of the masses, their redirection into managerial channels, by and large preceded the reduction of the home capitalists and capitalist institutions to impotence; and the undermining of the capitalists abroad proceeds along with the process of completing the reduction of the capitalists at home. This account is, however, too rigidly schematized. In actual fact, the reduction of the home capitalists began, by a partial voluntary abdication along with the curbing of the masses—the capitalists themselves seeing in this partial abdication their sole desperate chance of avoiding the more immediate and drastic Russian pattern (which it did, but as it turns out with no long-term difference in the process as a whole, except for the better chance it gives *individual* capitalists to integrate themselves into the new order). The exile of Thyssen and the earlier retirement of Schacht signify the recognition by German capitalism of the error in the original hope that Nazism was the savior of German capitalism, the understanding that Nazism is merely a variant pattern in the liquidation of capitalism.

As in the case of Russia, so with Germany, the third part of the managerial problem—the contest for dominance with other sections of managerial society—remains for the future. First had to come the death blow that assured the toppling of the capitalist world order, which meant above all the destruction of the foundations of the British Empire (the keystone of the capitalist world order) both directly and through the smashing of the European political structure which was a necessary prop of the Empire. This is the basic explanation of the Nazi-Soviet Pact, which is not intelligible on other grounds. The future conflict between Germany and Russia will be a managerial conflict proper; prior to the great world-managerial battles, the end of the capitalist order must be assured. The belief that Nazism is "decadent capitalism" (which is besides *prima facie* implausible in that not Nazi Germany but France and England have displayed all the characteristics which have distinguished decadent cultures in the past historical transitions) makes it impossible to explain reasonably the Nazi-Soviet Pact. From this belief followed the always-expected war between Germany and Russia, not the actual war to the death between Germany and the British Empire. The war between Germany and Russia is one of the managerial wars of the future, not of the anti-capitalist wars of yesterday and today.

In the United States, by virtue of relative geographical isolation and enormous resources, the revolution lags somewhat behind, but is already well enough advanced to indicate the same general direction and outcome. New Dealism, both in its practical measures and in its ideology, can now be seen to be a managerial movement and belief, at a more primitive level, with more capitalist hangovers, than Bolshevism or Nazism. This the "Tories" (that is, the capitalists) have, from shortly after the beginning, recognized, and attested in 1940 by overwhelming and "principled" opposition to Roosevelt's re-election. How ridiculous to attribute this opposition to a failure on the part of the Tories to understand "their own true interests"! The Tories include many shrewd and intelligent men. They oppose New Dealism because they see that New Dealism in its consequences is directed against capitalism and thus against themselves. And already, plainly, the power is shifting from the capitalist hands into those of the managers and administrators, and their bureaucratic colleagues. The locus of sovereignty, already, has nearly completed its shift from parliament (Congress) to the administrative boards and bureaus. Private enterprise—necessarily the decisive base of capitalism, for the capitalist is the private owner—gives way to the state. New Dealism is not Nazism, any more than Nazism is Bolshevism. There is not a formal identity among the three; but they are nonetheless linked historically. They are, all three, variant patterns of the way toward the same goal, differing in their stage of development as well as in their local background; they are three of the possible routes from capitalist society to managerial society. And in the war to come—which has, in reality, already started—the social transformation in the United States will leap forward.

We may, from the point of view of the managerial revolution, discover the historical significance of the first two world wars. In brief: the war of 1914-18 was the last great war of capitalism; the present war is the first great formative war of managerial society.

The first world war, we might say, was a final convulsive effort by capitalism to find a cure for the diseases which were already, below the skin, eating its substance away. Instead of a cure, as so often results from such desperate efforts, the disease was only spread and made mortal. The course of the war itself showed that capitalism was ending its days, by: the outright breaking off of an important section of the world (Russia) from the capitalist structure; the cumulative weakening of capitalist institutions in all nations together with the growth of new (managerial) institutions; the fact that, unlike the previous wars of capitalism, the war of 1914-18 was unprofitable for both victors and losers, whereas earlier wars were invariably profitable for the victors and often for the losers as well; the demonstrated inability to devise a workable peace. From 1928 on, a renewed and far more devastating crisis set in, as shown not merely by the unparalleled economic depression, but equally plainly by the consolidation of Stalinism and Nazism, the rupture of the state from its traditional capitalist limits in all other nations, and the beginning of the breakup of the political order (Manchuria, Ethiopia, Spain, the spread of Germany, and finally the new war).

The political division of the world into a comparatively large number of sovereign national states, each with its armies and forts and currencies and tariffs and civil bureaucracies, is no longer workable for modern society with its complex division of labor and its needs for wider planning, control and trade exchanges. But in the Versailles peace, capitalism demonstrated that it was unable to smash the traditional political structure. The preservation of capitalism in the victorious powers (above all in England, the heart of capitalist society) meant the continuation of capitalist—nationalist divisions, indeed their exaggeration; but such divisions, the last generation has proved, cannot any longer endure. The process of changing the world political structure involves also a change in the world social structure. The second world war comprises major initial steps in both these changes.

Already the world system of managerial society emerges: a comparatively small number of "super-states," fighting for and dividing the world among themselves. An economic map suggests the probability that the outcome will be three great super-states, each based upon one of the three main areas of advanced industry: northcentral Europe; the United States, especially northeastern United States; Japan together with the east coast of China. In the future conflicts the managerial super-states of tomorrow cannot, in reality, hope to achieve a definitive military conquest of each other. The struggle will actually be, not for control over the central areas of advanced industry—the European area will be ruled by Europeans, the East Asian by Asiatics, the United States area by Americans—but for prime shares in the rest of the world.

The world conflict, however, is not at all divorced from internal social transformation. On the contrary, as so frequently in history, war speeds up and spreads the revolution. Those nations (Russia, Germany) which have gone furthest toward the managerial structure, carry their new institutions with their tanks and bombs. Their influence acts also by contagion in the nations which they have not conquered by direct military means. Within their own borders, they are forces to speed the rate of social change in order to keep going—a fact well symbolized by the increasing "radicalization" of Hitler's speeches during the course of the war. And the opposing nations are compelled to adopt the managerial methods in order to meet the challenge.

The United States, for example, approaches the world conflict socially unprepared. Already it is discovering that the institutions of capitalism do not permit it to compete adequately with its great rivals on the economic, military and ideological fronts. The economic integration of Latin America, essential to the survival of the American super-state, is blocked by the fact that from a capitalist point of view such integration is not profitable. The building of an adequate military machine is prevented by the same cause. And, ideologically, the concepts and slogans and beliefs of capitalism are unable to arouse the masses. Since it is unlikely that the United States will decline its potential place in the new world system, as the isolationists in effect advise, we may feel sure that at an ever-increasing rate the United States will take those means necessary for the fulfillment of its "destiny": that is, will move evermore rapidly toward the managerial social structure. The managerial revolution is a world social revolution. Against a world revolution, even a six-ocean Navy would doubtless prove not enough.

12

Who Shall Decide?
WILTON IVIE

In a social group, be it a family, a village, or a nation, decisions must be made which will result in actions and affect circumstances. Who shall make these decisions? This question always comes up whenever any discussion of social planning is suggested. People with different backgrounds and varying social outlooks present different answers, and each tends to distrust the answers proposed by the others. Conflict and indecisions regarding the proper answer to that question have often been major factors in frustrating social action.

Many believe that decisions should be made by some constituted authority—a monarch, a magistrate, a priest, a general, a 'czar' or other form

From *The Technocrat*, 212 (December, 1964), pp. 2-5. Reprinted with permission.

of boss. Others prefer that the decisions be made by a council or tribunal, fearful of placing their full trust in a single personage. Others favor a congress or parliament made up of selected representatives of the people. And there are those who think that social decisions should be made by a popular referendum of all the people. These are all forms of decision by opinion. They have all been tried to a greater or lesser extent, and in no instance have the results been outstandingly successful in terms of lasting human benefits.

Of course, there are other forms of decision-making which are even less intellectual than decisions by opinion, among these are decisions by oracle, by chance, or by intuition. These forms are often employed by individuals, usually by the uneducated but not always so. They are also employed extensively by various cultist groups. And, on occasion, they appear at the highest levels of government.

Decision by oracle may be arrived at by reference to such things as the arrangement of the stars and planets at a given moment, a look at the intestines of a freshly-killed fowl, or the speculative interpretation of a dream; or one may consult an ouija board or a divining rod. A great many people still consult a horoscope or some other oracle as a guide for their actions.

Others rely on intuitions or hunches. They trust how they feel about something rather than what they think about it.

Decision by chance has the particular virtue that it is impersonal and non-mysterious; while it is non-intellectual, it avoids subjectivity. It is relied on heavily in gambling. Even the government uses it at times, such as when it selects names for the military draft. It is also used frequently in making minor decisions, such as flipping a coin to decide who shall pay the dinner check, or who shall take a certain risk, or for breaking a tie score in a game. Artillery commanders sometimes use chance to select the sequence of targets during a barrage rather than following an intellectually logical scheme (which might be deciphered and evaded by the enemy).

There are times when decision by chance is as useful and effective as any other means, and it is an expedient way to avoid deadlock. We cannot accord the same validity to decisions by oracle or intuition; they are too slippery in their approach and too much influenced by subjectivity.

Different personality types have different attitudes toward the making of decisions. The strongly opinionated type wants authoritative decisions firmly made and tenaciously adhered to; he tends to become the diehard defender of fading causes or ways of life. The opportunist thinks in terms of immediate personal gain or advantage; he favors decisions by whatever means that are likely to bring him, or his side, those benefits. To the opportunist, a majority vote is a fine thing—if he is on the winning side.

Chicanery, force, and violence serve his purpose when other means fail. The opportunist is without scruples and often reaches a high pinnacle of success—for a while.

The liberal is unable to decide who shall make the decisions, being uncertain what decisions should be made or how they should be arrived at. He is afraid of anything that is decisive. So, the liberal ends up by deciding not to decide and loses out by default.

Historically, most decisions have been in the form of authoritative decrees. This form has prevailed on all levels of decision-making. The authority making the decisions may be self-sufficient and arbitrary in his power; that is, his word is law. Or he may be guided by some code, which may circumscribe his authority, more or less, while at the same time it may reinforce his power. The code may be in the form of ecclesiastical commandments, a book of laws, a list of military regulations and directives, the profound pronouncements of past leaders, or traditions arising out of past customs. In any case, the immediate authority in power makes the decisions and usually there is no provision for dissent or appeal. Most people in the world today, as has always been so, have their lives governed by the decisions of various authorities, and regarding such decisions they usually have no safe choice other than obedience. Authoritarianism has traditionally prevailed at all levels of decision-making.

In the family, there was an authoritative voice, usually that of the male parent or patriarch, and this voice demanded unquestioned compliance.

On the job, there has been a boss who made the decisions and issued the orders. Under certain circumstances, one had the choice of obeying those orders or quitting the job, but such a choice is more likely to be recent than to be traditional. A stint at the whipping post was often the penalty for disobedience on the job.

In military formations, authority has always been rigid and stern. Disobedience has often proven fatal.

Most churches have been highly authoritarian, and this authoritarianism has penetrated into every phase of private and public life. The decisions of ecclesiastical authorities have usually had the implied direction, or at least sanction, of the prevailing deity or deities. These authorities have often possessed stern means of effecting obedience, even to punishment by burning alive.

The communities—tribes, villages, landed estates, and such—have had their authorities in the form of chiefs, burgomeisters, feudal lords, and war lords. Even today in many places, authorities of this sort make decisions and issue them in the form of decrees to their subjects. Police forces remind the people that they are not free agents.

The nations of the world have had their rulers, who often governed as despots, at best as benevolent administrators; and these rulers made many authoritative decisions affecting their people, but without the participation or consent of those people.

Decisions affecting life and death, peace and war, favor and punishment, fame and dishonor, fortune and poverty, salvation and damnation have been decisions of authority. No matter how stupid or demanding were the decisions of the authorities, it was usually safer for the subjects to obey them than to dissent. Authoritarians have always dealt severely with dissenters.

The most 'colorful' periods in history, when viewed in retrospect anyway, have been those centered in certain dynamic personalities who, by one means or another, worked their ways into positions of sovereign authority under propitious circumstances and fomented a great to-do in their respective areas. Among the more prominent of such personalities, we might mention: Rameses II, Cyrus the Great, Alexander the Great, Attila the Hun, Mohammed, Genghis Khan, Peter the Great, Napoleon Bonaparte, Adolph Hitler, and Josef Stalin. It also happens that these personalities usually gained their fame through, or in association with, military conquests and massive slaughters of people.

Parenthetically, we might mention that these 'colorful' periods of history were not a complete loss to mankind. The social dynamism and technology that were developed to advance power and conquest sometimes were adaptable to constructive uses afterward. Further, these events usually disrupted the status quo and caused events to take a different turn. Sometimes, out of the adaptation that followed, came social advancement.

Even in modern America, we are conditioned in many ways to acknowledge authority and to subject ourselves to it. We begin with parental authority in the home; then, we meet it in many other forms—in school, in church, on the playing field, on the streets, on the job, and perhaps in military service. However, in America, we tend to be lax in our respect for authority and, on many occasions, to accord it only nominal recognition. We are constantly seeking ways of evading its decisions, defying authority or otherwise frustrating it. Because of this tendency, our society is accused by some of being afflicted with moral decay.

Another form of social decision has been achieved through a council of authorities rather than by the will of one authority. This procedure is primitive in its concept and application, and it was often used among the early tribes. It has been applied, off and on, by modern nations and institutions. The authoritative councils have normally consisted of the aristocracy or the more privileged members of the social group, hence it represented the interests of a small elite minority.

The decisions of councils are often the result of a compromise among several opinions of what should be done or not done. Consequently, they are usually more restrained than the decisions of a single authority and tend to be downgraded by compromise. Only under circumstances of emotional excitement or severe emergency is a council likely to become dynamic in its decisions.

In recent times, there has been a tendency among nations to decentralize their decision-making. A parliament, often composed of hundreds of members, is selected to present, debate, and vote on proposals for action. This has proved to be a long, laborious, frustrating process. Such decisions, when they are not completely stymied, usually are of a very low order. There is also a tendency among the factions to make deals, to exchange favors. A quick decision can be made only under the duress of a *force majeure* or an enthusiasm for war.

A more diffuse form of decision by opinion is that of a popular referendum—a democratic decision. An issue is put up for vote by those who are interested enough to qualify for voting and to go through the ritual of voting. One serious handicap to this process is the strong urge on the part of the voters to turn down any proposal for social improvement which threatens to cost them money. However, this procedure is seldom as democratic as it would appear on the surface. The wording of the question is usually rigged by a minority interest and presented at a time when the outcome of the vote is fairly certain—a trick means of gaining popular approval for something already decided on by a few.

In the United States, it is generally assumed that the people vote for the kind of government they want, but that is not exactly true. Technically, they do not even vote directly for their president; they vote for electors who, in turn, are tacitly committed to vote for indicated candidates, the exact rules varying with the different states. Moreover, the public has little voice in choosing the candidates; it usually ends up with their having a choice between two men chosen by the respective political party 'machines.' And they have less choice concerning the policies of the president. Once elected, the president is under no real obligation to heed the desires of the people and often acts contrary to his campaign promises.

Decisions by oracle, by chance, by intuition, and by opinion have had a recognizable effect on the superficial aspects of human history; but nothing profound or lasting can come from those sources. All that can be seriously claimed as progress in man's way of life has been the result of decisions of quite another kind—decisions imposed on man by objective factors in his environment. The physical needs, comforts, and conveniences of mankind have compelled decisions that were useful albeit not always in conformity with prior opinions and beliefs.

In agriculture, animal husbandry, mining, transportation, health care, and other departments of practical activity, man slowly learned that the decisions had to conform to certain objective principles and facts. Although the factual information was often intermixed with opinion and superstition, nevertheless it was the factual knowledge that prevailed in the end. Slowly, very slowly, factual knowledge gained preeminence while opinion and beliefs faded away. It is gradually being learned that man has no right to decide by opinion that which can be determined by facts. The modern agriculturist of today, for example, does not consult oracles as to when and how to sow his seed; rather, he relies on his knowledge of soil, moisture, weather, pest control, and fertilizer to provide him with good crops. He no longer makes sacrifices to the gods nor beats the drums for rain.

More and more, man's decisions are being taken out of the realm of opinion, intuition, hocus pocus, and authoritarian decree. They are being made in accordance with facts pertaining to the environment and with accumulated scientific knowledge and technological know-how. Man is beginning to understand what he can do within the framework of his physical environment with the knowledge and equipment he has at hand. When his knowledge in a given area is deficient, he now seeks more facts rather than consults opinions or occult revelations.

It is the man who has command of the technical information who makes the real decisions in the functional phases of modern life. He is the only one who understands what needs to be done and how to do it. The politicians and financial manipulators who pretend that the right of decision is theirs are helpless without the technical men. In belated and reluctant recognition of this situation, the president of the United States recently appointed a scientific advisor to his staff.

We hear propaganda uttered to the effect that technical men are all right in their specialized fields but that they should be kept away from the councils where decisions pertaining to human relations and human values are involved. It is argued, when issues pertaining to government, education, social programs (such as population control), and morality are discussed, the scientist should be kept in the background as a mere consultant, not take a hand in making the major decisions. Presumably, the making of such decisions is to be the privilege of the hocus pocus artists—the politicians, the financial promoters, the witch doctors, the lawyers, and the guardians of ancient traditions.

Up to date, such people have held the privilege of making the major decisions and the results have been tragic. Their mistakes have accumulated to the point where mankind virtually faces annihilation at the push of a button—or what might be worse, be catapulted into a prolonged social debacle brought on by irresolvable conflicts within his society.

Technocracy holds that all decisions pertaining to the functional operation of the society—the production and distribution of goods and services, research, and governance—should be made by technical men and women. This does not mean that the technical people should leave their technical positions and go into politics, law, business promotion, public relations, and moral philosophy. Rather, it means that the scientists, technologists, engineers, and technicians shall continue to operate as such and that the decision-making of the society be moved into their functional realms. The public relations people would then have a secondary role, that of explaining to the people at large the significance of science in words that they understand.

Politics, legal hocus pocus, magic, and philosophy have no place in the human use of this materialistic world in which we live. No other 'world' is of any use to us, except possibly as a subjective titillation of the imagination.

All of man's gains in standard of living, in health and longevity, and in control of matter and energy have come through knowledge and application of observable data. Science continues to point the way to the future.

All scientific indicators point to the probability that the next social state shall be a Technocracy.

Part Three

Class Struggle and Class Rule

Part Three

Class Struggle and Class Rule

A. American Syndicalism and Marxism

The predominance of the American Federation of Labor since the late nineteenth century, with its tacit acceptance of the existing industrial system and willingness to eschew political separatism or revolution for collective bargaining and bread-and-butter demands, has given American labor history a uniquely conservative cast. Shortly after the turn of the century, however, the AFL's claim to speak for all workingmen was challenged vigorously by a new union with markedly different economic and political goals. The Industrial Workers of the World was organized in Chicago, in 1905, and from the first carved out a reputation for violent general strikes, riots, free speech crusades, and stormy court battles.[1] The Wobblies, as they were dubbed, broke the truce with industrial America. They were earnest, impatient advance agents for "One Big Union"—the framework for a proletarian utopia which would eradicate capitalism and the wage system.[2] Early divisiveness over tactics ended with rejection of Daniel DeLeon's call for a separate labor party, as well as total denial of the value of participation within the traditional party structure. The IWW chose, instead, to follow William D. Haywood (1869-1928), whose hard-fought struggles for unionism in the mining fields of the Rocky Mountain West had convinced him that the only hope for industrial justice lay in "direct action."[3] Haywood policies included an adaptation of radical French unionists' use of general strikes, industrial sabotage, and violence.[4]

Direct action appealed to the Wobblies because, for most of them, normal political activity was not an open alternative. The IWW's strength rested with the disfranchised: women, migrant workers, aliens, and Afro-Americans.[5] These were elements of the population which were not truly represented, either by the trade union movement or the two major political parties; distrust of both coursed through IWW thinking. "Direct action," wrote one Wobbly, "means industrial action directly by, for, and of the workers themselves, without the treacherous aid of labor misleaders or scheming politicians."[6] The union's organizers found willing followers among unskilled, migratory laborers, and they profferred a bitter gospel of class antipathy and impatience with the gradualism of the democratic process.[7] If the remedy they espoused was an impractical panacea granting power to a single class, their motivations originated in actual conditions and problems which American society had consistently neglected to confront. The Wobblies' fury was traceable to the dramatic changes wrought by rapid industrialization: the development of impersonal employer-employee relationships; the lessened socio-economic mobility of unskilled and semiskilled workers; real and imagined fears of what immigration would do to the labor market; and the relentless anti-union pressures exerted by the great corporations.[8]

Although the union's leaders threatened mass violence, warning that every strike was a small revolution and a dress rehearsal for a big one, and employers charged them with heinous crimes and portrayed them as madmen, the IWW was never as serious a threat as its leaders or detractors maintained. Its membership never exceeded 100,000.[9] Its insistence on direct action did lead to sporadic violence, but the promised industrial armageddon never came. One journalist who investigated Wobbly activities at the height of labor tensions in the Pacific Northwest during World War I concluded that employers' claims of planned violence were greatly exaggerated, as were Wobbly claims of success.[10] Aside from its historical importance as precursor of the industrial unionism of the Congress of Industrial Organizations, the IWW's chief legacy was a lesson in deep irony: the example of a movement undeniably seeking social justice and enlarged democracy, but relying on, and in the end, defeated by the instruments of class hatred and terrorism.[11]

The IWW still clings to a paper existence, with a small office in Chicago. Its real life ended by 1924, the "One Big Union" shattered by internal disputes over wartime tactics and methodical government suppression.[12] Big Bill Haywood, finally won to the belief that the fate of the world's workers rested with the new Soviet experiment, slipped out of the United States, dying disillusioned and lonely in a Moscow hotel in 1928.[13]

A tug-of-war between patriotism and pacifism not only contributed to the decline of the IWW, it tore a gaping hole in the unity of world socialism after 1914.[14] The trend toward factionalism was speeded by the Bolshevik seizure of power in war-weary Russia. Suddenly, Marx's prophecy of a worldwide proletarian upheaval appeared on the verge of fulfillment. All of Europe seethed with discontent; Germany displayed the symptoms of political disintegration. Radicals everywhere turned to watch the great Russian drama unfold. In the United States, a vocal group of Marxists within the Socialist Party called for immediate cooperation with the triumphant Russians. They were aided in their fight by the fact that large numbers of rank-and-file Socialists were furious with their leaders for apparently compromising principle by silently approving the American war effort. One group broke with the Socialists in 1919 to form a Communist Party; another faction, after unsuccessfully attempting to seize control of the Socialist Party, founded a Communist Labor Party the same year.[15] Many socialists, including Benjamin Gitlow, torn by the magnetic appeal of Bolshevik success on the one hand and a natural preference for Eugene V. Debs's strategy of eventual victory through the winning of a political majority, found themselves pressured into joining the communist movement by the Moscow-directed Russian Federation.[16]

From its inception, the American communist movement was spellbound by the Soviet success story. This was enough, in the early years, to make Russian suggestions gospel; this tendency to look to the Soviet Union for guidance was helped by the fact that initially most of the members of the American Communist Party were recently arrived, unassimilated immigrants from Eastern Europe.[17] A political organization frankly determined to provoke revolution could not expect a warm reception in the United States during the twenties, and the communists quickly decided to go underground. This was a crucial decision, for it set, in the formative stage, the party's future pattern as a secret, tightly organized conspiratorial agency dedicated to violent revolt rather than open political action.[18] When the Russian Revolution failed to fire similar uprisings throughout the Western nations, the communists settled back to confidently await a more propitious time for action. A lack of public support forced increasing reliance upon Moscow for financial and ideological aid, until the American movement was virtually a dependent Soviet colony.[19]

The Great Crash of 1929 and the years of severe economic dislocation and political indecision which ensued appeared to offer the communists that long-awaited opportunity. When hesitancy meant hunger and the promised plateau of permanent prosperity was transformed into bread lines and soup kitchens, some frustrated Americans saw in communism the scientific certainty, order, and equity others found in technocracy or fascism.[20] Yet even the bleak depression years proved insufficient for the growth of mass support for communism in the United States. At its peak, the party could claim fewer than 100,000 members, despite the party organs' "fuzzy, Whitmanesque . . . 'we-too-sing-America' " refrain.[21] This signal failure to capture a large American following testified to the inability of the communists to break with Lenin's definition of a party as a small group of full-time revolutionaries.[22] Party leaders, having weathered a decade of government and public hostility, could not bring themselves to modify the organization's reliance on centralized control and share power with the rank and file. Converts expecting the vicarious thrill of conspiratorial disclosures found, instead, that party meetings consisted in boring reports and inordinate demands on their time.[23] As Gitlow correctly recalled, party members lost their individual liberty the precise moment they enlisted in the "Cause"; a party member was a soldier, "a deployable resource."[24]

In other significant ways, the communists found themselves unable to knead American realities into their rigid dogma. According to Marxist assumptions, as revised by the Comintern, party recruits would come from the disinherited masses. Depression conditions seemed ideal for this development, but though the party did experience growth in the early 1930's, the new members were mainly former white-collar workers and as often college graduates as public school dropouts. Usually they embraced communism, not because of economic misery, but because of a sense of alienation and a decided predilection for absolutist ideology.[25] The traditional American emphases on the individual in a universe of choices, able to act freely in concert with others to modify the present or shape any future were contradicted flatly by Marxism. Freedom of choice was canceled out by submission to the inevitability of economic determinism; an open future was supplanted by an ironbound destiny.[26] American communism was and is profoundly antidemocratic. Its threat to both democracy and national security remains that of a foreign power's instrument, probing for gaps and strains in the American promise.[27]

NOTES

1. Joyce L. Kornbluh, ed., *Rebel Voices: An I.W.W. Anthology* (Ann Arbor: University of Michigan Press, 1964), p. v.

2. *Ibid.*

3. Morris Hillquit, *History of Socialism in the United States* (5th rev. ed.; New York: Russell & Russell, Inc., 1965), pp. 333-341; Paul F. Brissenden, *The I.W.W.: A Study of American Syndicalism* (2nd ed.; New York: Russell & Russell, Inc., 1957), pp. 226-228; Robert Hunter, *Violence and the Labor Movement* (New York: Macmillan Company, 1914), p. vii.

4. Hunter, *Violence and the Labor Movement,* p. vii; Patrick Renshaw, *The Wobblies: The Story of Syndicalism in the United States* (Garden City: Doubleday & Company, 1967), p. 68.

5. Kornbluh, *Rebel Voices,* p. 35.

6. Justus Ebert, *The I.W.W. in Theory and Practice* (Chicago, n.d.), p. 59.

7. Robert L. Tyler, *Rebels of the Woods: The I.W.W. in the Pacific Northwest* (Eugene: University of Oregon Press, 1967), p. 91.

8. Abe C. Ravitz and James N. Primm, eds., *The Haywood Case: Materials for Analysis* (San Francisco: Chandler Publishing Company, 1960), p. 2.

9. Renshaw, *The Wobblies,* pp. 22-23.

10. Robert Bruere, "The Industrial Workers of the World," *Harpers Magazine,* 137 (July, 1918), p. 256.

11. Renshaw, *The Wobblies,* p. 26.

12. *Ibid.,* pp. 22-23; Brissenden, *The I.W.W.,* p. x; Ralph Chaplin, *Wobbly: The Rough-and-Tumble Story of an American Radical* (Chicago: University of Chicago Press, 1948), pp. 205-228.

13. Chaplin, *Wobbly,* pp. 285-288; Renshaw, The *Wobblies,* pp. 240-242, 248-251; David H. Grover, *Debaters and Dynamiters: The Story of the Haywood Trial* (Corvallis: Oregon State University Press, 1964), pp. 1-5.

14. David Herreshoff, *American Disciples of Marx: From the Age of Jackson to the Progressive Era* (Detroit: Wayne State University Press, 1967), pp. 158-160.

15. David J. Saposs, *Communism in American Politics* (Washington, D. C.: Public Affairs Press, 1960), pp. 2-3.

16. Irving Howe and Lewis Coser, *The American Communist Party: A Critical History, 1919-1957* (Boston: Beacon Press, 1957), pp. 1-40; Saposs, *Communism in American Politics,* pp. 6-7.

17. Saposs, *Communism in American Politics,* p. 4.

18. Herreshoff, *American Disciples of Marx,* p. 186.

19. *Ibid.;* Saposs, *Communism in American Politics,* pp. 228-229; David J. Saposs, *Communism in American Unions* (New York: McGraw-Hill Book Company, Inc., 1959), vii and *passim.*

20. Maurice Parmelee, *Bolshevism, Fascism, and the Liberal-Democratic State* (New York: John Wiley & Sons, Inc., 1934), *passim.*

21. Nathan Glazer, *The Social Basis of American Communism* (New York: Harcourt, Brace & World, Inc., 1961), p. 3; David A. Shannon, *The Decline of American Communism: A History of the Communist Party of the United States Since 1945* (New York: Harcourt, Brace & Company, 1959), p. 267.

22. Theodore Draper, *American Communism and Soviet Russia: The Formative Period* (New York: Viking Press, 1960), pp. 194-195.

23. *Ibid.,* pp. 196-197.

24. Clinton Rossiter, *Marxism: The View from America* (New York: Harcourt, Brace & Company, 1960), p. 249; Glazer, *Social Basis of American Communism,* p. 4.

25. Draper, *American Communism and Soviet Russia,* p. 201; Glazer, *Social Basis of American Communism,* pp. 186-189.

26. Rossiter, *Marxism,* p. 248; H. B. Mayo, *Democracy and Marxism* (New York: Oxford University Press, 1955), p. 290.

27. Edward E. Palmer, ed., *The Communist Problem in America: A Book of Readings* (New York: Thomas Y. Crowell Company, 1951), *passim.*

13

Industrial Socialism
WILLIAM D. HAYWOOD AND FRANK BOHN

... In North America the workers behold a great mass of laws, old and new, which they have been carefully taught to respect and obey. These laws were made by the political and legal servants of the masters. They were created for the purpose of protecting property which existed long before the law gave the owners a "right" to it. Yet all the rights which the capitalists claim are based on these laws. As soon as the workers determine to abolish them, or ignore them, the capitalists' "right" to what the workers have produced will cease to exist. . . .

The world is ruled by force. The foundation of this force is control over a large number of people. The capitalists rule the world today because they have organized the workers in the shops and control them. They own and direct the industries . . .

The workers thus live under an awful tyranny. They are ruled without their consent. The government which oppresses them is the government of the shops, the mines, and the railroads. This government declares when they shall work and when they shall be idle. All of the profits taken by the capitalist class are in reality taxes paid by the workers. These taxes are not voted by the workers. They are seized by the employers. The idea that we have freedom in America is ridiculous. What the capitalists call "freedom," is nothing but freedom to enslave the working class. This they can now do without let or hindrance.

We have compared the trust to an industrial state. Many states make up the Nation. In the same way many trusts compose our present great nation of industry. So the Nation is coming to be governed as an empire. J. Pierpont Morgan is now the chief ruler of this empire. He is the emperor of the trusts. Under him there are kings and dukes who rule separate trusts and corporations. This great government of industry is said, upon very good authority, to have brought on the panic of 1907 in order to seize several great corporations which were fighting it. During this panic it grabbed hundreds of small businesses.

Selected passages from *Industrial Socialism,* Charles H. Kerr, Chicago, 1911.

No capitalist, even though he might possess ten millions or twenty millions of money, can today start any new business of his own unless he goes to Wall Street, appears at court, and gets the consent of the Emperor of America. Whatever small separate industries exist, still remain alive because the industrial empire does not wish to crush them out too fast. To do this would be to raise a cry of revolt among the middle class. Until now the workers have been so enslaved, so helpless, so deadened, that the Wall Street magnates have not even thought of their opposition seriously. But it would not do to go too far and too fast. So some small business men are still permitted to enjoy a hand-to-mouth existence.

The Industrial Empire and the Goverment at Washington. Morgan and his associates on Wall Street use the government at Washington as a tool to serve their ends. They rightly despise the President, the members of the Supreme Court and Congress, for these politicians are far beneath them in power and importance. What laws Wall Street wants are passed. In case of a strike, the governor of a state is used to control the militia and crush the strike. The federal and state judges issue injunctions, that is, they make such new laws as the trusts want. The powers of the separate states are usually quite strong enough to deal with the divided and blinded working class. But if these do not suffice, then the powers of the National Government are used. Grover Cleveland, a Democratic President, broke the great A. R. U. strike in 1894. Theodore Roosevelt, a Republican President, broke the Goldfield Miners' strike in 1907. The Republican state of Pennsylvania has established a standing army of its own in order to have it ready to shoot working people. The Democratic legislature of Florida, in the spring of 1911, refused to pass a law forbidding the employment of children under eight years of age. All the Democratic and Republican officials, from dog-catcher to President, are but the hired agents of the empire of Industry.

The Real Government of the United States. America is governed from Wall Street, New York. This is the real seat of public power. Under its tyrannical laws all of us are forced to live. When labor raises its head it is quickly clubbed into submission. The industrial oligarchs are now attempting to destroy freedom of speech and of the press. Professors in the universities and colleges and teachers in the public schools do not attempt to tell the truth about government. Such as do quickly lose their positions. Clergymen and priests do not dare preach the truth about the working class in their sermons, for the industrial empire is gaining control of the churches. All of the newspapers in the larger cities, except the Socialist papers, are owned out and out by the capitalists. They are used to keep the workers in ignorance and to entertain them with pictures, cheap sporting news and sensational reports of scandals.

Thus the trusts control the army, the navy, the police, the political government, the schools, the press, the church, and even the theaters. The industrial empire is a power with its forces encamped in every city and state of the land, armed not only with the weapons which slay the body, but also with those mightier weapons which destroy the free mind of the working class.

Is all hope lost?

Let us see.

Capitalists cannot live without wage-workers. Where one class exists there the other will be found. Furthermore, there is sure to be trouble between the two. The master is always scheming to get more profits out of the worker. The worker fights for more wages from his boss. The less one gets the more there is for the other. Hence we have, between the capitalist and his worker, what is known as the *Class Struggle.*

At first this struggle does not seem to be important. The small capitalist and his workers associate together and may for a time be good personal friends. This small capitalist is not very rich nor is the worker very poor. The personal relationship between the two prevents violent outbreaks. At this stage of production, especially in America, the more greedy and calculating workers were constantly "rising" and becoming small capitalists.

But with every step in the growth of industry, peace between the capitalist and worker becomes less likely. Soon the capitalist lives an altogether different life from the worker. He associates only with his own kind. He builds himself a palace and travels about the world. Meanwhile the worker continues to work and sweat in the shop. Neither he nor any of the members of his family meet the capitalist or his family. The capitalist's children go to college. The worker's children go to work.

The Growth of the Class Struggle. And thus the two classes come to be wholly separated as regards every aspect of life. The capitalist who never works comes to despise work and the workers. The worker naturally hates the capitalist who is taking such huge profits and paying such low wages. But at first the worker's opinions are not clear in his own mind. In fact, few workers even now understand the real problem which confronts them.

The Problem of Labor. However, it was very early discovered that the only way for the workers to make head against the capitalists was to organize. The purpose of labor unions has been to control, or partly control, the conditions of labor and the division of labor's product. That is, the workers seek, through their unions, to help govern the industries, instead of letting the capitalist do just as he pleases. Every demand made by organized labor upon the capitalists is in the nature of a proposed law for the shop. When the capitalist surrenders and gives in to the demands of the workers the law is passed . . . .

Industrial unionism has been developed to meet the conditions confronting the workers since the coming of the latest machines and the organization of the trusts.

The revolutionary industrial union is very active, always fighting. The prosperity of a modern labor organization is measured by its activity. Activity for improved conditions or against the lowering of existing standards of living means that the membership is in arms against the exploiters.

Action against exploitation requires agitation, publicity, strikes, boycotts, political force—all the elements and expressions of discontent. Discontent is life. It impels to action. Contentment means stagnation and death. . . .

The political government of capitalism has served its purpose. Its day is done. The Socialist Party can seize it, prevent its doing further harm to the workers and at the proper time throw it on the scrap heap where it will repose with the outworn tools for the protection of which it was organized.

We have already described the new government—the government of industry. Its development began with the organization of industrial corporations. At the present time it is rapidly becoming centralized. Its capital is at New York City. There its executive and legislative departments are located. It is a plutocracy, a form of government by the great rich. It is rapidly becoming an empire.

This industrial government makes the real laws of the land. It determines who shall and who shall not work and how long and for what wages. That is, it has the power to say who shall live and who shall not live. It legislates as regards the amount of protection the worker shall receive while at work. It holds in its hands the powers of both the industrial and political governments. It has decreed, in order that profits may be increased, that the workers shall suffer slavery, starvation, disease and death.

The workers' government of the future will realize Socialism. No government is created in a day. Any new system of society, with its peculiar government, must grow through many years to its final and perfected form. In this Socialism cannot be different from other forms of government. Socialism cannot be realized until the workers, through their industrial government, own and manage the means of production. This government is now developing—in the workshops, of course. Wherever the organized workers gain partial control over the shop in which they work, we have the growth of industrial democracy. If the workers have been employed twelve hours a day and they force their employer to grant them the ten-hour day, they are passing an important law of the shop. That law springs from the power of the workers to govern the shop.

Suppose that the workers of the whole Nation demanded and enforced the eight-hour day. That would be a mightier law in the interest of the working class than all the laws ever passed by Congress and the state legislatures.

With the growth of the organized industrial and political power of the workers, the class struggle will become ever keener. The government of the capitalists will make war on the workers. The battle will rage throughout the land, in every city and town, in every shop and mine. It will continue until the workers are strong enough to gain complete control of the Nation's industries. The trust is organized industry. The labor union will become organized industrial society.

The Class Struggle in Politics

In their war upon the working class, one of the most effective weapons of the capitalists has been the physical force wielded by their political government. Everywhere the workers have been fooled into supporting this government. The Republican and Democratic parties and the various reform parties are maintained to keep the workers divided. Whichever of these capitalist parties is victorious, the workers are always defeated. Democratic, Republican and reform politicians alike use the powers of government in the interests of the master class, wherever the workers seek to control the shop. Whenever the workers strike they are brutally clubbed, stabbed and shot by police and soldiers. Whenever they declare a boycott they may be put in jail. Injunctions prevent them from picketing a struck shop and talking to the strike breakers. The courts seize the funds of the union and turn them over to the capitalists.

Fortunately the male workers have the right to vote. At first they foolishly try to defend themselves by defeating this or that obnoxious politician of the old parties. They vote for such politicians as call themselves "the friends of labor." But they soon find out again that "the friends of labor" out of office, become the enemies of labor when in office. So finally, in every country under the sun, the workers are forced to organize a party of their own. . . .

Until Marx it was generally thought that history was made by great men. Great men won battles, made treaties of peace, created constitutions and laws, ruled nations, and saved humanity from destruction. Marx and Engels showed, through their study of history, that this was a childish view of life and of government. The great facts of history—its wars, its governments, its art, science and literature—these were created by a deeper social force. This force, said Marx, was the economic or material force. People lived as they did and acted as they did, because they made their living in a certain way. If they used small, rude, tools, and the soil they worked was poor, their ideas would be much different from what they would be if they used larger and more productive tools upon richer soil. The nature of man's social life depends chiefly upon the physical conditions under which he is living. This same principle is true in matters of morality. An individual, or nation, or a class, will finally come to think that right which is to his material advantage. Nations make war in order to add to their possessions. Individuals engage in such work or business, as will yield them the largest pay or profits. A class will fight to the death with another class over profits or wages.

In war, killing people and burning cities is thought to be a patriotic work. If successful it is considered to be right and fine. In industry the capitalists will enslave small children, and the profits wrung from their pitiful toil goes to build churches and universities and support Christian missions. The murderous capitalist who robs cradles to get his gold comes to be praised as most "benevolent," "virtuous," "religious," etc.

When the worker, either through experience or a study of Socialism, comes to know this truth, he acts accordingly. He retains absolutely no respect for the property "rights" of the profit-takers. He will use any weapon which will win his fight. He knows that the present laws of property are made by and for the capitalists. Therefore, he does not hesitate to break them. He knows that whatever action advances the interests of the working class is right, because it will save the workers from destruction and death. A knowledge of economic determinism places the worker squarely on his intellectual feet and makes him bold and independent of mind.

14

I Confess
BENJAMIN GITLOW

. . . Dependence on the Russian Communist Party—and more specifically, on the ruling clique and the dominating person within it from time to time— became the condition *sine qua non* for every non-Russian member of the Comintern. Matters concerning the German, French, English, American or any other Communist party were first thrashed out inside the Russian Communist Party by its Political Bureau, and the decisions reached by a half a dozen Russian leaders were handed down to the Communist party in question through the channels of the Comintern. Hence, the policy of every Communist Party became dependent in large measure on the exigencies of the foreign policy of the Russian Soviet Republic, which was the prime concern of the Russian Political Bureau surely since Brest-Litovsk and more definitely and increasingly so since Rapallo, until today it is exclusively so. Official Communism has thus rapidly crystallized into no more than merely the international instrumentality of the Russian Soviet government. That was not apparent when Communism was still in the state of turbulent solution that was being shaken constantly by political winds; now, however, with its stabilization and crystallization under Stalin's personal dictatorship, it is clear that this characteristic of Communism was inherent from the start. This essential characteristic of Communism—I mean, of course, Leninist Communism in practice, not in theory—must be clearly borne in mind, if you are to understand what took place in the American Communist Party from the moment of its emergence as an open political party out of the fusion of Number One and Number Two early in 1923.

We all accepted, without any reservations, the right of the Russian Bolshevik leaders to boss our party. At the same time, we the leaders of the American Communist Party fought each other. Since basic policies were decided upon not by us but by our bosses in Moscow, ours was a struggle for power rather than for principles. In that respect, we were of course no different from Tammany Hall shysters or from any other politicians, for we all became the victims of that strongest of all the social passions, the politi-

Selected passages from Benjamin Gitlow, *I Confess,* Dutton, New York, 1940. Reprinted by permission of Mrs. Benjamin Gitlow.

cal passion. Yet the fashion among us Communist politicians—and we believed it to be far more than merely a fashion of thought, we believed it to be an incontrovertible truth—was to proceed on the premise, more readily assumed than practice, that in the Communist movement the individual factor was of negligible, if any, importance. The individual, we contended when arguing the matter with our aloof sympathizers of the Liberal Left, merely reflected social conditions. In the face of daily experiences with individual Communist leaders of opposing factions who ruthlessly connived to wrest power from us or to keep us from wresting power from them, we insisted to our Liberal friends that pure objectivity was the determining factor in all Communist politics. Therein, indeed, was the crux of the difference between lowly bourgeois politics and the politics of the proletariat's revolutionary priesthood—meaning ourselves, of course. We did not lie with malice aforethought; we lied subconsciously, to ourselves as well as to others; nevertheless, we lied. The truth is, that in the struggle for power inside the Communist Party, the personal ambitions of individuals, their selfish interests, their animal instincts of self-preservation, always come to the forefront and all but completely overshadow the political issues and the principles, which indeed serve mostly as the rationalization for the struggle. In that the Communist Party must be very much like any other political party, bourgeois or proletarian. What makes it worse than any bourgeois party, however, in that respect, is the injection of pseudo-revolutionary amorality; the effect of that is to cast into limbo the last vestiges of human decency as mere "bourgeois prejudices." It is this which flavors Communist politics with horrible bitterness, for the strife among the "comrades" proceeds with all rules suspended and any weapon at all in use, all the way from deceit, chicanery, doubledealing, patronage and bribery, to character assassination and outright assassination, if possible. Anything goes. It is this which makes every Party debate between the leaders a small-scale but highly intense civil war. Indeed, the ethics of civil war against the bourgeoisie and its White Guard defenders are merely applied to the strife among the leaders inside the Party. . . .

The years 1925 and 1926 witnessed a development of the Communist movement in all directions. The membership, in spite of the factional warfare, was devoted to the Party and fanatical in its belief in Communism. The greatest ambition of a Party member was to serve the cause and become a professional revolutionist—a paid Party official or organizer. The members were highly disciplined. They functioned like privates in a military organization. Orders given were carried out. Personal or family considerations were never taken into account; to take them into account was to be considered a petty-bourgeois, the greatest insult to a Communist. The Party was dynamic, intensely active in whatever it did. This was possible because our members gave every moment of their spare time to the Party.

This is difficult for one who has not been active in the Communist Party to understand. It can best be described by a typical Party member's daily routine, a rank and file comrade, a union member, who works during the day. In the morning he buys his Communist newspaper and reads it going to work. He may arrive a little earlier than his shopmates in order to spread Communist leaflets around without being noticed. At noon he will be engaged in some noon day activity of the Party or of his Communist trade union faction. After work, instead of going home, he will rush to Party headquarters, to attend committee meetings of the Party or of the Trade Union Educational League, of his trade union faction, and the like. Later, after eight o'clock, he may have to attend a union meeting or a meeting of his Party branch. After the meeting he probably will go back to Party headquarters to get instructions for the next day's activities.

A Party member is always meeting, for he belongs as a rule to the following organizations: The Communist Party, the Trade Union Educational League, the union of his trade, the Communist fraction in that union. The International Labor Defense, the International Workers Aid, and a fraternal organization. In all the organizations to which he belongs there are Left Wing organizations organized by the Communists into fractions of Communist Party members. All of them hold meetings. The Communist Party member must attend them all. Besides, he must attend the Party school, help circulate the Party papers, attend the caucus meetings of his faction, and be present at all the general important meetings called by the Party. In addition, all the organizations, and the organizations within the organizations to which he belongs, have special committees, with the result that the Communist Party member is always hurrying from one committee meeting to another. Sometimes an active rank and filer attends half a dozen meetings in the evening, until late into the night. Saturday afternoons are particularly crowded with numerous meetings, with perhaps an occasional demonstration thrown in. At night either his attendance is required at a Communist lecture or forum, or else he must be present at a Communist ball or entertainment. On Sunday, too, meetings and conferences take place, followed by Communist lectures and other affairs in the evening. In the summer time, if the Communist Party member finds it possible to take a few week-ends off or to take a vacation for a few weeks, he will invariably go to a Communist summer camp, where as part of his vacation enjoyment he will engage in innumerable Communist camp activities for the Party, the *Daily Worker* and the multitudinous campaigns in which the Communists are active raising money.

A Communist's life is in and of the Movement. He is like a squirrel in a cage, always running around in circles. He is so busy, so feverishly active, that it is impossible for him to see what is going on around him. His world is the Party and its incessant round of meetings. His personal associations are almost completely confined to Communists. He reads the Communist press and the numerous party tracts and magazines. A Party member even speaks a language peculiar to the Communists and foreign to others. The Communist Party members talk and think almost alike, because they keep absorbing the phrases, arguments and expressions which the Party lavishly feeds them through its press, propaganda and cultural departments.

The fanatical zeal of the Communist Party member is founded on his belief in the power of the Soviet Union and in its ultimate victory over the capitalist world. To the Communist Party member the Soviet Union is a worker's paradise, the most desirable place in the world to live in. Not only does the Communist Party member give every moment of his time to the cause but every dollar he can spare as well, often giving much more than he can afford. In fact, the contributions Communist Party members are called upon to make are out of all proportion to their earning power. There are the dues to the Party, to the union, to the Trade Union Educational League, to the International Labor Defense, to the Workers International Relief, to the Left Wing in their union, to the Communist fraternal organization, to the workers' club, besides contributions to the Party branch, the *Daily Worker,* the special appeals of the National Office for funds, and the numerous financial drives constantly carried on by the Party. In some of these drives, like support of the *Daily Worker,* members are assessed from time to time as much as a day's pay. In addition, there are always tickets to buy and sell, dozens of them every week, for every kind of affair. The Party member gives freely, happy to be able to do so. The individual Communist is a generous contributor; the Party bureaucrat, an extravagant spender. We would not hesitate to spend twenty-five thousand dollars for a single demonstration, if we deemed it politically necessary. I doubt if Chinese "bandit generals" ever taxed the Chinese peasantry more heavily than Communist officials tax the Party membership.

Courageous and disciplined, the rank-and-filers of my days were ready to give up their lives for the Party. They carried out unflinchingly the Party's order to go out on dangerous demonstrations, to do picket duty in strikes, to defy injunctions, to resist the police. The Party member would not hesitate at any time to give up his job, to leave his home and family, to engage in Party activities in some remote part of the country or anywhere in the world. Yet in most cases all this was done not only as a free sacrifice, but also in large measure as an investment in a future career. All rank and file Party members considered themselves potential political leaders of the working class. We developed this leadership psychology by impressing the members with the idea that they represented the vanguard of the working class. Hence, imitating us, their leaders, they became adept in political intrigue and trickery. The result was that Party members did not trust one another. Whenever Party members met they generally talked deprecatingly about other members. The Party was a regular gossip factory, in which the most intimate personal relations of the members and leaders were discussed and all kinds of rumors about them circulated. And of course, being embryo politicians, Party members magnified their own importance and exaggerated the extent of their activities and achievements. If they were unable to make headway, they would exaggerate the difficulties confronting them out of all proportions to the actual facts, because a Party member who did not succeed in carrying out an activity assigned to him was subjected to the harshest kind of criticism. They were afraid of this criticism and did everything to avoid it.

Many Party members were given over to fads. In Russia the men and women wore leather coats and caps. The Communists in America followed suit by wearing caps and leather coats. A Communist girl could be recognized in a crowd by her swaggering walk, her bobbed hair, her low-heeled shoes, her leather coat and boyish cap. Communists were a boisterous and jolly lot. After midnight, the meetings over, they would swarm into their favorite cafeterias, to discuss and wrangle in a more care-free vein over the problems they had been discussing, or to digest over the coffee cups the latest factional developments in the Party. This was especially true of the New York Communists, who had a night life all of their own, never getting to bed before two or three o'clock in the morning. One who joined the Party was soon caught in the Communist whirlpool. Family ties had to be broken almost immediately, the non-Communist friends dropped and one's social life completely changed. If a man was married to a non-Communist, in many instances, he would be separated from his wife and family before very long and would be found living with a girl Party member. . . .

Friendship and Politics

The Communist Party is an impersonal organization in which nothing is left to chance. All human relations are mangled, in keeping with the Procrustean standards of political schemes and plans. Long before it could hope to attain the expropriation of capitalist property, the Party had expropriated our very souls, controlling not only our behavior in public but our private actions and our thoughts. If we had friends prominent in public life, the party was bound to know about it and to determine our relations with them. . . .

In addition to being a branch or "section" of the Communist International, the Communist Party also acted as an agent of the Soviet government. Indeed, it is the link between the American Communist Party and the Soviet government that accounts for the tight grip of the Party upon its membership. The typical American Communist regards himself by virtue of his membership in the Party as an important cog in the world-wide Communist machine that serves the Soviet government. He is compensated for his opposition to the United States government by being impressed with his importance to the government of the Soviet Union. It is this tie-up with a mighty government that holds the Party and the leadership together more than any other single factor. Of course, the Soviet government has repeatedly argued that it and the Communist International are two separate entities. But their separation is as real as, say, the separation of the President of the United States from the U. S. State Department. Soviet spokesmen have always insisted that the Soviet government and the Russian Communist Party are two entirely different organizations, like, let us say, the United States government and the Republican Party during a Republican administration. Yet in Russia the Communist Party is the state even more so than the Nazi Party in Germany and the Fascist Party in Italy. Stalin, the head of the Russian Communist Party, is the recognized ruler of the Soviet government, and has been for years, even though the nominal head of the government is that political nonentity, Mikhail Kalinin. The Communist Party of the Soviet Union directly considers all the policies of the Soviet Union and its decisions then become the laws of the state. In its turn the American Communist Party has always argued that it had no connections whatsoever with the Soviet government, but the fact of the matter is that the American Communist Party is in the same relation to the Soviet government as the paid agents of Nazi Germany in the United States are to the government of the Third Reich.

Before the Soviet government was recognized by the United States, visas were issued in this country for the Soviet government by the Society for Technical Aid to Soviet Russia. This was a Russian organization which was run by the members of the Russian Federation of the Communist Party. Its affairs were subject to the control and decisions of the Party. Individuals who desired to visit the Soviet Union would get approval for their visas either from this organization or from the Party. If the Party O. K.'d them, the procurement of visas was facilitated. Very often the Party would direct-ly notify the Soviet government that it was opposed to certain persons obtaining visas. In one case, that of Abraham Cahan, Editor of the *Jewish Daily Forward*, the Party held up the granting of a visa to him for a long time, and when a visa was granted to him, the Soviet government made sure that his trip in Russia would be supervised and carefully watched by the G. P. U. At the same time, the Party has always served as an agency of informa-tion on American visitors to the Soviet Union. The Soviet government was supplied with a detailed report on particular visitors. When Party members traveled to the Soviet Union they received special credentials from the Party which were recognized by the customs officials and the G. P. U. agents on the border. Presentation of such a Party credential, which was typed on a small strip of white silk, stamped with the Party seal and sewed into the lining of one's coat, immediately gave the bearer special consideration. Furthermore, Party members who went to the Soviet Union to settle perma-nently or for a period of years obtained transfers to the Communist Party of the Soviet Union only after the American Party received the membership request of the Russian Party and approved of the transfer.

The opening of the Amtorg Trading Corporation, the Soviet's trading corporation in the United States, gave the Party many advantages. In staffing the Amtorg with technical help, bookkeepers, stenographers, trans-lators, salesmen, advertising personnel and publicity agents, the Party was consulted, the important, confidential and well-paying positions being filled by Party members. Several hundred Party members were employed by the Amtorg. These workers became in fact part of the Party bureaucracy, their jobs depending definitely upon the good will of the Party. The Party mem-bers working in the Amtorg were organized into an Amtorg Nucleus, but this nucleus was kept a strict secret. The head of the nucleus was the confidential liaison officer between it and the Party. Party members in the Amtorg had to pay whatever assessments or taxes were levied upon them by the Party. Failure to do so would have meant loss of their job. But the influence of the Party in the Amtorg did not apply only to Party members. Others who sought jobs in the Amtorg did not hesitate to court the favor of Party leaders, and many who were job-conscious rather than class-conscious joined the Communist Party in order to obtain jobs. When Soviet trade or technical missions came to the United States, it was a rule that the Amtorg sought to obtain from the Party not only advice and other help for these missions but that Party members were also given posts on the missions as translators, interpreters, guides and the like. Party members who obtained these jobs consulted with the Party on what they could do to be of service to it and from time to time gave special reports to the Party on matters of importance. Moreover, the heads of the Amtorg very often conferred with the members of the Party Secretariat on political matters pertinent to their activities. Jay Lovestone and I had a number of conferences with Saul Bron, head of the Amtorg, on how a movement could be started in the United States Congress for the recognition of the Soviet Union. At another time, when the Amtorg arranged an exhibition in New York City, employing Party members almost exclusively in taking care of the various phases of the exhibition, we were requested by the head of the Amtorg to discourage Party members from attending the exhibition, because they wanted to create the impression that it was a bourgeois affair.

But the Party was tied to the Soviet government by stronger strings as well. Most important of these was the G. P. U. Directly upon the request of the G. P. U., the Party supplied it with Party members who could be added to its espionage staff. These Party members became full-fledged G. P. U. agents, employed and paid by the Soviet government. These agents were the link between the Party and the G. P. U. Contacts were made for them by the Party Secretariat, who from time to time advised them how to proceed. A Party member who became a G. P. U. agent dropped out of Party activity the moment he was selected. He became subject to the severe discipline which the G. P. U. imposes upon its agents. Only very few of the Party leaders knew when a Party member became a G. P. U. agent, and they kept this information strictly confidential. Every time the Party was called upon by the G. P. U. to help, it was paid for any expenses involved far above what was actually spent, the surplus going into the Party treasury. But we, the Party leaders, who greatly cherished every opportunity to be of service to the G. P. U., aid in its work and be in its confidence, knew that the G. P. U. kept a close watch on us, too. It was an open secret among us, the Party leaders, that the G. P. U. was supplying Moscow with a complete record of all the leaders of the American Communist Party along with reports on the activities of the Party as a whole. But it was impossible really to find out whether the G. P. U. agents who came to the United States, many of whom were unknown to the Party leadership, favored or disapproved of the Party leaders and their activities. However, we all knew that the Soviet government did not consider our Party merely a section of the Communist International, which the leaders of the Soviet government dominated, but that they looked upon the American Communist Party as one of its agencies.

Nor were the Party's services to the Soviet government confined to the borders of the United States. The Soviet government utilized members of the American Communist Party over a far-flung area that included China,

Japan, Germany, Mexico and the countries of Central and South America. Charles Krumbein, a leader of the American Party, was sent to England, presumably to work for the Profintern. Jack Johnstone went to India, from where he was deported by the British government. H. M. Wicks went on special missions to Germany and Central America. Earl Browder headed a bureau, known as the Pan-Pacific Trade Union Secretariat, with headquarters in Hankow, China. Party members traveled as representatives of the Communist International and the Profintern to the four corners of the earth, not only to carry out the particular policies of the Comintern and Profintern, which were adopted as part of the intricate policies of the Soviet government in the spheres controlled by these two organizations, but the representatives of these two organizations also served directly as G. P. U. and all sorts of other agents of the Soviet government as well. This was strikingly brought out by the activities of the Soviet government in China during the rise to power of the Kuomintang in 1924-1927. Not only were Russian Communists poured into China, but also Communists from other countries. They made up the trusted corps of confidential representatives who watched out for Soviet interests and helped guide Soviet policy through the difficult maze of Chinese politics. . . .

The Bolshevik rulers of Russia are extreme nationalists. All their actions are predicated on Russian national interests. But what the Bolsheviks have been taught by Lenin they have never forgotten, and that is that propaganda is a very valuable and effective weapon. The Bolsheviks have never been parsimonious with their propaganda machine. They have spent lavishly for propaganda, with the result that they have impressed millions of people with the belief that in Russia a new society is being built which is greatly benefiting the people, and that the Russian form of dictatorship surpasses all democracies in the freedom and liberty its people enjoy. They go further and seek to gain the loyalty and support of the masses throughout the world for the Soviet Union, by instilling in them a patriotism for the Soviet Union as the fatherland of the exploited and oppressed people of the world. The *Pravda* greeting the Eighteenth Party Congress on March tenth, 1939, bore this out, when it declared:

The exploiters and oppressors in all countries feel and know that the decisions of the Eighteenth Congress of the Bolsheviks will make the Soviet Union—*the fatherland of the working people and the oppressed of the whole world*—even stronger, more powerful, will hasten the triumph of Communism throughout the world.

No other government in the world enjoys or can afford to maintain the kind of propaganda machine the Soviet government maintains in the name of Communism and for the liberation of mankind from exploitation and oppression. The Communist propaganda machine is built up on the basis of idealism. It does not depend upon the sending of paid agents from the Soviet Union to other countries, as the Nazis do, to carry on its propaganda. In all countries it has Communist parties made up of the countries' nationals, which constitutes the kernel of its propaganda machine in that country. But its propaganda agents are not confined to the Communists, for many liberals and other well-intentioned people are impressed with the Soviet's virtues and become its most ardent supporters and propagandists. Besides, through the activities of the Communist Party machine, the Soviet government is able to maintain contacts for information and all other purposes it deems necessary in the key industries of the country, in the newspapers and agencies of public information, in the schools and colleges, in the government, and even in the armed forces. Moreover, Communists seek support for the foreign policies of the Soviet government from the government of the United States, while simultaneously organizing for the ultimate aim of turning the United States into a Communist totalitarian state.

In every country where the labor movement has fallen under the spell of the Communists, the people as a whole have had to pay very dearly for it. . . .

The short-lived vigor shown by American fascism during the 1930's issued from two sources: the total despair of a small section of the lower middle class, with a consequent willingness to try any remedy which would salvage private property; and the example and financial help of the Italian and German corporate states. Unlike the indigenous rightist extremism which some writers traced back to the Know-Nothings and Populists, fascist groups derived what strength they could muster not from a Protestant rural population, but from the urban concentrations of the Eastern seaboard and the Great Lakes.[1] Fascist ideologues and agitators hammered at six basic themes: the need to reassert national pride, with a corresponding suspicion of anything smacking of international co-operation; social discipline, to be enforced by revitalizing traditional family ties and invoking the full powers of a corporate state; substitution of an authoritarian elite for representative government; economic policies allegedly beneficial to small merchants and persons with fixed incomes, who distrusted both big business and organized labor; emphasis on an international conspiracy of financial interests, somehow identified with both Zionists and communists; and a strident insistence on measures for preserving the Nordic stock, including, as Madole makes clear, the eradication of other races.[2]

Although the subject of hysterical warnings from leftists, fascism in the United States has never constituted a sustained, popularly supported challenge to democracy. Its message of hate and nonsense was spread, however, by groups attaining a semblance of political importance in the worst years of the depression. Most successful and lasting was the National Union for Social Justice, headquartered in Royal Oak, Michigan, and totally dominated by the controversial Roman Catholic priest, Father Charles E. Coughlin.[3] Coughlin established a national reputation, and gathered a large following, with his weekly radio sermons—sermons which were indiscriminate mixtures of religion, politics, and racism. Beginning as a champion of Franklin Roosevelt—he once compared FDR to Christ—Father Coughlin soon grew petulant when it became clear that the new president had no intention of making him his chief economic advisor.[4] While recognizing the radio priest's influence, Roosevelt rendered Coughlin only small favors, turned a deaf ear to his apoplectic denunciations, and shrewdly permitted Coughlin to isolate himself from both political and church support. As his strength slipped away, Coughlin shifted his message ever further toward extremism. He moved from a neo-Populist call for free silver, which had generated a mild responsiveness in the farm belt, to an aggressive defense of corporate-statism.[5]

Coughlin envisioned a New America patterned after the New Germany of Adolf Hitler and Mussolini's resurrected Roman Empire. He used his magazine, *Social Justice,* to spell out his program for a fascist state.[6] His support, drawn chiefly from urban, disillusioned Irish and German Catholic merchants and professional persons, shrank perceptibly as he attempted to excuse nazi and fascist aggression in Europe.[7] By the time of American entry into World War II, his once impressive following had dwindled to a small clique composed of authoritarians and badly misled or deranged individuals who were convinced of Coughlin's messianic credentials. The nation's salvation, wrote one such supporter, would come "when you become dictator of our land . . . [,] as indeed you must because you are the only virulent [sic] leader standing between us and communism."[8] Coughlin no doubt agreed, but whatever hopes he may have harbored were ended by an embarrassed church hierarchy's order to cease political activities.[9]

Mussolini's clumsy efforts to enlist Italian-Americans in the fascist cause—through appeals to their heritage and, when these failed, blackmail or threats—made little headway in the early 1930's and ended at war's beginning. The experience of the Friends of the New Germany was identical.[10] Facist activities in the United States were confined to fifth-column efforts and minor disturbances created by street-corner orators like William Dudley Pelley, Gerald Winrod, and Joe McWilliams, whose legions included the economic wreckage of the Great Depression and scattered with the first shots fired at Pearl Harbor.[11]

From the beginning, American fascism claimed only a thin veneer of respectability. There is little evidence to show that the pro-fascist writings of Lawrence Dennis or Ezra Pound had any significant influence, and the tentative nazi sympathies of some America-Firsters, like Charles A. Lindbergh, Jr., disappeared in the rush of patriotism which accompanied American involvement in the war.[12] Today, American fascism is represented by tiny groups such as the American Nazi Party and the National Renaissance Party, preaching a paranoiac message of bitterness and violence.

NOTES

1. Seymour M. Lipset, "Social Stratification and 'Right Wing Extremism'," *British Journal of Sociology,* X (December, 1959), pp. 348-349; Victor C. Ferkiss, "Populist Influences on American Fascism," *Western Political Quarterly,* 10 (June, 1957), p. 350; and Paul S. Holbo, "Wheat or What? Populism and American Fascism," *Western Political Quarterly,* 14 (September, 1961), p. 735.

2. Ferkiss, "Populist Influences on American Fascism," pp. 350-351; and Holbo, "Wheat or What?," pp. 729-730.

3. Craig A. Newton, "Father Coughlin and his National Union for Social Justice," *Southwestern Social Science Quarterly,* 41 (December, 1960), p. 341.

4. Authur M. Schlesinger, Jr., *The Politics of Upheaval* (Boston: Houghton Mifflin Company, 1960) pp. 76-83.

5. James P. Shenton, "The Coughlin Movement and the New Deal," *Political Science Quarterly,* LXXIII (September, 1958), p. 371.

6. *Social Justice,* I, n.s. (April 4, 1938), pp. 11, 14; *Ibid.,* II, n.s. (December 19, 1938), p. 14.

7. Newton, "Father Coughlin," p. 344; Shenton, "The Coughlin Movement and the New Deal," p. 360.

8. Quoted in Shenton, "The Coughlin Movement and the New Deal," pp. 362-363.

9. *Ibid.*

10. Ferkiss, "Populist Influences on American Fascism," p. 371.

11. *Ibid.,* pp. 361-362, 371; John Roy Carlson, *Under Cover* (New York: Books, 1943), *passim.*

12. Ferkiss, "Populist Influences on American Fascism," pp. 361, 367-368; Charles A. Lindbergh, "Aviation, Geography and Race," *Reader's Digest,* XXXV (November, 1939), pp. 64-67; and Victor C. Ferkiss, "Ezra Pound and American Fascism," *Journal of Politics,* 17 (May, 1955), p. 173.

15

How Long Can Democracy and Capitalism Last?

CHARLES E. COUGHLIN

If the World War was fought to make the world safe for democracy, there are many signs to indicate that the next war will be fought to make the world safe either for fascism, socialism, communism, or social justice. Needless to say, despite all the protestations of pacifists, of members of the League of Nations and of devotees of the policy of "peace-at-any-price," there will be another war before the present generation passes out of existence.

I am speaking not only as a churchman who still has faith in the prophetical words of Christ, Who reminded us that there will be wars and rumors of war even until the end of the world. I am venturing to speak as a layman who is confronted by the imponderable fact that the world is prepared for a war hitherto undreamed of.

The purple ink of the signers was not dried on the Treaty of Versailles before Italy, France, England, Russia, Japan and Turkey were found to be spending more money on armaments than they spent previous to 1914. Despite their avowals to the contrary, there is not one nation, including our own, which has removed the causes that produce war. Foreign trade at a profit, commercial greed, national hatred—this trinity of major vices is still regulating the policies and fashioning the programs of influential diplomats.

More than that, the internal unrest evident in every nation is still to be conjured with. It is still the psychology of many governments that this internal unrest can be dissipated by focusing its wrath upon an external peril.

Whatever causes or motives will be alleged to set Europe, Asia and America aflame with the fires of war, it is apparent that perhaps only England and the United States will even whisper the slogan of "save democracy."

Modern democracy, as we know it, was cradled almost in the same year as was modern capitalism. Together they matured and grew old, within the short span of one hundred and fifty years. The span of the life of feudalism was longer by hundreds of years. The monarchical form of government was a Methuselah, compared to democracy. In fact, all forms of government last

From *Today,* Vol. III (December 29, 1934), pp. 6-7.

only as long as the economic systems under which they are regulated. Perhaps this thought will suggest, to some historian of economics, a new angle of approach to a subject that is as hoary as the hills. I wonder if our democratic form of government is crashing because capitalism has decayed— or is it the other way about? That is a question similar to the priority of the egg or the hen.

But what was the essential thought associated with modern democracy? In theory, it was supposed to be a government by the people, contradistinguished to the monarchical form, which is a government by a king or by an individual. In modern times, it has never been possible to have a complete and perfect government by the people. The closest we ever came to realizing this ideal was many hundreds of years ago, when the some twenty thousand citizens of Athens, not counting the seventy thousand resident slaves of the city, assembled to participate in the initiation, the legislation and the execution of laws.

Our democracy is limited to the indirect initiation, legislation and execution of law. Our voters have little or no opportunity to write bills or to determine policies. There was never a better example to prove this statement than in the days of President Wilson, when the people elected him on the platform of "He kept us out of war!" only to awaken to the black reality that it was he who inveigled us into war.

Moreover, the revolution within the ranks of democracy, and its dissolution, are still in progress here in the United States. Our democratic government was conceived to consist of three distinct major activities: Congress initiated and passed laws, as the legislative branch. The office of the President, assisted by his Cabinet and appointed officers, was designed to execute these laws, while the courts and the judiciary were planned to determine legal application of laws.

Now—in the past two years especially—we discover that the Chief Executive, his secretaries and his appointees (who were neither chosen nor elected by the people) are found to be initiating laws. We even discover that Representatives and Senators, during the past two elections, appealed to the electorate for votes on the ground that "they would support Roosevelt." Call this democracy, if you will. But it is not the same kind of democracy which was conceived by Jefferson, Washington and Adams. To put it mildly, it is an evolutionized form of democratic government. Or to express it harshly, it is a revolution which has silently gone on with little and negligible protest coming from the mass of the American people. Evidently, they like it, or at least they have grown leg-weary of trying to keep apace with the wolfish politicians who, since the days of Andrew Jackson, have misrepresented them too freely.

These thoughts are only opinions and personal observations. But in sequence, I am prompted to remark that if democracy even in America is showing signs of weakening, it is partially due, in its last analysis, to the decadence of capitalism. It is my opinion that, although we have democracy in name as our form of government, it is really a plutocracy, by which the capitalist class, through sheer force of intellect and indisputable power of wealth, succeeds in dominating the minds of the Representatives. That accounts for the fact that so many thousands of laws are passed to protect property rights. That accounts for the fact that the original Constitution of our nation was legally perverted, in that we permitted the financial class to coin and regulate the value of money, which prerogative originally belonged to Congress. That accounts for the fact that wealth is monopolized in the hands of a few; for the fact that, even in the prosperous year of 1929, 71 per cent of our population was existing below the American standard of living; and for the fact that, in this year of 1934, more than 83 per cent of our people are legally deprived of a just share of the wealth which they and their ancestors helped create.

Incidentally, in his letter, *Quadragesimo Anno,* Pius XI, who is the highest ranking official in the Catholic Church, both in dignity and in power, particularly criticizes the economic system of capitalism for the following reasons, which I will paraphrase:

1. Modern capitalism violated right order because it so employs the working of wage-earning classes as to divert business and economic activity to its own advantage, without any regard to the human dignity of the workers, the social character of economic life, social justice or the common good.

2. It is evident that, in our days, capitalism not only accumulates wealth but also immense power and despotic economic domination into the hands of a few; and that those few, who are frequently not the owners but only the trustees and directors of invested funds, administer these funds at their own pleasure. (It is absolutely erroneous to say that the public utility corporations, for example, are owned by hundreds of thousands of stockholders; that the steel corporation has 500,000 owners, and General Motors 300,000 owners. As a matter of fact, most of the stock in the public utilities, in the steel industry and in the motor industry is controlled by a very small group of men whose representatives outvote the hundreds of thousands of so-called stockholders.

3. This capitalistic power has become particularly irresistible because it was exercised by those who held and controlled money and who governed and determined the allotment of credit. For that reason, upon bended knee, industry and labor and agriculture in the past were forced to beg a supply of

life blood, so to speak, for the entire economic body. These financiers grasped, as it were, in their hands the very soul of production, so that no one dared breathe, let alone live, against their will.

4.   Free competition is a further characteristic note of modern capitalism. This permits the survival only of those who are the strongest, and means that those who fight most relentlessly, careless of the Commandments and of social justice, are the victors.

5.   Modern capitalism has always been identified with the dictatorship of economic domination. It was chiefly due to this phase of modern capitalism that fierce battles arose to acquire control of the nation, so that its resources of power, of light, of water and of money, as well as the House of Representatives, could be abused in the struggle for existence.

It was the same economic dictatorship which could not brook a rival; for by its very nature it created wars amongst the nations.

6.   A well-known characteristic of modern capitalism is unbridled ambition—ambition for domination, which has succeeded the desire to profits. As a result of this, the whole economic life has become hard, cruel and relentless.

Furthermore, the multiplication of Federal and state officers, the intermingling and scandalous confusion of duties and offices of civil authority, have been created under capitalism to protect the privileged classes. No wonder our government sometimes is regarded as only a slave bound over to the service of human passion and greed—a slave who, if he attempts to rebel, is confronted with capital on strike until, finally, the nation must come whimpering to the hand of the banker who holds the lash.

7.   From modern capitalism, as from a poisoned fountain-head, there flows that stream of detestable internationalism by which several families dominate affairs not only in America, but also in the central banks of Europe, and fly from their mastheads the flag which bears this emblem: "My country! 'tis where my fortune is." It is an internationalism which cares not for the righteousness of social justice or of human rights, but only for the protection of its private property. This was made evident by capitalistic France who, recently wedded her destinies to those of communistic Russia.

These seven points form the platform of a rather strong indictment against capitalism.

It was recently admitted by those who are supposed to dwell within the holy of holies at Washington that Mr. Roosevelt is determined to protect and cultivate the capitalistic system. My personal opinion is that he has set himself to accomplish a task which is not more difficult than removing in a sieve the water from the Atlantic Ocean to the swimming pool of the New York Athletic Club. By no means do I subscribe to the opinion that, if capitalism is worn out beyond repair, we then must adopt communism or socialism or even fascism. I simply mean that capitalism has become so identified with abuses which encumber it that its nature is merged with the abuses. Their removal means the burial of capitalism.

To my mind, the capitalistic system is indisputably united to a financial system by which private individuals coin and regulate the value of money, and control credit and currency. It is a system which, by its very nature, gains control over industry. Its essential policy is to exist for profits in dollars and cents. It cares not how it makes these profits, so long as the stockholders or owners of industry receive constant dividends, even while factory doors are closed and laborers are forced to live in non-productive idleness. It even clings to the heresy that profits or interests should be gained from destructive and nonproductive borrowings, such as war bonds and relief bonds.

Although capitalism was originally conceived as an economic system by which the present generation could borrow from the future generations, at interest, for productive purposes, this definition has been lost sight of. The term "productive purposes" has been changed to "profitable purposes," and the "profitable" has been interpreted in money of some sort which must accrue to the lender.

Under capitalism, industry—which consists of the investor, the scientist and the laborer—can be profitably engaged only while producing dividends for owners of the machines.

Now, this theory of economics was wonderful in those days when our great problem was that of production. At that time, the scientist and the laborer were constantly at work, endeavoring to balance the law of supply and demand. When the disciples of Watt, Fulton and Edison became so successful in designing and perfecting mechanical devices which permitted the almost instantaneous production of the necessities and conveniences required by our people, then the laborer who was paid only while he worked, and not on a basis of a share in the profits for what he produced, was forced to become the enemy of capitalism, because this economic theory never entertained seriously within its definition the concept of distributing equitably, to the laborer, a share in the wealth which was created.

Thus, I believe that the economic system of tomorrow will not be that type of socialism which desires to nationalize not only natural resources, but also all productive industry. Nor will it be capitalism wedded to the theory of private financialism and production for a profit. It will be a new system based on the belief that wealth is not money, but that wealth is created by the union of capital and labor; and that this wealth must be distributed, even through the intervention of the government, in such a way that every laborer who cooperates in producing this wealth shall have that share of it which will enable him to enjoy, according to his merits, the things which we are capable of growing and of manufacturing as a nation.

Of course, this new system, which I have so often referred to over the radio as social justice, can never be instituted and reduced to practice unless the majority of the citizens adopt the principle of religious stewardship. By this, I mean that no man has absolute ownership over anything in this world. That "the earth is the Lord's and the fulness thereof" must not be forgotten. Because He created us, He is in a manner bound, by a sort of justice, to provide us with the food and the shelter and the necessities which our nature demands. It is His divine economy that no men so control the earth and its fulness that thousands or millions of our fellow-creatures are deprived of its usage, provided they are willing, in a social manner, to work for their own sustenance.

But capitalism, denying the doctrine of stewardship and identifying all wealth with money which is privately controlled and privately used, controls the wealth and the world itself when the big problem confronting us today is not one of production, but of distribution. It is my opinion that capitalism cannot face or solve this problem, because its nature has become identified with its abuses.

16

Fascism for America
LAWRENCE DENNIS

Conservatives like Messrs. Hoover and Ogden Mills have repeatedly warned us of the fascist danger implicit in the trends of the Roosevelt New Deal. Only this week a group of moderate socialists, rendering a report in the name of the Methodist Federation for Social Service, admonished the Nation that Senator Long, Father Coughlin, and General Johnson, all of

From Annals of the American Academy of Political and Social Science, Vol. 180 (July, 1935), pp. 62-73.

whom either now are or recently have been supporters of the New Deal, constitute a serious fascist menace. Moderate socialists generally will be found to concur in the generalization that present trends in this country are towards fascism. As for the orthodox Communists, any one who is familiar with their current writings and utterances is aware that one of their dogmas is that the reign of a fascist antichrist is likely to be the culminating phase of the decline of capitalism and the prelude to the opening of the communist millennium. Indeed, about the only important leaders who do not openly express this fundamental agreement as to the imminence of fascism, and even as to its actuality in a modified form, are our three outstanding leaders—President Roosevelt, Senator Long, and Father Coughlin—and their followers, these leaders being charged by their conservative and liberal critics with fascist tendencies.

The Liberal Diagnosis

Now, I entirely agree with the Hoovers, the Norman Thomases, and the Communists that our three foremost political and spiritual leaders are moving in fascist directions. But I do not agree with the critics of these leaders that fascism is per se something to be feared or fought. It appears to me that prevailing social forces the world over make a fascist trend the inevitable alternative to chaos or communism. I cannot be sure at present whether our momentarily outstanding leaders will lead us on to fascism or to chaos. They are not clear in their own minds, as yet, as to ends and means. Therefore it seems to me that instead of denouncing a trend we are clearly powerless to arrest, those of us who can think and still have a chance to think out loud ought to try to clarify the issues so that the wills of the leaders and their followings may be clarified as to choices of ends and means. It is significant that I, an apologist for the authoritarian state and a critic of liberal democracy, should be trying to fix the thought of constructive minds on the analysis of present trends with a view to creating informed judgments and making enlightened choices, while the rabble of the liberal intelligentsia is largely occupied with organizing emotional demonstrations and unloosing floods of impassioned words against the fascist trend which is sweeping the world.

Now, although I agreed with the diagnosis by Messrs. Hoover and Mills that we are moving toward fascism under the leadership of Messrs. Roosevelt, Long, and Coughlin, I cannot accept their prescription of a fight to preserve and reinvigorate the old system. Believing it doomed, I see no sense in fighting for it. Fighting for lost causes imposed on mankind the most futile and criminal sort of warfare. British mercantilism which was doomed in 1775, and the Southern planter system with its accompaniment of Negro slavery which was doomed by 1850, each fought on American soil two futile wars for two doomed or lost causes. Why? Well, largely because certain sincere and worthy people felt it to be a matter of duty and honor loyally to fight for a system under which they had been fairly well off.

Most of us here today, quite as much as Mr. Hoover and Mr. Mills, have been fairly well off under the liberal-capitalist system. Like all the other doomed systems of the past, it has glorious traditions which can be made to evoke dynamic responses from large numbers of people. But if it is an order doomed by the irresistible trend of prevailing social forces, why fight for it?

Every time I read an utterance of Mr. Hoover or exponents of his orthodox and traditional liberal capitalism, I think of the British loyalists of the Stuart dynasty since 1688. It is pathetic and romantic to want a boat to row you over to bonny Prince Charlie, and a construction in distress can be almost as full of pathos as an exiled prince in distress. All that is needed now for the loyalists of the liberal American Constitution is a few good ballads. I offer this suggestion to the Republican National Committee. But I see the captains of industry, along with the realistic leaders of radical reaction to prolonged depression, climbing on the fascist band wagon.

The Communist Diagnosis

As for the communist diagnosis of the present phase of capitalist decline, particularly as to the proposition that it obviously indicates fascism in the interest of the elite of the present order, I am in substantial agreement. The Hoover conservatives say that we are going fascist and that it will be the end of liberal capitalism. To this I say "Check." The Communists say that we are going fascist because it will be the only salvation of the elite of the present order. To this I say "Double check."

With the rest of the communist thesis as to fascism, I disagree. The communist contention that any possible fascist formula will be doomed to early disaster, I find utterly unprovable. I also deny the communist assertion that any fascist formula would necessarily prove detrimental to the welfare of the people. This latter proposition, of course, raises issues of ultimate values rather than of facts, so it cannot be argued out. Naturally, I reject many of the communist values, one of the most important of which is that human welfare demands the liquidation of the elite of the old order. Liquidation, as you know, is a euphemism for experiences like being stood up before a Communist firing squad.

I find the bourgeoisie of this country too numerous and too strong to be liquidated except in one of the bloodiest and most prolonged civil wars the world has ever known. Aside from the consideration that I should not like to be liquidated, I cannot but feel that the liquidation of so large and useful a group of persons would be a greater loss to the rest of the community than the advantages any dictatorship of triumphant proletarian revolutionary leaders could possible vouchsafe to the community.

So I am against the Marxian class struggle. I am in favor of a middle-class revolution and against a proletarian revolution. The middle-class revolution has already begun. I call it fascist. I hope it can be more productive of human values than the middle-class revolutions of England in 1648 and 1688, of America from 1776 to 1825, or of France from 1789 to 1815.

I am prepared to make a concession to the communist thesis which I cannot make to the liberal thesis. I am prepared to admit that, given a conceivable combination of circumstances and events, the radicalism of Lenin, as it might be made explicit and effective by a regime of competent, professional, power-hungry, revolutionary leaders, having a high order of military and administrative genius, could be made to work. I am unable to see how the radicalism of Adam Smith, John Locke, and John Stuart Mill, now the conservatism of Herbert Hoover, can possibly be made to work in the world of Mussolini, Hitler, and Stalin. I consider any one of the last three named leaders fitter to survive in the present struggle for existence. I would remind any who may not be clear on this point that fitness to survive is not an ethical quality.

Failure of the Present System

The reason why my money is not on the liberals and why my sympathies are not with their ideologies is due to a complex of facts implicit in the present situation and of personal preferences. I find the liberal theory and practice inadequate both to what I consider to be social requirements and to my own personal requirements. I am wholly uninterested in explanations of its failures or in prescriptions for its recovery. It has failed. It has proved inadequate. Therefore, by the ineroxable law of the survival of the fittest, it is doomed.

In the present crisis of liberalism which began in 1914, the exponents, the theorists, and the practitioners of liberalism have had their innings. They and their system have failed. I cannot and do not have to prove that a new system will work better. For a new system inevitably to emerge out of the crisis of the present system, it is necessary only to have it established that the present system is inadequate. The growing ranks of the recipients of state relief and of the frustrated elite of the middle classes, are going to be more and more swayed in their emotional reactions and impulses to action by the simple logic I have just stated: When a system fails or proves inadequate, a new one is indicated. There is only one argument that can defeat that logic, and that argument is turning the failure or the inadequacy of the system challenged into success and adequacy.

The liberal leaders have had their chance since 1914. They have been slipping one by one into the abyss. They have failed. The people are not interested in the excuses or sympathetic to pleas for a second chance. They have ears now only for leaders who promise a new system. New leaders will enjoy power only as long as they move in the direction of a new system. Mr. Roosevelt can hold his prestige only as long as people believe in the New Deal.

Let me emphasize the fact that we face the situation of a system which has been giving increasing signs since 1914 that it no longer works tolerably well. It came out of all the wars of the nineteenth century stronger than it went in. It is therefore nonsense to say that war is the cause of the depression or the world crisis of liberal capitalism. Liberalism won the Napoleonic wars but lost the late World War. Liberalism in England, America, and continental Europe had won innumerable wars up to 1914.

Government Financing of the System

Need I run over a bill of particulars to substantiate the proposition that the present system no longer works, and that the changes now being inaugurated in this country are not reforms calculated to restore the system to normal operating efficiency? The banks could not reopen and they could not now stay open without Government intervention. Public order could not be maintained if the state failed to increase public expenditure to provide work and relief for the growing number of the destitute and unemployed. Although surplus bank reserves are over two and a quarter billion dollars, or enough to support an expansion of commercial loans in excess of twenty billion dollars, bank loans to industry and commerce have been almost steadily shrinking during the past two years. Banks do not lend and investors do not put idle funds into new enterprises or construction because under present conditions the prospects of getting a return are not good enough.

The measure of recovery from the panicky lows of 1933 which we momentarily enjoy in the lull before the next crash is proportionate to and dependent on the amount of Government money actually being disbursed to prevent banks from being closed, to pay for labor that private enterprise will not hire, and to give money to farmers and other producers which they could not obtain in the open market. Not only the unemployed, but the banks, the railroads, agriculture, and industry are all on the dole. Profits are being obtained by certain producers through the Government financing of curtailment of production. But for this Government financing on credit of curtailment of production, prices would have continued their fall until every bank, insurance company, and large debtor in the country would have gone into insolvency.

Two things are certain: (1) The Government cannot go on financing a curtailment of production without lowering the national standard of living and without thereby increasing the violence of popular discontent; (2) the Government cannot go on financing curtailment of production, the maintenance of artificial price levels, the solvency of insolvent railroads and financial institutions, and a growing army of destitute unemployed all by the process of borrowing.

The orderly processes of the liberal-capitalist system call for adjustment of the financial difficulties through bankruptcy, mortgage foreclosures—putting the country through the legal wringer, in other words. The system calls for adjustment of market, price, and wage difficulties by letting prices and employment be determined by the free play of supply and demand without Government subsidy to production curtailment or to subsistence of the unemployed. There is not a serious-minded man in the country who would long keep his head on if he tried to put the country through the wringer of orderly capitalist readjustment. Therefore I say the system is doomed and no longer works. The plea of the conservatives for a return to the Constitution is absurd when the strict enforcement of constitutional property rights would precipitate civil war.

Every economic adjustment today rests on Government interventions in new and innumerable forms. Therefore I say we are headed toward fascism, communism, or chaos. It is not yet fascism or communism because the bases of Government intervention do not at present constitute a system which can be rationally defined or successfully maintained. In other words, the underlying scheme of Government intervention does not constitute a stable system of social administration. It seems to work only because the scheme of Government intervention now in operation is a sort of toboggan—the toboggan slide of the dollar and national credit to the vanishing point. When we hit bottom, we shall have chaos or fascism. I should like to see fascism before we hit bottom.

Briefly, there is no recovery of the orderly capitalist sort, here, in England, in France, or in Canada. There cannot be such recovery without a revival of private investment in adequate volume. There cannot be a revival of private investment in adequate volume under present conditions of closed world markets, artificial maintenance of prices, and colossal government expenditures for relief. Liberalism can stand off the final crash only as long as strong liberal governments like those of the United States, England, and France can coast along down the toboggan of inflation. But on that route, liberalism will have a one-way ride.

Liberalism in Germany survived the postwar inflationary ride only as long as the financially sound liberal countries like the United States and England could support the international financial structure. When liberalism in America, England, and France takes this last ride, there will be no other financially sound liberal countries to maintain the integrity of liberal-capitalistic institutions with the aid of foreign loans and financial arrangements. As I see it, liberalism in America is on its last ride down the dollar toboggan.

Liberalism cannot achieve a governmental pattern of intervention which can be stabilized and made permanently to work, and there's the rub. Granted this generalization which I think I have sufficiently established, we have the alternatives of some form of authoritarian state to do a job of economic or social planning, or chaos. I do not have to prove that state planning will succeed; I have only to prove that without state planning, conditions are intolerable.

Ends and Means

Broadly summarized, the issues are matters of ends and means. The ends of the liberal-capitalist state are mainly those of good policing, the protection of life and property, and the enforcement of contrasts, with a little welfare in the form of education, sanitation, and traffic regulation thrown in, all on the broad assumption that individuals can best plan their economic activities without other government intervention. The ends of the authoritarian state are some sort of planned social order, made explicit and effective by the state.

There is a plan under both the liberal and the authoritarian scheme of things. But the plan of the liberal scheme of things results mostly from the play of individual and competitive initiatives in a relatively free market and field of economic choices. The plan of the authoritarian scheme of things has to result from the planning of a central authority, which must always be really a council of *persons,* charged with this function. Hence the epithet "dictatorship" attaches so easily to the planned state.

Now fascism, as a term, differs from communism, as a term, for the purposes of this discussion, largely in the following respect: The communist plan is, for the moment, whatever the Communist council of elders or cardinals of the international Communist faith, assembled in Moscow, decide and promulgate; while the fascist plan is whatever the fascist council in a given nation decides.

As yet there is no fascist council planning government intervention in this country. Consequently, any fascist plan for America which I might offer you would of necessity have to be largely the creation of my imagination. A Communist, on the other hand, could give you a plan for America fresh from the pigeonholes of the Moscow Communist Party bureaucracy. The ends of a planned society can be many and different in different societies. The means of an authoritarian state, however, are always essentially governmental. Therein communism and fascism are alike. But in this connection "governmental" must be understood as referring to everything that enters into the enterprise of achieving a centrally planned scheme of social organization. Hence, both the communist and the fascist states are properly called totalitarian.

I shall try briefly to lay down certain broad generalizations as to both ends and means of an ideal fascist authoritarian state for this country.

Public Welfare

The fundamental ends of government and public administration, whether under fascism, liberalism, communism, or any other "ism," are obviously public order and the realization of some idealized scheme of public welfare. I have little patience with those liberal, fascist, or communist critics of other political systems who assume that those systems are conceived and operated by wicked and insane leaders whose chief motivation in the exercise of political power is the gratification of irrational personal caprices at the expense of the welfare of the people they govern. Order and public welfare, I believe, are the ends of every government in operation today. But there are different schemes of maintaining order, and there are different values and hierarchies of values to make up the content of any scheme of public welfare. The ideologies and the methodologies of welfare differ.

The weakness of the liberal scheme is that it can no longer maintain order without concerning itself with economic government in ways which are admittedly incompatible with the basic tenets of liberalism. And the trouble with the liberal scheme of welfare is obviously that too many people are dissatisfied with it. Liberalism stands condemned, not of an indifference to welfare, but of failure to work out its ideologies and methodologies of welfare. As I have already stated, this amounts to saying that the liberal plan no longer works. The alternatives are chaos or an authoritarian plan.

Security of Labor

The ends of public order and welfare today must mean, among other things, certain types of specific government enterprise like the following: First, the state must assure employment and a tolerable standard of living to the people. This of course could be achieved by a military mobilization of all the people in economic enterprises of appropriate sorts to provide the requisite elements of goods and services to make up some scheme of the good life.

Such a program of military mobilization would obviously mean complete communism and the end of private property rights. If private property rights are not to be entirely expropriated by the state in such an undertaking, then, broadly speaking, the state must make up all the deficiencies or shortcomings of the private ownership and management which it allows to continue operative. This would mean at the present time that the American state ought to invest on new construction or capital goods about ten billion dollars a year, in addition to the three or four billion that private ownership and management are now investing.

The present government building program is hopelessly inadequate for the purpose of taking up unemployment, as the figure of over ten million unemployed proves. The trouble with present government spending, a trouble which a fascist state must remedy, then, is that the state is spending not too much but too little, and is not financing its spending on a pay-as-you-go basis. The liberal state cannot finance adequate spending on a sound basis, for the reason that if Mr. Roosevelt is to play politics he cannot increase taxation and lower wages enough to put the unemployed to work and keep them at work on a soundly financed basis. He therefore rides the dollar toboggan of inflation, and goes on smiling and fishing with the Astors.

The present pattern of government interference to raise prices and wages, to spend money without taxing, and to subsidize nonproduction, makes it impossible to achieve adequate spending and employment on a sound basis. Wages and prices must fall. Production must rise. Interest rates must be made more secure by assurance of currency stability and stable operating costs. Profits must be made possible by allowing costs to be brought into the right relation to selling prices in the given market. But both interest and profit return, in the net, must be pared down to a small percentage by the process of high but orderly and equitably distributed taxation. The public budget must balance year in and year out—something which cannot be achieved under our liberal system, which excludes the possibility of an executive budget and leaves the treasury exposed to organized raids of minority pressure groups.

Government could, under a fascist set-up, force the insurance companies and the institutional investors to finance at low rates of interest a large part of the present capital—goods deficiency. But in so far as new investment would have to be for purely government account, just that far government should have the will and the power to levy a current income without borrowing to match its current outgo.

The success of the government in achieving sound financing of its enterprises would depend largely on the realization of the second end of state intervention, namely—control. A state which has to fight minority group pressures in the electoral campaign and minority economic interests in the courts cannot plan orderly economic processes. Contrary to liberal premises, the result of the play of minority and private interests in the electoral and court games is not a conspiracy of welfare but a conspiracy of chaos.

Private Property Rights

If private property is to survive, it must accept any measure of control necessary to the realization of the plan adopted. This means the end of the liberal system of property rights. The new regime of property must not mean the right of a property owner to do with his property whatever the courts decide he can do consistently with a charter or bill of rights adopted three hundred years ago. Law must be made and interpreted by those who have to cope with the problems of management. The function of the courts must be that of clerks carrying out the latest decisions of those charged with responsibility and vested with power.

The new regime of property must mean that a private property right is only a right to do what the state from day to day may decide may be done with private property. The investor could be assured of his principal intrusted to an approved investment agency, and whatever rate of interest, if any, it might be found necessary to offer to secure sufficient savings. The manager or enterpriser could be allowed to retain something in the nature of profits as a bonus for efficient and successful management. Ownership and management would lose their present legal rights to win court victories over the state and to obstruct its policies, but in exchange they would derive from a benevolent state a degree of security from labor trouble and competitive practices which only a strong executive state can afford.

Limiting the Judiciary

The most fundamental reason, perhaps, why a liberal state cannot make a success of economic planning inheres in the liberal system of charter rights and judicial revision of laws and administrative acts. It may be said that under a system of executive control, individuals would be without judicial protection against administrative abuses. I need only reply that under the liberal state system, individuals who cannot afford expensive judicial process have no judicial protection, as a practical matter, against great corporations. And to the big business men who are afraid of administrative abuses of power which cannot be checked by judicial intervention, I would say that they are going to have a lot more to fear from the lobbies of pressure groups making organized raids on the treasury and more from irresponsible labor agitators, all acting within the framework of complete legality to sabotage their productive system.

The notion that nine old men removed from the responsibilities of making executive decisions and meeting crucial problems can be the pillars of order and security in the present situation is naive. Security and order today must be executive problems so far as the state is concerned. The theory that order can be maintained by court enforcement of rights and contracts is knocked into a cocked hat by the Supreme Court's gold decision, as it is by every other significant economic change of the past fifty years of the rise of great corporations and growth of increasing inequality as between legal persons before the courts and the chambers of legislature.

Equity is done; law is made and interpreted by our corporate directorates. Their imperium can only be brought effectively under that of public interest if it is freely granted that the end of the state is to control the major economic processes and not merely to umpire the competitive pursuit of profits under juridical norms appropriate to a seventeenth-century English village in which a free market was possible and from which important monopolies could be excluded.

The Sphere of Control

Control, of course, is not bounded by the confines of the economic interests. The fascist state, however, is concerned mainly with effective control of capital and labor. A type of fascism could well arise to seek control in the field of cultural interests and activities not affected with important economic interest. I should deplore the growth of such a type of fascism. I am not prepared to delimit the functions of the state as the liberals are—in theories which strangely differ from practices.

Broadly stated, the individual can and should be left a large field of choices in respect to occupations, uses of leisure time, and uses of resources not required for public ends. The field in which the state has to be most authoritarian and restrictive of liberty is a field which will only affect seriously two or three thousand corporations and the five or ten thousand men who have hitherto had too much freedom of choice of policies for self-enrichment.

The point I want to stress is that so far as the millions of stockholders, bondholders, depositors, and insured having an interest in corporate affairs are concerned, fascism will not materially modify their rights or liberties, for the very good reason that, as it is they have *de facto* no rights or liberties to be modified except the rights to sell their rights of ownership if they can find a buyer and to take what management gives them. These rights will undoubtedly be left to them.

State intervention, of course, will often penalize owners under fascism. Mistakes and rascality of management have done the same under liberal capitalism. Wherein would the right of an insuree in the Metropolitan Insurance Company have been modified if the state had told its managers that they could not put $25,000,000 into an office building in New York at a high rate of interest but that they must put that sum into slum clearance projects at a low rate of interest? There must be much state interference with corporate management under fascism, and there should be little state interference with personal habits. Economic and not sumptuary control is the need. But economic control must not mobilize cultural instruments of the control, like radio, press, school, and church, against the state. The state must have a monopoly of those uses of power which can make or break successful social planning.

This leads me briefly to speak of the problems of means under a fascist authoritarian state. The ends, as we have already seen, are order and welfare, which I would express more concretely by saying as high a standard of living as the people want to pay for with their labor and available resources. The means, however, are the more characteristically fascist features of the new system. I can only run over certain important fundamentals.

Concentration of Power

As to the political or governmental scheme of things, the keynote is concentration of power, or centralization of control. This means scrapping the principle of separation of power. Government is no longer a matter of checking and balancing or playing a game of the individual versus a state which is constantly suspected of having designs on his liberty and welfare. Individuals who have been beaten by the depression in the free market do not want liberal liberties to do things they cannot as a practical matter do, and liberal liberties for others to do things to them which the others can and actually do, and which the victims do not like to have done to them.

The liberal critics of fascism are apt to stress the question of liberty. With a curious lack of historical sense and of a sense of humor, they forget that the cry for liberty has always been the cry of the leaders of the "outs." Our liberal critics can be quite sure that any successful revolution will leave a lot of people with more liberty than they had before. Our liberal friends can also be sure that the people who want a New Deal or a new system are not entirely enchanted with their present liberties. Liberty is a word to be used by people fighting for something they do not have; it is not a good propaganda word for people to play with who are fighting to keep something they have and which their opponents are after.

Senator Long's followers really want to share other people's liberties by sharing their wealth. Every social revolution is a fight for liberty. The members of the Liberty League are on the defensive, and the leaders of the Long and Coughlin forces are on the offensive. My money is usually on the offensive. The elite of the present order can assure their leadership or liberties only by giving up the defensive and joining the offensive on the technological problems of social organization and production.

The political instrument of government must be directed by an executive council representing a mandate from the people to do a managing job. This means the end of the parliamentary or congressional system, under which governmental decisions and policies are the result of power group pressures.

Economic Reorganization

I forbear to go into the details of economic reorganization. They are too vast and complex for easy generalization. Two concrete types of change occur to me to mention. First, the state must nationalize credit or banking, so as to have unlimited financial facilities without incurring interest charges. This will mean that private property interests will take the form of rights to own for use or for an income, which income will never be contractually rigid but always subject to change without notice, according to the indications or the necessities of economic change. The investor will buy a right of an investment trust or company entitling him to whatever income it will be found possible and convenient to the state to have him paid.

The enterpriser will buy a right to use his skill in management to earn a profit under conditions rigidly regulated by the state in the public interest. Labor will be forced to accept organization and discipline under leadership responsible to the state. Strikes will be eliminated, along with lockouts. Any unit of capitalistic management not prepared to operate a property satisfactorily to the state will find itself relieved of management by the state and its rights assigned to another management, subject to such equitable arrangements as may be possible.

Government will be understood by all to be an instrument in the hands of a managing committee representing a political party pursuing certain popularly approved ideals of national interest. Fascism will differ here, as elsewhere from the reform movements and the specific panaceas of the period, in that fascism will have but one panacea—good government. That means government by the right people, for the right objectives, and with the right methods for the realization of these objectives. It is essentially totalitarian or all-embracing, for the simple reason that the close integration of modern social organization makes it necessary that government should have this quality if it is to maintain public order and promote public welfare.

Opportunity of the Political Parties

Present trends must put the state sooner or later in the complete control of some combination of power groups with a will to use the state in the pursuit of some set of ends not embraced within the liberal ideologies. I see no chance that that combination will be the professional Communist leaders in this country, at least not unless we have a big war and a military mutiny. I should like to see our two major political parties accept the major fascist premises and each propose to do for the American people a job of social planning for a period of years with all the power and all the revolutionary changes necessary to insure success.

Ideally, both parties should make a national appeal and promise a government by the best people—experts—for the achievement of a stated set of objectives. The country should be told what each party proposes to achieve in the way of larger objectives. A bloodless and glorious social revolution could result from giving a mandate to either party to do such a job.

I am, however, pessimistic as to the emergence of the indicated formula in any such ideal manner. My pessimism is founded on the fact that the leaders of both parties, with few exceptions, are not thinking in terms of a situation the important facts of which are that one system is in collapse and that another system is indicated. The conservatism of the best people ought to express itself in an attempt to save their leadership by saving the situation. Instead, their conservatism is expressing itself in attempts to save a system, to save traditions, and to save rights which will soon have no value because they will not be enforceable under changed economic conditions.

The Mind of the Masses

Many of the conservatives believe or seem to believe that the American people are attached to a given system and ideology. This is a delusion peculiar to the lawyers and the instructed classes. Ninety percent of the American people have no grasp whatever of the ideological content of the system. They have not read the Federalist papers, Rousseau, Montesquieu, Adam Smith, or Blackstone. If they are moved by words or symbols, like "Constitution," "liberty," "democracy," "representative government," and so forth, it is purely a result of early emotional conditioning and the association of a given feeling with a given word, without the occurrence of any understanding process. All these words or symbols can be incanted by any demagogue committed to any enterprise. A fascist dictatorship can be set up by a demagogue in the name of all the catchwords of the present system, just as a Communist dictatorship was set up in Russia in October 1917 in the name of democracy and other catchwords of the liberals.

It is also a mistake to suppose that the American people are averse to government regimentation, or orderly organization and procedure. We are the most organized, standardized, regimented, and docile people in the world so far as the processes of mass direction and management are concerned. People who fall into this erroneous generalization about the American people fail to see that most of our government is now done by large corporations and cultural associations rather than by the state. The state can easily include the corporations and most of the cultural associations within its scheme of social control without having the masses of people notice the difference. The $25,000-a-year vice-president of a big bank or a big university is as much the yes-man of the power hierarchy on which his job depends as any communist or fascist party official, and he has about the same liberty of basic dissent.

I am not showing a contempt but a high respect for the masses in advancing these heterodox generalizations about them. The people have too much sense to take symbols and verbalisms, like the "Constitution" and "liberty," as seriously as our educated liberals and lawyers do. Both Senator Long and Father Coughlin, in harping on the calamities of our present situation and in clamoring for changes, are in far closer harmony with the logic of mass needs than are our intellectual exponents of liberalism, or conservatism, as you may care to call it, who are invoking symbols and verbalisms not as instruments of action but as deterrents to revolutionary action. The people want public order and the elements of subsistence. Liberty with these, yes; liberty without them is nonsense.

Character of Coming Fascism

Revolutionary change is indicated. It is beginning. Its velocity and momentum will accelerate. The elite of the present order have their chance now to reform their thinking and lead the trend. Whether our coming fascism is more or less humane and decent will depend largely on the contributions our humane elite can make to it in time. There need to be no acute class struggle, if the elite of the present order in both parties will but recognize that a planned economy can best be planned in the interests of the dominant elite, if it is also planned to give the masses the maximum output of human satisfactions. The larger the total product, the larger the cut for ownership and management. The problem can be that of organizing for the maximum social income as a part of organization for class advantage. It can also be a class struggle between the "ins" fighting to defend their liberties, and the "outs" fighting to capture them. It will depend largely on the decision of the "ins" during the next few months.

17

The Program of the National Renaissance Party

JAMES MADOLE

During the past several months we have been asked by large numbers of people to explain exactly what principles the National Renaissance Party is fighting for, and how we differ from the programs of the orthodox Republican and Democratic Parties. This article is designed to answer all these questions.

To begin with, the National Renaissance Party believes in subordinating the interests of the individual citizen to the interests of the national community as a whole. The nation represents the totality of the American

From *National Renaissance Bulletin* (October, 1953), pp. 3-4.

people; their hopes, their needs, and their ideals . . . and as such the welfare of the nation must always supercede the private interests of any race, class or individual. Whereas our doctrine of Racial Nationalism welds the nation into a united and compatible Iron Front based on the ancient ties of blood and race, the poisonous Jewish doctrines of Democracy, Liberalism and Communism seek to foment class warfare, disunity and revolution within the borders of all national states. Until the power of the Jew is crushed there can never be peace between, among, or within nations.

Secondly, we believe that the individual has only fulfilled his duty to the national community when he has founded a successful home and family. The healthy Christian concept of the home and family is the backbone of Western Civilization. A man who will not fight for his wife and family will certainly not fight for his native land either. Hence, just as individually healthy cells constitute a healthy human body, so do individually healthy family units insure a healthy, united and strong national community.

During the past century the White Race has undergone a steadily declining birth rate in contrast to the ever increasing fecundity of the colored hordes in Africa and Asia. This situation is partly due to economic conditions in both America and Western Europe where the combination of inflationary prices, greedy industrialists and rapacious labor czars make it necessary for young married couples to remain in their jobs in order to eke out the barest existence. Naturally when both husband and wife are forced, through economic necessity, to spend their days working in offices and factories, the conditions are hardly suitable for raising even the most meagre sized family.

We believe that strong, healthy family units can be established by providing loans to newly married couples who have first passed a strict medical examination to insure that they are not suffering from any hereditary physical or mental disease which might prove detrimental to their progeny. The child must always be the paramount concern of the Racial Nationalist State since the national youth represents the seed bed of the rising generation from which shall arise the elite Aryan leadership of the NEW AMERICA. We can insure the propagation of a strong, virile race only by prohibiting racial intermarriage and by permitting only those who are physically and mentally sound to marry. The racial purity of a nation and its freedom from hereditary disease are just as closely related as body and soul. To restore the Christian home, marriage loans should be granted without interest, to be repaid to the State at the rate of 3 per cent monthly so long as the wife is in paid employment, and at the rate of 1 per cent thereafter. A reduction of 25 per cent will be made from each marriage loan for every child that is born of the union. This will vastly increase the Aryan birth rate in America and open up many jobs now held by married women to unemployed men.

Thus the National Renaissance Party is primarily concerned with the welfare of the national community as a whole and with the supreme task of the national community which is the protection and preservation of our most valuable Aryan racial elements. As opposed to this, the worthless Democratic and Republican Parties are solely concerned with the accumulation of gold and votes. The Republican Party serves the interests of International Finance, the Democratic Party serves International Jewry; but neither serves the interests of the American people as a whole. To clarify the issues we will outline the complete 9-point political, racial and economic program of the National Renaissance Party.

1.   To encourage racial nationalism among the peoples of Europe, Africa and Asia as an antidote to the spread of International Communism. We must disassociate American foreign policy from the decadent British and French colonial empires against which the entire land mass of Africa and Asia is in revolt. We must also repudiate the operetta-state of Israel unless we wish to drive the entire Middle East into the open arms of Soviet Russia in order that our political windbags in Washington may appease a howling pack of New York kikes, whose sole contributions to American culture have been syphilis and usury.

2.   To enforce a strict policy of racial segregation in America in order to preserve and advance the culturally dominant White Aryan Race which brought the cultural and social benefits of Western Civilization to our shores in 1492. (By the "Aryan Race" we refer to the Nordic, Celtic, Anglo-Saxon, Latin and Slavic people.)

3.   To bring about a gradual deportation of those racial elements which cannot be assimilated with the culturally predominant White Race. Laws must be passed to rigidly prohibit racial intermarriage. (Those racial elements which cannot be assimilated in an Aryan racial community are the Porto Ricans, Negroes, Jews and Asiatics.)

4.   The Jewish Race, which constitutes the motivating financial and intellectual force behind Communism, shall be deprived of their American citizenship and hence barred from all political and professional posts. Marriage between Jews and members of the dominant White Race shall be forbidden. (During the past 20 years the Jews have managed to obtain a tremendous hold on American politics, art, culture and commerce. No people on earth with a vestige of pride in itself and its national honor will tolerate such a domination of the KEY professions by members of a com-

pletely ALIEN race. At the same time, the Jews are a determining factor in those political parties which have sought to undermine the last vestiges of racial and national pride in America. The Jew constitutes an alien virus in our national blood stream and as such he must be purged from our cultural, economic and political life.)

5. To bring about the withdrawal of the United States from the United Nations in order to prevent further exploitation of American resources and man-power by foreign parasites. (In regard to foreign trade, America must develop a policy of preserving the American market for the American farmer and manufacturer. America must "Buy American" and subsidize, if necessary, American scientific ingenuity toward the end of producing chemically many of these products which are not found here in America but upon which this nation is dependent.)

6. The alliance of German scientific and military genius combined with American technology, mass production technique and manpower could dominate both the American and European continents. Therefore our foreign policy must have the threefold objective of realizing a German-American alliance in Europe; a Moslem-American alliance in the Middle East; and a Japanese-American alliance in Asia.

7. The creation of an American Corporate Economy wherein labor and management will be equally represented in an Economic Dept. of the Federal Government. All disputes will be settled by impartial labor tribunals. (Labor and management exist to serve the interests of the State, which represents the totality of the American people. Class warfare and inflationary prices create universal economic chaos hence prices and wages must be stabilized by the State in order to meet the needs of the American people as a whole.)

8. The abolition of parliamentary government by a national-minded elite.

9. The use of all educational facilities to imbue the American youth with an intense feeling of racial and national pride as a sure antidote to the international poison of World Communism.

Part Four

The Politics of Alienation

Part Four

The Politics of Alienation

A. Political Fundamentalism

Paradoxically, America's swift rise to world power and unprecedented affluence has promoted "one of the most extraordinary social-psychological phenomena in modern times": a political mentality nourished by insecurity and nostalgia.[1] Despite the preoccupation of historians with reform in this century, the far right had displayed a continuity and persistence which deserve very serious consideration. Even the so-called Progressive era was not spared nativist "Law and Order" crusades, and the First World War provided new incentives to hysterical, indigenous right-wing extremism. In 1915, a former salesman, preacher, and college teacher turned fraternal organizer, William Simmons, resurrected the Knights of the Ku Klux Klan.[2] The Klan's overt racism and penchant for vigilante activities appealed to that segment of the American population afraid of alleged fifth-column conspiracies and willing to equate labor unrest with subversion. Helped along by sensational publicity and an ingenious organizing campaign, membership in the Klan was counted in the millions and spread throughout the United States by the early 1920's.[3] National power drew men who saw the organization as a great potential political instrument. A carefully staged coup on the eve of the national convention in 1922 replaced Simmons with Hiram Evans, "a roly-poly, glad-handing cut-rate dentist from Dallas, Texas," who remained the Klan's chieftain past the height of the group's influence, until 1939.[4]

The Klan's role as spokesman for reaction was divided among a number of organizations during the depression years. The Townsend Plan attracted some support, as did William Lemke's lame third-party coalition with Coughlin's Union for Social Justice. Of more lasting importance was the Share-Our-Wealth movement launched by Huey Long. Long's assassination in 1935 left his following in the covetous hands of Gerald L. K. Smith. A descendant of four generations of fundamentalist preachers, Reverend Smith had left the ministry in 1934 to help in the establishment of a national Share-Our-Wealth organization, justifying his leader's iron grip on Louisiana to thousands of people as "the dictatorship of the surgical theatre."[5] Smith lost control of the Long organization and found himself repudiated by Lemke and Townsend when he sought a political alliance with them in 1936. Undaunted, he formed the Committee of One Million the following year, dedicating it to a nationalist assault on communist influences in American life. His favorite targets were the New Deal and the Congress of Industrial Organizations.[6] Identified with isolationist elements, Smith turned an about-face after Pearl Harbor, urging a total American commitment to the Pacific theatre, where he thought he discerned a secret alliance between Japan and the Soviet Union. Smith's secret society, the Inner Circle, initiated the publication of *The Cross and the Flag* in 1942.[7] By 1943, Smith was leading a temporarily potent America First Party. At the insistence of a group of liberal congressmen, Smith found himself the subject of an investigation conducted by the House Un-American Activities Committee in 1946, but the committee's majority and its chairman, Martin Dies, agreed with Smith that it was communism, not the far right, which needed to be exposed.

Smith and his congressional allies, like John Rankin of Mississippi, who claimed that the paramount issue was an internal communist menace— "They have been flooding into this country by the hundreds of thousands .... They have wormed their way into every department of this Government "—were reinforced, then almost eclipsed, by the efforts of Wisconsin Senator Joseph McCarthy.[8] McCarthy won national attention when, in a speech delivered at Wheeling, West Virginia in February of 1950, he produced a list he claimed contained the names of confirmed communists in high government positions.[9] The total number on McCarthy's famous list changed on several occasions; although a noisy affair, the Senator's crusade netted few facts not already in the hands of responsible public officials.[10] Nevertheless, many frightened citizens followed McCarthy's lead, seeing communists and their sympathizers everywhere. McCarthy reached the pinnacle of his power in 1952, turning his talents for innuendo and guilt-by-association to good use in that year's presidential race. Observers who believed that his censure and sudden death would end anticommunist hysteria were in for a rude shock. Not only Gerald L. K. Smith's Christian Nationalist Crusade, but groups led by Carl McIntire, Billy James Hargis, Ezra Taft Benson, and Robert Welch emerged in the 1950's and 1960's, dedicated to the same goals.[11]

From the days of Ku Kluxery to the present, the far right projected a naive readiness to meet complexities with oversimplifications, new issues with worn clichés.[12] Those attracted to the extreme right shared some important characteristics: they were severely disoriented persons, seeking an easy route through a world of perplexities, driven to warn their fellow citizens that in the interests of national salvation, "in politics we must return to absolutes."[13] These extremists were deeply alienated from the political mainstream, often either personally or professionally damaged by a shifting socio-economic environment.[14] Often from the lower middle class or fixed income brackets, such persons felt isolated from social control, ineffective, aware of their slipping social status, and desperate in the search for clues to the changes and cures for their grievances.[15] The social system somehow had locked them out. As Hargis complained, "Everything is so impersonal now. The government takes care of you with a check . . . . The government can't do anything about spiritual needs."[16]

This sense of dispossession meshed with a residue of traditional moralism to form an ideology which one analyst has termed igorance made politically operative.[17] Rightists insisted upon equating their personal disaster with some sort of national peril. Convinced that his world was *the* world, the rightist preferred survival to democracy.[18] His status was uncertain; the national fate, therefore, swayed in the balance. The impersonal political, economic, social, and intellectual forces of the contemporary era, in short, were transformed into personal, spiritual matters. Or as one extremist explained it, "They're trying to kill us just as Christ was crucified."[19] Their political struggle was an apocalyptic one, and it invited the application of a rural Protestant frame of reference.

Thus the political fundamentalists have clothed their frustrations and biases in religious and patriotic terms. Racism, anti-intellectualism, impatience with the inconclusiveness of limited war, a taxpayer's resentment over growing costs of foreign aid and welfare measures—all were restated as "fundamentals" of a program for national salvation.[20] In the credo of the rightists, the nation must return to individualism, by which rightists apparently mean small shopkeeper capitalism. Collectivism (their term for social welfare legislation) is un-American. The United States is a republic, not a democracy; social disorder is directly traceable to democracy's emphasis on equalitarianism. Rightists dismiss the intricacies of modern diplomacy by decreeing the impossibility of compromise. The United States, it is argued, stands as the last bulwark of Christianity against a worldwide conspiracy of godless communism, and already its power is sapped by an establishment composed of traitors and communist sympathizers in league with the Kremlin. So great is the danger of national collapse, it is urged, that the saving remnant of pure Americans must adopt the instruments of their avowed enemies: cell groups, secrecy, fronts, and preparation for ultimate violence (seminars, alerts, forums).[21]

In a movement possessed of paranoiac fears of master plots and legions of fellow travelers, the opportunities for demagogic influences and rash "direct action" are great. It is ironic that political fundamentalism, seeking to combine patriotism and Christianity, somehow ends by equating that Christianity with a dogma of hate, confusing the interests of the forgotten man with elitism, and attempting to protect liberty by constraining any opposition.[22]

NOTES

1. Gilbert Abcarian and Sherman M. Stanage, "Alienation and the Radical Right," *Journal of Politics,* 27 (November, 1965), p. 779; Alan Barth, "Report on the Rampageous Right," *New York Times Magazine,* (November 26, 1961), p. 25; Stanley Alderson, "McCarthyism in Perspective," *Contemporary Review,* 186 (November, 1954), p. 269; Richard Hofstadter, *The Paranoid Style in American Politics, and other Essays* (New York: Alfred A. Knopf, 1965), *passim;* and Daniel Bell, ed., *The Radical Right* (Garden City: Doubleday, 1963), *passim.*

2. John M. Mecklin, *The Ku Klux Klan: A Study of the American Mind* (New York: Harcourt, Brace & Company, 1924), pp. 3-15; David M. Chalmers, *Hooded Americanism: The First Century of the Ku Klux Klan, 1865-1965* (Garden City: Doubleday, 1965), pp. 28-38.

3. *Ibid.*

4. Chalmers, *Hooded Americanism,* pp. 101-104.

5. Maxine Block, ed., *Current Biography: Who's News and Why, 1943* (New York: H. W. Wilson Company, 1944), pp. 707-708.

6. *Ibid.,* pp. 708-709.

7. *Ibid.,* pp. 709-710.

8. *Congressional Record,* 79th Cong., 2nd Sess. Vol. 92, Part 2 (March 15, 1946), p. 2330.

9. *New York Times,* February 21, 1950.

10. Alderson, "McCarthyism in Perspective," p. 269.

11. Mark Chesler and Richard Schmuck, "Participant Observation in a Super-Patriot Discussion Group," *Journal of Social Issues,* XIX (April, 1963), pp. 18-30; J. Allen Broyles, "The John Birch Society: A Movement of Social Protest of the Radical Right," in *Ibid.,* pp. 51-62.

12. Abcarian and Stanage, "Alienation and the Radical Right," pp. 782-784; Lloyd J. Averill, "Political Fundamentalism in Profile," *Christian Century,* 81 (August 12, 1964), p. 1009.

13. *Ibid.,* p. 1010.

14. Abcarian and Stanage, "Alienation and the Radical Right," p. 795; Murray Levin, *The Alienated Voter* (New York: Holt, Rinehart & Winston, Inc., 1960), p. 59.

15. Chesler and Schmuck, "Participant Observation," p. 24; see an alternate approach in Everett C. Ladd, Jr., "The Radical Right: The White-Collared Extremists," *South Atlantic Quarterly,* 65 (Summer, 1966), pp. 314-324.

16. Quoted in John K. Adams, "Saving America, Incorporated," *Nation,* 193 (September, 1961), p. 194.

17. Ladd, "The Radical Right," p. 323.

18. Averill, "Political Fundamentalism in Profile," p. 1011; Edgar Schein and Harold Proshansky, "American Political Extremism in the 1960's: Introduction," *Journal of*

Social Issues, XIX (April, 1963), pp. 1-2; Chesler and Schmuck, "Participant Observation," p. 24; Broyles, "John Birch Society," p. 53; Barth, "Rampageous Right," p. 131.

19. Quoted in Chesler and Schmuck, "Participant Observation," p. 26.

20. *Ibid.,* p. 20; Barbara B. Green, Kathryn Turner, and Dante Germino, "Responsible and Irresponsible Right-Wing Groups: A Problem in Analysis," *Journal of Social Issues,* XIX (April, 1963), p. 3.

21. R. H. S. Crossman, "Radicals on the Right," *Partisan Review,* Vol. 31 (Fall, 1964), p. 559; Abcarian and Stanage, "Alienation and the Radical Right," pp. 779-781; Daniel Bell, "Some Comments on Senator Goldwater," *Partisan Review,* 31 (Fall, 1964), pp. 584-586; Chesler and Schmuck, "Participant Observation," p. 19; Green, Turner, and Germino, "Responsible and Irresponsible Right-Wing Groups," pp. 13, 15, and 17.

22. Averill, "Political Fundamentalism in Profile," p. 1009; Chesler and Schmuck, "Participant Observation," p. 27.

18

The Klan's Fight for Americanism

HIRAM W. EVANS

The Ku Klux Klan . . . has made a place and won a record for achievement which are almost, if not quite, unique in the history of great popular movements. It has not merely grown from a handful to a membership of millions, from poverty to riches, from obscurity to great influence, from fumbling impotence to the leadership in the greatest cause now before the American people. All these are important, but not vital.

What is vital is that in these years the Klan has shown a power to reform and cleanse itself from within, to formulate and vitalize fundamental instincts into concrete thought and purposeful action, to meet changing conditions with adaptability but without weakness, to speak for and to lead the common people of America and, finally, to operate through the application of practical patriotism to public life with increasing success, and along the only constructive lines to be found in the present welter of our national thought. . . .

The greatest achievement so far has been to formulate, focus, and gain recognition for an idea—the idea of preserving and developing America first and chiefly for the benefit of the children of the pioneers who made America, and only and definitely along the lines of the purpose and spirit of those pioneers. The Klan cannot claim to have created this idea: it has long been a vague stirring in the souls of the plain people. But the Klan can fairly claim to have given it purpose, method, direction and a vehicle. When the Klan first appeared the nation was in the confusion of sudden awakening from the lovely dream of the melting pot, disorganized and helpless before the invasion of aliens and alien ideas. After ten years of the Klan it is in arms for defense. This is our great achievement.

The second is more selfish; we have won the leadership in the movement for Americanism. Except for a few lonesome voices, almost drowned by the clamor of the alien and the alien-minded "Liberal," the Klan alone faces the invader. This is not to say that the Klan has gathered into its membership all who are ready to fight for America. The Klan is the champion, but it is not merely an organization. It is an idea, a faith, a purpose, an organized crusade. . . .

From *North American Review*, 223 (March, 1926), selected passages from pp. 33-63.

The Klan [speaks] for the great mass of Americans of the old pioneer stock. We believe that it does fairly and faithfully represent them, and our proof lies in their support. To understand the Klan, then, it is necessary to understand the character and present mind of the mass of old-stock Americans. The mass, it must be remembered, as distinguished from the intellectually mongrelized "Liberals."

These are, in the first place, a blend of various peoples of the so-called Nordic race, the race which, with all its faults, has given the world almost the whole of modern civilization. The Klan does not try to represent any people but these.

There is no need to recount the virtues of the American pioneers; but it is too often forgotten that in the pioneer period a selective process of intense rigor went on. From the first only hardy, adventurous and strong men and women dared the pioneer dangers; from among these all but the best died swiftly, so that the new Nordic blend which became the American race was bred up to a point probably the highest in history. This remarkable race character, along with the new-won continent and the new-created nation, made the inheritance of the old-stock Americans the richest ever given to a generation of men.

In spite of it, however, these Nordic Americans for the last generation, have found themselves increasingly uncomfortable, and finally deeply distressed. There appeared first confusion in thought and opinion, a groping and hesitancy about national affairs and private life alike, in sharp contrast to the clear, straightforward purposes of our earlier years. There was futility in religion, too, which was in many ways even more distressing. Presently we began to find that we were dealing with strange ideas; policies that always sounded well, but somehow always made us still more uncomfortable.

Finally came the moral breakdown that has been going on for two decades. One by one all our traditional moral standards went by the boards, or were so disregarded that they ceased to be binding. The sacredness of our Sabbath, of our homes, of chastity, and finally even of our right to teach our own children in our own schools fundamental facts and truths were torn away from us. Those who maintained the old standards did so only in the face of constant ridicule.

Along with this went economic distress. The assurance for the future of our children dwindled. We found our great cities and the control of much of our industry and commerce taken over by strangers, who stacked the cards of success and prosperity against us. Shortly they came to dominate our government. The *bloc* system by which this was done is now familiar to all. Every kind of inhabitant except the Americans gathered in groups which operated as units in politics, under orders of corrupt, self-seeking and un-

American leaders, who both by purchase and threat enforced their demand on politicians. Thus it came about that the interests of Americans were always the last to be considered by either national or city governments, and that the native Americans were constantly discriminated against, in business, in legislation and in administrative government.

So the Nordic American today is a stranger in large parts of the land his fathers gave him. Moreover, he is a most unwelcome stranger, one much spit upon, and one to whom even the right to have his own opinions and to work for his own interests is now denied with jeers and revilings. "We must Americanize the Americans," a distinguished immigrant said recently. Can anything more clearly show the state to which the real American has fallen in this country which was once his own?

Our falling birth rate, the result of all this, is proof of our distress. We no longer feel that we can be fair to children we bring into the world, unless we can make sure from the start that they shall have capital or education or both, so that they need never compete with those who now fill the lower rungs of the ladder of success. We dare no longer risk letting our youth "make its own way" in the conditions under which we live. So even our unborn children are being crowded out of their birthright!

All this has been true for years, but it was the World War that gave us our first hint of the real cause of our troubles, and began to crystallize our ideas. The war revealed that millions whom we had allowed to share our heritage and prosperity, and whom we had assumed had become part of us, were in fact not wholly so. They had other loyalties: each was willing— anxious!—to sacrifice the interests of the country that had given him shelter to the interests of the one he was supposed to have cast off; each in fact did use the freedom and political power we had given him against ourselves whenever he could see any profit for his older loyalty.

This, of course, was chiefly in international affairs, and the excitement caused by the discovery of disloyalty subsided rapidly after the war ended. But it was not forgotten by the Nordic Americans. They had been awakened and alarmed; they began to suspect that the hyphenism which had been shown was only a part of what existed; their quiet was not that of renewed sleep, but of strong men waiting very watchfully. And presently they began to form decisions about all those aliens who were Americans for profit only.

They decided that even the crossing of salt water did not dim a single spot on a leopard; that an alien usually remains an alien no matter what is done to him, what veneer of education he gets, what oaths he takes, nor what public attitudes he adopts. They decided that the melting pot was a ghastly failure, and remembered that the very name was coined by a member of one of the races—the Jews—which most determinedly refuses to melt. They decided that in every way, as well as in politics, the alien in the vast majority of cases is unalterably fixed in his instincts, character, thought and interests by centuries of racial selection and development, that he thinks first for his own people, works only with and for them, cares entirely for their interests, considers himself always one of them, and never an American. They decided that in character, instincts, thought, and purposes—in his whole soul—an alien remains fixedly alien to America and all it means.

They saw, too, that the alien was tearing down the American standard of living, especially in the lower walks. It became clear that while the American can out-work the alien, the alien can so far under-live the American as to force him out of all competitive labor. So they came to realize that the Nordic can easily survive and rule and increase if he holds for himself the advantages won by strength and daring of his ancestors in times of stress and peril, but that if he surrenders those advantages to the peoples who could not share the stress, he will soon be driven below the level at which he can exist by their low standards, low living and fast breeding. And they saw that the low standard aliens of Eastern and Southern Europe were doing just that thing to us.

They learned, though more slowly, that alien ideas are just as dangerous to us as the aliens themselves, no matter how plausible such ideas may sound. With most of the plain people this conclusion is based simply on the fact that the alien ideas do not work well for them. Others went deeper and came to understand that the differences in racial background, in breeding, instinct, character and emotional point of view are more important than logic. So ideas which may be perfectly healthy for an alien may also be poisonous for Americans.

Finally they learned the great secret of the propagandists; that success in corrupting public opinion depends on putting out the subversive ideas without revealing their source. They came to suspect that "prejudice" against foreign ideas is really a protective device of nature against mental food that may be indigestible. They saw, finally, that the alien leaders in America act on this theory, and that there is a steady flood of alien ideas being spread over the country, always carefully disguised as American.

As they learned all this the Nordic Americans have been gradually arousing themselves to defend their homes and their own kind of civilization. . . .

The plain people realize also that merely stopping the alien flood does not restore Americanism, nor even secure us against final utter defeat.

America must also defend herself against the enemy within, or we shall be corrupted and conquered by those to whom we have already given shelter.

The first danger is that we shall be overwhelmed . . . by the aliens' "mere force of breeding." With the present birthrate, the Nordic stock will have become a hopeless minority within fifty years, and will within two hundred have been choked to death, like grain among weeds. Unless some means is found of making the Nordic feel safe in having children, we are already doomed.

An equal danger is from disunity, so strikingly shown during the war and from a mongrelization of thought and purpose. It is not merely foreign policy that is involved; it is all our thought at home, our morals, education, social conduct—everything. We are already confused and disunited in every way; the alien groups themselves, and the skilful alien propaganda, are both tearing steadily at all that makes for unity in nationhood, or for the soul of Americanism. If the word "integrity" can still be used in its original meaning of singleness of purpose or thought, then we as a nation have lost all integrity. Yet our old American motto includes the words " . . . divided we fall!"

One more point about the present attitude of the old stock American: he has revived and increased his long-standing distrust of the Roman Catholic Church. . . .

The real indictment against the Roman Church is that it is, fundamentally and irredeemably, in its leadership, in politics, in thought, and largely in membership, actually and actively alien, un-American and usually anti-American. The old stock Americans, with the exception of the few such of Catholic faith—who are in a class by themselves, standing tragically torn between their faith and their racial and national patriotism—see in the Roman Church today the chief leader of alienism, and the most dangerous alien power with a foothold inside our boundaries. It is this and nothing else that has revived hostility to Catholicism. By no stretch of the imagination can it fairly be called religious prejudice, though, now that the hostility has become active, it does derive some strength from the religious schism.

We Americans see many evidences of Catholic alienism. We believe that its official position and its dogma, its theocratic autocracy and its claim to full authority in temporal as well as spiritual matters, all make it impossible for it as a church, or for its members if they obey it, to cooperate in a free democracy in which Church and State have been separated. It is true that in this country the Roman Church speaks very softly on these points, so that many Catholics do not know them. It is also true that the Roman priests preach Americanism, subject to their own conception of Americanism, of course. But the Roman Church itself makes a point of the divine and unalterable character of its dogma, it has never seen fit to abandon officially any of these un-American attitudes, and it still teaches them in other countries. . . .

The hierarchical government of the Roman Church is equally at odds with Americanism. The Pope and the whole hierarchy have been for centuries almost wholly Italian. It is nonsense to suppose that a man, by entering a church, loses his race or national loyalties. The Roman Church today, therefore, is just what its name says—Roman; and it is impossible for its hierarchy or the policies they dictate to be in real sympathy with Americanism. Worse, the Italians have proven to be one of the least assimilable of people. The autocratic nature of the Catholic Church organization, and its suppression of free conscience or free decision, need not be discussed; they are unquestioned. Thus it is fundamental to the Roman Church to demand a supreme loyalty, overshadowing national or race loyalty, to a power that is inevitably alien, and which at the best must inevitably inculcate ideals un-American if not actively anti-American. . . .

Another difficulty is that the Catholic Church here constantly represents, speaks for and cares for the interests of a large body of alien peoples. Most immigration of recent years, so unassimilable and fundamentally un-American, has been Catholic. The Catholics of American stock have been submerged and almost lost; the aliens and their interest dictate all policies of the Roman Church which are not dictated from Rome itself.

Also, the Roman Church seems to take pains to prevent the assimilation of these people. Its parochial schools, its foreign born priests, the obstacles it places in the way of marriage with Protestants unless the children are bound in advance to Romanism, its persistent use of the foreign languages in church and school, its habit of grouping aliens together and thus creating insoluble alien masses—all these things strongly impede Americanization. . . .

Finally, there is the undeniable fact that the Roman Church takes an active part in American politics. It has not been content to accept in good faith the separation of Church and State, and constantly tries through political means to win advantages for itself and its people—in other words, to be a political power in America, as well as a spiritual power. Denials of Catholic activity in politics are too absurd to need discussion. The "Catholic vote" is as well recognized a factor as the "dry vote." All politicians take it for granted. . . .

This is the general state of mind of the Nordic Americans of the pioneer stock today. Many of them do not understand the reasons for their beliefs so fully as I have stated them, but the state of mind is there beyond doubt, and the reasons are true at all vital points. It is inevitable that these people are now in revolt. This is the movement to which the Klan, more through Providence than its own wisdom, has begun to give leadership.

The Ku Klux Klan, in short, is an organization which gives expression, direction and purpose to the most vital instincts, hopes and resentments of the old stock Americans, provides them with leadership, and is enlisting and preparing them for militant, constructive action toward fulfilling their racial and national destiny.... The Klan literally is once more the embattled American farmer and artisan, coordinated into a disciplined and growing army, and launched upon a definite crusade for Americanism! . . .

We are a movement of the plain people, very weak in the matter of culture, intellectual support, and trained leadership. We are demanding, and we expect to win, a return of power into the hands of the everyday, not highly cultured, not overly intellectualized, but entirely unspoiled and not de-Americanized, average citizen of the old stock. Our members and leaders are all of this class—the opposition of the intellectuals and liberals who held the leadership, betrayed Americanism, and from whom we expect to wrest control, is almost automatic . . .

First in the Klansman's mind is patriotism—America for Americans. He believes religiously that a betrayal of Americanism or the American race is treason to the most sacred of trusts, a trust from his fathers and a trust from God. He believes, too, that Americanism can only be achieved if the pioneer stock is kept pure. There is more than race pride in this. Mongrelization has been proven bad. It is only between closely related stocks of the same race that interbreeding has improved men; the kind of interbreeding that went on in the early days of America between English, Dutch, German, Huguenot, Irish and Scotch.

Racial integrity is a very definite thing to the Klansman. It means even more than good citizenship, for a man may be in all ways a good citizen and yet a poor American, unless he has racial understanding of Americanism, and instinctive loyalty to it. It is in no way a reflection on any man to say that he is un-American; it is merely a statement that he is not one of us. It is often not even wise to try to make an American of the best of aliens. What he is may be spoiled without his becoming American. The races and stocks of men are as distinct as breeds of animals, and every boy knows that if one tries to train a bulldog to herd sheep, he has in the end neither a good bulldog nor a good collie.

Americanism, to the Klansman, is a thing of the spirit, a purpose and a point of view, that can only come through instinctive racial understanding. It has, to be sure, certain defined principles, but he does not believe that many aliens understand those principles, even when they use our words in talking about them. . . . [The] Klansman believes in the greatest possible diversity and individualism within the limits of the American spirit. But he believes also that few aliens can understand that spirit, that fewer try to, and that there must be resistance, intolerance even, toward anything that threatens it, or the fundamental national unity based upon it.

The second word in the Klansman's trilogy is "white." The white race must be supreme, not only in America but in the world. This is equally undebatable, except on the ground that the races might live together, each with full regard for the rights and interests of others, and that those rights and interests would never conflict. Such an idea, of course, is absurd; the colored races today, such as Japan, are clamoring not for equality but for their supremacy. The whole history of the world, on its broader lines, has been one of race conflicts, wars, subjugation or extinction. This is not pretty, and certainly disagrees with the maudlin theories of cosmopolitanism, but it is truth. The world has been so made that each race must fight for its life, must conquer, accept slavery or die. The Klansman believes that the whites will not become slaves, and he does not intend to die before his time.

Moreover, the future of progress and civilization depends on the continued supremacy of the white race. The forward movement of the world for centuries has come entirely from it. Other races each had its chance and either failed or stuck fast, while white civilization shows no sign of having reached its limit. Until the whites falter, or some colored civilization has a miracle of awakening, there is not a single colored stock that can claim even equality with the white; much less supremacy.

The third of the Klan principles is that Protestanism must be supreme; that Rome shall not rule America. The Klansman believes this not merely because he is a Protestant, nor even because the Colonies that are now our nation were settled for the purpose of wresting America from the control of Rome and establishing a land of free conscience. He believes it also because Protestantism is an essential part of Americanism; without it America could never have been created and without it she cannot go forward. . . .

19

We Take Our Stand
GERALD L. K. SMITH

We have named this magazine *The Cross and the Flag* because we want it to symbolize the highest and most dynamic ideals. This is a patriotic, crusading journal which recognizes the fact that the ethical, moral, and spiritual teachings of Christ constitute the fountainhead of all worthwhile modern civilization.

We expect the worst from our foes, because we propose to use this magazine as a weapon with which to deal blows to the enemies of our traditional American way of life.

The reader may not be able to find in this editorial the symbol and name of everything we shall fight for, but if you keep right on reading, by the time you have finished this you will have a pretty fair idea of what we propose to support and oppose.

In the first place, we are 100 percent for an American victory and every sacrifice necessary to win that victory for America. We invite you to read our war platform on page 14. We have a very definite definition of victory, which appears elsewhere in this issue. *The Cross and the Flag* will never say nor do anything to lend aid and comfort to the enemies of America, whether they be on the battlefield, outside America, or among the agents of subversion inside America. America's attitude toward the Nazis, the Fascists, and the Japs is a fixed military policy which has been approved by the overwhelming majority of our Congress.

Now that we have made these facts clear, for the record, we assert that even though America is at war we old-fashioned Americans do not propose to be city-slicked by boondoggling bureaucratic politicians, Communists, British imperialists (the Union Now gang), and a thousand and one other porch climbers, confidence men, and snake-oil salesmen who are working day and night on conspiracies designed to compel us to swallow a hundred poison pills in the name of wartime emergencies.

We are not complaining about bloodshed, taxes, or any of the sacrifices that go along with the legitimate conduct of a war to save and defend America. We are talking about bureaucratic fakers, brain-trust screwballs

From *Congressional Record,* Vol. 88 (March 26, 1942), pp. A1203-4. Editorial from *The Cross and the Flag* (April, 1942) submitted for inclusion in the *Record* by Representative Woodruff of Michigan.

and political mechanics whose conscience and self-respect are about as calloused as the operator of a French guillotine. We are talking about ruthless political racketeers, propagandists, and character assassins who never hesitate to translate blood into ballots and defense bonds into boondoggling. *The Cross and the Flag* knows that many of these fakers and political confidence men are right on the pay roll of the United States Government. Some of them are awfully close to the White House, and many are in both Houses of Congress. The editors expect the worst from these people. We expect to be called appeasers, turtles, copperheads, Fascists, anti-Semites, racketeers, fifth columnists, rumor mongers, and even candidates for the Cliveden set.

A fraternity of smear artists has sprung up in America which has mastered the science of character assassination. The moment we old-fashioned Americans assert ourselves over the air or by the publication of a magazine these character killers turn on the heat. They issue bulletins, they bark over the air and suddenly the plain old-fashioned American, whether he be Charles Lindbergh or Gerald Smith, is aware of the fact that 10,000 mysterious enemies have descended upon him with scandalizing persecution, physical threats, editorial scorn, picket lines, and protest meetings. His patriotism is impugned and his Americanism is questioned.

We see a man like Walter Winchell monopolize an international radio network for a given period of time each week presuming to interpret Americanism at the rate of five thousand luscious "lotion" dollars per week. Walter Winchell has a background of scandal mongering, underworld gossiping, and now steps up to assume the role of a superpatriot. Political pull and White House favoritism make it possible for him to become a commissioned officer in the United States Navy, although to this date he continues to draw from the Jergens Lotion Corporation, the motion-picture industry, and others, a salary estimated at from $250,000 per year up. This man is no special evil in himself; he merely typifies the mattery [sic] festering of an evil element within our borders. Let Mr. Winchell, the great patriot, explain to us over the air some night why he presented, some months ago, to every Member of Congress a book written by the notorious Red, John Spivak. Let Mr. Winchell explain why he recommended the works of this Red propagandist de-luxe to the elected Representatives of the United States. We agree with Congressman Vinson, chairman of the Naval Affairs Committee of Congress, who said in effect, "Let Winchell put on the uniform and enter the Navy or take off the uniform and get out of the Navy."

We don't like the idea of the President of the United States playing politics with a wartime Cabinet. We think he should demonstrate a willingness to fill his Cabinet with men representing all the major political elements in our Nation. We agree with the American Legion of Michigan, which, by resolution, called on the President to remove five of the impotent, ineffective members of his Cabinet. We don't like the idea of Harry Hopkins being so powerful that every high official in the United States has to siphon his ideas through this ailing pink.

We are impressed with the editorial challenge of men like David Lawrence, editor of the United States News, who accuses Donald Nelson of toying with Soviet technique—in setting up industrial committees. If David Lawrence is wrong, he should be rebuked. If David Lawrence is right, then Nelson should be curbed or dismissed.

We don't like the way the administration has ignored the sensational findings of Congressman Martin Dies, in his exposure of reds, pinks, and Communists on the pay roll of our wartime Government. We are opposed to the theory that America must flatter and cajole the Communists in America merely because we are military allies of Russia.

We recognize the priorities emergency, but because we know something of the background of Leon Henderson we think that some place in this set-up there are certain Marxists who are getting a real thrill out of seeing the great middle class crucified in the name of this emergency. Every day we see creative minds being nailed upon the cross. Forty-four thousand automobile dealers, with an average of 12 dependent employees each, totaling over 500,000 men, are virtually in the bread line. Add to these 100,000 little manufacturers making nondefense material who have been closed up; add to these tire dealers, advertising agencies, and 10,000 correlated business enterprises, and you witness a crucifixion of middle-class individuals surpassing even the liquidation of similar groups during and following the Russian Revolution.

The Cross and the Flag admits the necessity of radical adjustments due to a shortage of war materials, labor, and factory facilities, but we are bold to assert that the most serious thing about this crucifixion of the middle class is not only the fact that our bureaucrats apparently don't care what happens to these people but they actually appear to delight in their annihilation. Thousands upon thousands of these people are friends of the crusade represented by this magazine.

Over 50,000 members of the Congress of Industrial Organizations in Detroit alone, are affiliated with our committee. There are still millions of Bible-reading, church-going prayerful workers in America, who don't like the idea of being led around by the nose by a former playmate of Nikolai Lenin—Sidney Hillman; and there are still millions of American workers who don't fall for this Walter Reuther bunk (it is to be remembered that Victor and Walter Reuther took a two-year intensive course on industrial organization at Lenin University in Moscow).

If we are to be governed by a long-term President, we hold the conviction that the people should have a chance to express themselves concerning his administrative policies oftener than once every 4 years.

We don't like the idea of Madam Litvinoff and Ambassador Maxim Litvinoff running around over the country addressing a series of red-sponsored rallies under the guise of Russian relief. Our Congress has appropriated nearly $50,000,000,000 to be used by the President of the United States for foreign countries in the prosecution of this war. That should be enough to give them all the relief they need without conducting these propaganda rallies under the guise of relief.

We want a "he-man" civilian defense program.

We will get along without sugar, we will eat sorghum molasses, we'll jack up the car, we'll send our sons off to battle for America, but we are not afraid or ashamed of the words "America First" whether we are at war or at peace. We hate nazi-ism, fascism, communism, shintoism, and imperialism.

The state of mind, represented by this journal, is just too old-fashioned to understand why the Agricultural Adjustment Administration proposes to burn and plow under this year 2,000,000 acres of Kansas wheat.

We know that a set of highbinders in Washington are trying to sneak us back into the British Empire in the name of this so-called new world program, and we know that a similar outfit is going to try to get Earl Browder out of the Federal penitentiary and elect him to Congress while another set of Red stooges, and propagandists work on a scheme to make us part of an international imperialistic empire to include Russia—Communist Russia.

We won't swallow that stuff; in fact *The Cross and the Flag* holds the conviction that if our President and his coordinates and the administration in Washington don't put a stop to such tricks our beautiful America will be made the victim of a paralyzing disunity which is exactly what we do not need in this awful hour.

Of course, we old-fashioned Americans expect to be made the victims of a highly organized smear campaign. We expect certain political strategists in Washington and elsewhere to put the finger on us. We expect to be made the scapegoats, because when the American people really wake up to what is going on in this country, the bureaucratic politicians, in an attempt to deflect and sidetrack the scorn of an indignant people, will attempt to make us the goats in a desperate effort to save their own hides. Well, it won't work. Bring on your house-wrecking crew and your character assassins, you who operate the political torture chambers of America, and give us the works; and for every Gerald Smith you annihilate and smear and cripple, 10,000 will rise up to take his place.

America is on the march. Protest is in the hearts of the people, not against our Government; we are devoted to the America of Washington and Lincoln, but we are against treason, waste, profligacy, bureaucratic arrogance, stupidity, and military defeats which have been the outgrowth of short-sightedness. We believe that the convictions expressed in this editorial are so universally accepted by the American people, that if the congressional elections were today we would send to Washington a Congress whose majority would O.K. this statement.

God bless you until next month.

20

Address Accusing Governor Stevenson of Aid to Communist Cause

JOSEPH R. MCCARTHY

We are at war tonight—a war which started decades ago, a war which we did not start, a war which we cannot stop except by either victory or death. The Korean war is only one phase of this war between international atheistic communism and our free civilization.

And we've been losing, we've been losing that war since the shooting part of World War II ended, losing it at an incredibly fantastic rate of speed, losing that war at the rate of 100,000,000 people a year.

And for the past two and a half years I've been trying to expose and force out of high positions in Government, those who are in charge of our deliberate planned retreat from victory.

Now this fight, this fight against international communism, should not be a contest between America's two great political parties. Certainly, after all, the millions of Americans who've long voted the Democrat ticket are just as loyal, they love America just as much, they hate communism just as much as the average Republican.

Speech by Senator Joseph R. McCarthy published in the October 28, 1952, issue of *The New York Times* © 1952 by The New York Times Company. Reprinted by permission.

Unfortunately the millions of loyal Democrats no longer have a party in Washington. And tonight, tonight I shall give you the history of the Democrat candidate for the Presidency who endorsed and could continue the suicidal Kremlin-directed policies of this nation.

Now I'm not going to give you a speech tonight. Tonight I'm a lawyer giving you the facts on the evidence in the case of Stevenson vs. Stevenson.

Let me make it clear that I'm only covering his history in so far as it deals with his aid to the Communist cause and the extent—the extent to which he is part and parcel of the Acheson-Hiss-Lattimore group. Now I perform this unpleasant task because the American people are entitled to have the coldly-documented history of this man who says "I want to be your President."

The issue which faces 150,000,000 American people tonight, very simply stated, is: Will communism win or will America win? And you, the people—you the people who are listening to me tonight on radio, television, here in the hall—will decide that issue on Nov. 4 because we shall win or lose depending on the leadership which we choose on that day.

I shall now try to fit together the jig-saw puzzle of the man who wants to be President on the Truman-Acheson ticket. And I don't call it Democrat ticket because it would be a great insult to all good Democrats in this nation.

That which I present to you tonight is only that part of his history on which I have complete unchallengeable documentation. Now Stevenson has not yet heard the speech but already he and his camp are denouncing it as a pack of lies. Tonight I give you the cold record, a full week—a week and a day—before election so that he may have a chance to explain this record—if he can.

Now these facts, my good friends, cannot be answered, cannot be answered by screams of smears and lies. These facts can only be answered by facts. And we call upon Adlai of Illinois to so answer those facts.

The time is short, so let me get about the task of looking at his record. The Democrat candidate has said, and I quote him verbatim. He said, "As evidence of my direction I have established my headquarters here in Springfield with people of my own choosing." In other words he says, judge me, judge me by the advisers whom I have selected. Good, let's do that. Let's examine a few of those advisers first.

First is Wilson Wyatt, his personal manager. Now Wilson Wyatt is a former head of the left-winger A. D. A., the Americans for Democratic Action. The A. D. A. has five major points in its program. Listen to these and remember them if you will:

No. 1: Repeal of the Smith Act, which makes it a crime to conspire to overthrow this Government.

No. 2: Recognition of Red China.

No. 3: Opposition to the loyalty oath.

No. 4: Condemnation of the F.B.I. for exposing traitors like Coplon and Gubitchev, and

No. 5: Continuous all-out opposition to the House Committee on Un-American Activities.

Let me speak to you about that platform. They publish it day after day.

Now, according to an article in *The New York Times,* and I have that—which I hold in my hand—the Democrat candidate's campaign manager Wyatt condemns the Government's loyalty program and here's the proof—it condemns the loyalty program in the most vicious terms. Strangely Alger—I mean Adlai—Adlai in 1952, now that he's running for President, says I will dig out the Communists using as my weapon the loyalty program which my campaign manager damns and condemns.

Next, and perhaps the key figure in the Stevenson camp is his speech writer, Arthur Schlesinger Jr., former vice chairman of the same A. D. A. Now, Schlesinger has been a writer, incidentally, for The New York Post, New York Post whose editor and his wife admit, admit that they were members of the Young Communist League.

Now in 1946, Stevenson's speech writer wrote . . .: "The present system in the United States makes even freedom-loving Americans look wistfully at Russia." I wonder if there's anyone in this audience tonight who's looking wistfully at Russia. And I wonder, also, if some calamity would happen and Stevenson would be elected, what job this man would have.

Perhaps the most revealing article written by Stevenson's speech writer appeared in The New York Times on Dec. 11, 1949, on Page 3, and listen to this if you will. I quote, he says: "I happen to believe—I happen to believe that the Communist party should be granted the freedom of political action and that Communists should be allowed to teach in universities."

Nothing secret, nothing's secret about it, it's in the New York Times Dec. 11, 1949. Stevenson's speech writer saying I think that Communists should be allowed to teach your children, my good friends. And he says, Oh but judge me, judge me by the advisers whom I select.

Now let's see how Stevenson's speech writer feels on the subject of religion. The answer is given in his review of the book of Whittaker Chambers. Whittaker Chambers, the man whose testimony convicted Alger Hiss. Chambers in his book, as you know, maintained that a belief in God was the hope of the free world—the feeling which most Americans have regardless of whether they're Protestant, Jewish or Catholic. Well, Schlesinger wrote about that. . . .

. . . He says: "The whole record, the whole record of history indeed gives proof that a belief in God has created human vanity as overweaning and human arrogance as intolerable as the vanity and arrogance of the Communists."

And I say all of these documents are available for my good friends of the press to examine each and every one of them.

Stevenson says, judge me by the people I choose as my advisers. Here you have the philosophy of his chief adviser, the philosophy of his speech writer, laid bare. This idea of course that religion should be ridiculed is one of the basic principles of the Communist party. Now if you couple—couple this ridicule of religion with his statement that Communists should be allowed to teach your children and you have a fairly clear portrait of the man.

Another of Stevenson's assistants is Richard (Barnard) DeVoto. Now DeVoto has violently attacked our strongest defense against communism, the F. B. I. In Harper's Magazine, as reported in the Daily Worker of Dec. 29, 1949, Page 7, this man DeVoto denounces the F. B. I. as "nothing but college-trained flatfeet" and he says this: "And I would refuse to cooperate with the F. B. I."

The Communist Daily Worker of Feb. 13, 1947, reports that Stevenson's man DeVoto headed a group seeking a permit for a meeting for the wife of Gerhardt Eisler, the Communist who had disappeared behind the Iron Curtain and who as of tonight is heading up the anti-Communist (sic) group in East Berlin. So much for that.

. . . one of the men selected by Stevenson as one of his ghost writers—is . . . James Wechsler. Wechsler and his wife both admit—both admit having been members of the Young Communist League and I hold in my hand an article from the The New York Times which states that Wechsler's the man who helped Stevenson write the speech here it is, helped Stevenson write the speech in which Stevenson ridiculed anti-Communists as men who hunt for Communists in the Bureau of Wildlife and Fisheries.

That's a speech also in which he condemned—condemned my exposure of Communists as low comedy.

Now I just doubt whether the mothers and wives of the 120,000 Korean casualties consider it low comedy. I think they may possibly consider it a high tragedy. I'd like to call Mr. Stevenson's attention to that. . . .

. . . Another part of the jigsaw puzzle of Stevenson's history is his membership over many years on the Central Committee of the World Citizens Association.

Now I know that you may find some good people in that organization. You may even find some good Republicans, but Stevenson was not merely a member of the group. Stevenson was one of the twelve-man policy forming committee.

And this is quite an outfit, really quite an outfit, and the time is so short I'll cover Point 5 in their platform. I hold that platform in my hand. Keep in mind that the twelve men including Stevenson drafted this platform.

Let me read plank No. 5: "National states must be subordinate to world civilization; their jurisdiction must be limited by world law, and any local legislation contrary to world law must be null and void."

Now what does this mean my good friends, what does this mean to the 150,000,000 American people? It means that a world organization such as the United Nations could veto any state or Federal law or any part of our Constitution. This becomes doubly significant in view of recent revelations that twelve of the men who were recommended by the State Department to the United Nations have been dropped because they refused to say under oath whether or not they were or had been members of the Communist Party.

Twelve of the men in this world organization that should have the power to veto your laws. Well, while Stevenson's own office has been stating that he was a member of this unusual organization for only 1941, I have here a copy of Who's Who which he gives in a signed statement admitting that he was a member until 1945. I have a copy of the letterhead of this organization, February, 1948, carrying Stevenson not as a member but as part of the Central Committee twelve-man governing body.

Why is this significant? Simply my friends, simply because you're asked to elect a Presidential candidate who proposed to fly the flag of a super-world government over the Stars and Stripes.

We now come to the much-discussed testimony by Adlai Stevenson in the trial of Alger Hiss. Now, my good friends, I haven't considered, I have not considered this part standing alone as overly important in the Stevenson record. It is only a link in the chain of events that proves a case in Stevenson vs. Stevenson.

Now what does impress me, however, is the deathly fear that Governor Stevenson displays when additional links tying him to Alger Hiss are brought forth. We find that he very cleverly attempts to imply that his knowledge of Hiss was casual, remote and that he is not vouching for Hiss' character at the trial.

And I hold in my hand a petition which has never been made public before, either in the New York courts, a petition by the Hiss lawyers when they asked the court to admit Stevenson's statement. You will recall Stevenson said, I will sign a statement but I will not go to New York and run the risk of being put under cross-examination.

And Senator McCarran's committee, unanimously a committee of four Democrats and three Republicans, a committee of four Democrats and three Republicans unanimously found that the I. P. R. was Communist-controlled, Communist-dominated and shaping our foreign policy.

Now let's take a look at a photostat of a document taken from that Massachusetts barn. One of those documents that was never supposed to see the light of day, rather interesting it is, this is the document that shows that Alger Hiss and Frank Coe recommended Adlai Stevenson to the Mont Tremblant conference which was called for the purpose of establishing foreign policy—post-war foreign policy in Asia.

Now as you know Alger Hiss is a convicted traitor. Frank Coe was the man (named) under oath before Congressional committees seven times as a member of the Communist party. Why, why do Hiss and Coe find that Adlai Stevenson is the man they want representing them at this conference. I don't know, perhaps Adlai knows.

Let me read this one small section of this affidavit to you, and the entire affidavit's available to the press. Here's the affidavit of the Hiss lawyer:

Gov. Adlai Stevenson of Illinois has been closely associated with Alger Hiss in the course of certain international diplomatic undertakings. They were together at the San Francisco conference of the United Nations at which the Charter of the United Nations was adopted and they were together at the London conference which preceded and prepared the agenda for the San Francisco conference.

They say this: "The testimony of Governor Stevenson would be of great importance to Alger Hiss." Now I want you to examine closely the statement Governor Stevenson made at Cleveland, Ohio, about two days ago, the twenty-third, in which he attempted to defend his support of the reputation of Hiss—Hiss the arch-traitor of our times. Stevenson said this last Thursday. I quote him. He said: "I said his reputation was good. I did not say that his reputation was very good."

. Now here we have a man who says I want to be your President, saying that Hiss' reputation was good but not very good.

Now I say, my good friends, that if he had such misgivings he should not have vouched for Hiss at all. There are no degrees of loyalty in the United States. A man is either loyal or he's disloyal. There is no such thing—there is no such thing as being a little bit disloyal or being partly a traitor. . . .

21

The Internal Threat to the American Way of Life
EZRA TAFT BENSON

My fellow Americans, we are in the midst of continuing international crisis. The outlook for world peace and security is dark indeed. The gravity of the world situation is increasing almost daily. The United Nations seem unable to settle the troubles of the world. In truth we are faced with the hard fact that the United Nations seems to have largely failed in its purpose. Yes, the days ahead are sobering and challenging.

We live today in an age of peril. It is an age in which we are threatened with the loss not only of wealth and material prosperity, but of something far more precious—our freedom itself. The very thing that distinguishes man from the beasts—his freedom to act, freedom to choose, is threatened as never before by a total and atheistic philosophy of life known as communism.

Never before in the history of our country has there been a greater need for all of our people to take a little time to discover what is happening in the world. Every day decisions are being made affecting the lives of millions of human beings. We now need, as much as during any crisis . . . courageous leadership. . . .

[All] of us need to join a crusade to develop men and women who talk straight, tell the truth and who are willing to take a course deserving of God's blessings.

From *Congressional Record,* Vol. 108 (February 19, 1962), pp. A1201-5.

A genuine leader tries to stay well informed. He is a person who acts on principle rather than expediency. He tries to learn from all human experience measured against revealed principles of divine wisdom. As a rule, a good leader is not easily deceived.

What has been lacking in our culture that has allowed the Communists to deceive so many of our people so many different times? Perhaps part of it has been ignorance, another part misinformation, and certainly an important part has been apathy-complacency. . . .

Just a short time ago Fidel Castro broadcast to the world his boastful confession that he has been a hard-core Communist all of his adult life. He gloried in the fact that he has been able to confuse and deceive many people simply by saying he was not a Communist. And because there were people in this and other countries who believed his false assertions, he was able to establish a Soviet beachhead only 90 miles from our shores. Americans must face the cold hard fact that Fidel Castro was encouraged and supported in his seizure of Cuba. Why? Simply because many Americans were led to believe the falsehood that he would resist Soviet influence and restore the basic freedom of the Cuban people. A few of us issued early warnings based on unimpeachable evidence. Two U. S. Ambassadors repeatedly warned that Castro was part of the Communist camp and that he was working for the Communist conquest of Cuba. These voices went unheeded.

This is merely a repetition of the same deceitful pattern which was used after World War II to have us tolerate revolutionary Communists in China, to accept them as agrarian reformers and allow them to seize and enslave some 450 million people on the Chinese mainland.

This is the same deceitful pattern which we have been asked to accept in the Congo, in Laos, in British Guiana. In fact, everywhere the Communist conspiratorial machinery is preparing for a seizure of power, we are assured there is no immediate danger from communism. We are told that the high political officials in these countries, who surround themselves with known Communist advisers are merely trying to reconcile the various political factions and make their governments more representative. Later, after each country is taken over by the Fidel Castros, we are then assured that these men betrayed the revolution. Research subsequently reveals that these men had been hard-core Communists for many years. Those who believed them, once more lament, "I wonder how they deceived us?"

To me, the important question is, "Are we going to let them deceive us any longer?"

To the true Communist, nothing is evil if it is expedient. Being without conscience or honor, he feels completely justified in using whatever means are necessary to achieve his goal: force, trickery, lies, broken promises, mayhem, and individual and mass murder.

Let us have no illusions about them. Their leader has told us bluntly their purpose is not alone to enslave us; they want to bury us.

What we face today is not just a cold war, not just a struggle for the control of land, sea, air, and even outer space, but total competition for the control of men's minds. Unless we meet it and defeat it, we shall almost inevitably one day face the loss of all that we hold dear.

In less than half a century this evil system has gained control over one-third of mankind and it is steadily pursuing its vicious goal of control over all the rest of the world. It is time, and past time, for us to be alarmed.

Latin America does not believe that suppression is the road to freedom.

Less than 15 years ago communism was not a powerful force in Latin America. Today it is not only strongly present there as an enemy to be reckoned with—it is openly allied with a government located on an island only about 90 miles south of Key West, Fla.

The only political party now functioning in Cuba is the Popular Socialist Party—the Communist Party under another name.

Cuba is being used as a funnel through which Communists are infiltrating other American republics.

True to Communist and dictator tradition, the Cuban Government has deprived its people of the rights of a free press, free elections, and the protection of other fundamental human rights.

How did this situation come about? How has it been possible for this completely warped philosophy in such a short time to reach its present position of influence in the world? How is it possible for communism to be here and now moving into Africa, pressing upon all of Asia, threatening the Middle East and increasingly becoming a danger in the Western Hemisphere?

There are, of course, many reasons. Some nations have failed to provide for the advancement and desperate physical needs of their people. Others have failed to recognize the worth of the individual. But is it not perhaps true, that the biggest reason of all is the failure of Western civilization to live up to its Judaic-Christian ideals? . . .

We must revivify Western ideals and in particular the ideals of our own great Nation. We must call back the spirit of the dauntless leaders of the past. We must meet our present-day challenge not with softness and complacency, but with the depth, wisdom, and daring that characterized America in the days of old.

We have a rich history to guide us. Think back with me a moment to the year 1823. In that year, James Monroe, of Virginia, was President. John Quincy Adams, of Massachusetts, was Secretary of State. These two men formed and announced policy which has profoundly influenced the development of our entire hemisphere.

Here was the situation that called forth this policy, known as the Monroe Doctrine, in 1823.

Several of what are now the Latin American republics had by force of arms newly won their independence from Spain and Portugal. Among them were Colombia, Mexico, Chile, and Brazil.

Meantime a number of the sovereigns of Europe were seeking to enforce the divine right of kings with the express purpose of putting an end to the system of representative government. France, accordingly, had proceeded to restore the rule of Ferdinand VII in Spain. Now these countries proposed to overthrow the new and independent governments in Latin America.

This our Government refused to permit. It said so plainly in the celebrated Monroe Doctrine. The heart of the Monroe Doctrine consisted of these words: "The American continents, by the free and independent condition which they have assumed and maintained, are henceforth not to be considered as subjects for future colonization by any European power."

And the Doctrine went on to spell out clearly just what was meant as follows:

The political system of the allied powers is essentially different . . . from that of America. We owe it, therefore, to candor, and to the amicable relations existing between the United States and those powers, to declare that we should consider any attempt on their part to extend their system to any portion of this hemisphere as dangerous to our peace and safety.

Now there is a statement which might well be engraved in all the capitols of all the countries in this hemisphere today. Every word in it is as applicable today as it was 138 years ago.

Surely if it were true a century and a half ago that European monarchy was essentially different from our American system of representative government, it is even more true today that the Communist system is totally different, totally incompatible, totally inimical to our free way of life.

We are eminently justified in declaring that we should consider any attempt on the part of the Communists to extend their system to any part of this hemisphere as dangerous to our peace and safety.

Moreover, the Monroe Doctrine went on: "Nor can anyone believe that our southern brethren if left to themselves, would adopt it (this system) of their own accord." Here again the words of the Monroe Doctrine ring true.

It is almost unthinkable that any people would knowingly and willfully take on themselves the yoke of Communist oppression. No nation has ever done so yet. If large masses of the Cuban people have done so it is because they have been duped or coerced.

This Monroe Doctrine has been the continuing policy of our Nation for almost a century and a half.

It has been reaffirmed by many American Presidents.

We are on solid, traditional American ground in demanding that the Communists should not attempt to extend their political system to this side of the Atlantic Ocean. . . .

The Communists bring to the nations they infiltrate a message and a philosophy that affects human life in its entirety. Communism seeks to provide what in too many instances a lukewarm Christianity has not provided—a total interpretation of life. Communists are willing to be revolutionary; to take a stand for this and against that. They challenge what they do not believe in—customs, practices, ideas, traditions. They believe heatedly in their philosophy.

But our civilization and our people are seemingly afraid to be revolutionary. We are too broadminded to challenge what we do not believe in. We are afraid of being thought intolerant, uncouth, ungentlemanly. We have become lukewarm in our beliefs. And for that we perhaps merit a bitter condemnation stated in the Book of Revelation 3:16: "So then became thou art lukewarm, and neither cold or hot, I will spue thee out of my mouth."

This is a sad commentary on a civilization which has given to mankind the greatest achievements and progress ever known. But it is even a sadder commentary on those of us who call ourselves Christians, who thus betray the ideals given to us by the Son of God Himself. Again, I ask, are we going to permit the atheistic Communist masters, fellow travelers and dupes to deceive us any longer?

There is a deception going on in our country this very moment which is just as dangerous to the United States as the false pretensions of Fidel Castro were to Cuba. It is amazing to me that some of our citizens seem to take special delight in ridiculing the warnings of Government investigators and the cry of alarm which comes from Iron Curtain refugees when they see how the United States is being led carefully down the trail of disaster.

Clear back in 1953 the Jenner committee published a report on June 30 of that year which should have sobered the entire country. The report stated:

1. The Soviet international organization has carried on a successful and important penetration of the U. S. Government and this penetration has not fully been exposed.

2. This penetration has extended from the lower ranks to top-level policy and operating positions in our Government.

3. The agents of this penetration have operated in accordance with a distinct design fashioned by their Soviet superiors.

4. Members of the conspiracy helped to get each other into government, and protected each other from exposure. (The first Communist cell in government was organized in the U. S. Department of Agriculture in the 1930's.) . . .

6. In general, the Communists who infiltrated our Government worked behind the scenes—guiding research and preparing memorandums on which basic American policies were set, writing speeches for Cabinet officers, influencing congressional investigations, drafting laws, manipulating administrative reorganization—always serving the interests of their Soviet superiors. . . .

12. Policies and programs laid down by members of this Soviet conspiracy and still in effect within our Government, and constitute a continuing hazard in our national security."

Eight years have passed since that warning was given, but the American people have not yet insisted upon the house-cleaning which is so long overdue. In this year, 1961, that fearless and distinguished American, J. Edgar Hoover, testified before the House Appropriations Committee and said (FBI appropriation hearing, March 6, 1961, p. 49.):

The Soviet intelligence services have reorganized, multiplied their contacts with the American people, and have become aggressively bolder in spearheading their espionage offensive against the United States.

Speaking of Communist front organizations, he said (FBI appropriation hearing, March 6, 1961, p. 49.):

They represent transmission belts through which the Communist Party furthers its conspiratorial designs. They have infiltrated every conceivable sphere of activity: youth groups; radio, television, and motion picture industries, church, school, education, and cultural groups; the press, nationality minority groups, and civil and political units.

Of course, such groups can have only one purpose and that is deception. The only way to avoid being deceived is to get the facts. Here are people who would try to hide the facts from us and replace the truth with a falsehood. They want us to believe that America is a failure, that her system of capitalistic free enterprise is doomed, that she must remedy her failures by adopting Marxist theories of collectivized control. I recognize these voices. I heard them in 43 nations which I visited in the past few years. I heard them often during my 8 years in Washington. None of them came to me in the name of communism or even socialism, but they came. And while many of us fought them and resisted them on every front, nevertheless, it was alarming to discover how many others were willing to believe and follow. Why do otherwise loyal Americans believe and follow? Because these voices came from masters of deception.

Now supposing a person came along and said, "I am in favor of doing away with competitive markets and private property, of setting communes in each locality, of taking all the land away from the farmers, of taking over all the steel mills, all the electric power plants, all the automotive industry, the banks, the railroads, the newspapers, the television and radio stations, all the mines, and so forth." I am sure such a proposal would meet with immediate and united resistance by the vast majority of the American people. But supposing this same person came and said: "It is in the public interest and to the benefit of each citizen if we make industry, the farms, and all means of production and distribution operate for the benefit of all the people and not just for the private profit of a few stockholders." Immediately this line of deception receives a wave of support. It is occurring today here in the United States. It occurred in England, France, and Eastern Europe as well as the Scandinavian countries. It occurred in Russia.

If you ask the individual who made this last statement whether or not he is a Communist or Socialist he will undoubtedly reply with great indignation that he is a loyal American—that he is very anti-Communist. He will generally say he merely wants to see our Nation achieve marvelous new goals which will make our present standard of living appear meager indeed.

When you ask this individual where his plan has been tried and proven successful, he will tell you it is a plan of the future and its virtues are yet to be demonstrated. And if you press him even further by pointing out that his program sounds exactly like the Marxist-socialism of Europe he may become extremely indignant and call you a reactionary who doesn't want to see the country progress.

Now this accusation, of course, is as false as it is unfair. All of us are anxious to see our country progress, but we want to know by what means. The whole American concept of progress, which has outstripped every other nation on earth, is based on certain fundamental principles which these men now ask us to abandon. Certainly we are entitled to challenge such proposals when they are asking us to give up what has worked so well and substitute something which they merely hope will work.

What are these fundamental principles which have allowed the United States to progress so rapidly and yet remain free?

First, a written Constitution clearly defining the limits of government so that government will not become more powerful than the people.

Second, an economic system which is characterized by:
Free enterprise—the right to venture, the right to choose;
Private property—the right to own, develop and enjoy; and
A market economy—the right to exchange and to profit.

Third, building an open society where each individual enjoys the greatest opportunity to improve himself, to travel, to become educated, to invent, to compete, to build, to speak, to worship, and to pursue happiness in whatever way the individual finds most satisfying and worthwhile.

Fourth, assigning government the role of referee rather than competitor—giving it enough power to provide peace, order, and security but not enough power to rob the people of their liberty or take away their property without due process of law.

Of course, it immediately becomes apparent that if certain people wanted to seize control of private property, if they wanted to nationalize the land, if they wanted to have the government take over all the industries, the schools, the transportation complex, and communications network, the way to do it would be by due process of law. Therefore, certain people have set out to do this very thing.

Is this possible? It is indeed, and every American should know it. . . .

The Communists use the Socialists to pave the way for them wherever possible. This is why Communists and Socialists are often found supporting each other, collaborating together and fighting for the same goals.

The paramount issue today is freedom against creeping socialism. . . . The Socialists know they cannot seize property and power by due process of law unless they are politically popular, therefore, they try desperately to avoid the taint of the Communists and present their program so that it appears moral, democratic, peaceful, and so gradual that the people will not resist it. . . .

All of this may begin to sound familiar to many American businessmen who have been watching similar influences of creeping socialism gradually using Government regulations or Government ownership to destroy the basic framework of economic freedom and private production in our own country.

We must ever keep in mind that collectivized socialism is part of the Communist strategy. Communism is fundamentally socialism. We will never win our fight against communism by making concessions to socialism. Communism and socialism must be defeated on principle.

When socialism is understood, we will realize that many of the programs advocated, and some of those already adopted in the United States, fall clearly within the category of socialism. What is socialism? It is simply governmental ownership and management of the essential means for the production and distribution of goods.

We must never forget that nations may sow the seeds of their own destruction while enjoying unprecedented prosperity.

The socialistic Communist conspiracy to weaken the United States involves attacks on many fronts. To weaken the American free-enterprise economy which outproduced both its enemies and allies during World War II, is a high priority target of the Communist leaders. Their press and other propaganda media are therefore constantly selling the principles of centralized or federal control of farms, railroads, electric power, schools, steel, maritime shipping, and many other aspects of the economy—but always in the name of public welfare.

For 30 years we have aided the cause of atheistic, socialistic communism by permitting Communists in high places in Government; by giving away vital military secrets; by squandering much of our material resources; by recklessly spending ourselves to near bankruptcy; by weakening our free enterprise system through adoption of socialistic policies; by wasteful bungling of our foreign affairs; by ever increasing confiscatory taxation and by permitting the insidious infiltration of Communist agents and sympathizers into almost every segment of American life.

Many people have wondered if the Marxist concepts of the Fabian Social Democrats have deeply penetrated the United States. In truth they have. British Social Democrats came to the United States in 1888 for a long visit to train Fabian groups in several of the leading universities. Eventually their followers were organized into the Intercollegiate Socialist Society in 1905. By 1916 this organization was becoming increasingly influential and its members were already climbing into the higher echelons of the Government. After World War I the society changed its name to the League for Industrial Democracy and continued to plant its most brilliant personalities in government, education, communications and policymaking bodies. There they remain today, occupying some of the highest offices in the land. Their records will show that they have consistently sponsored the basic ideas of the Social Democrats of Europe. Some of them have been exposed, as not only being sympathetic, and collaborating with their fellow Marxists of the U.S.S.R., but actually joining them. . . .

[T] he internal threat to the American way of life is in the secret alliance which exists between the more advanced Social Democrats and the hard-core Communist conspiracy. Occasionally this sympathetic alliance breaks out into the open, but most of the time it is maintained in the labyrinths of quiet secrecy. . . .

It would appear to me that when a mind has been trained to hold such bitterness against capitalism: to believe so blindly in the illusions of communism, it is no wonder that some of this same mentality have used their influence in scientific circles, in embassies, and in governmental positions to betray the interests of their own countries and collaborate with what has turned out to be the most formidable enemy freemen have ever faced.

I believe J. Edgar Hoover and the investigating committees of Congress know whereof they speak when they warn us of a serious internal threat to the American way of life. I hear that some people and more particularly the Communists and the Social Democrats don't want us to examine this internal threat, but I believe we should. I think we should study communism and study socialism so we can recognize the influence of each. We can leave the spies to the FBI, but learning how our enemies are trying to subvert us is everybody's job. I also recognize that it is not popular in some circles to be called an anti-Communist, but I consider communism a godless political and economic disease. I do not believe an American citizen can be patriotic and loyal to his own country, and its God-inspired Constitution, of freedom, without being anti-Communist.

Now I know that Moscow has ordered that all anti-Communists are to be attacked and discredited in every way possible. I know the Communist Party of the United States has issued a similar mandate. This does not disturb me at all. It should be expected. Meanwhile we should pursue a calm and steady course. We should expose to the light of public inquiry those forces which would destroy our country and our way of life. We should pay no attention to the recommendations of men who call the Constitution an 18th century agrarian document—who apologize for capitalism and free enterprise. We should refuse to follow their siren song of concentrating, increasingly, the powers of government in the Chief Executive, of delegating American sovereign authority to non-American institutions in the United Nations, and pretending that it will bring peace to the world by turning our Armed Forces over to a U. N. worldwide police force.

My own political and economic creed is a simple one. I commend it to you:

I am for freedom and against slavery.

I am for social progress and against socialism.

I am for a dynamic economy and against waste.

I am for the private ownership and against governmental ownership and control of the means of production and distribution.

I am for national security and against appeasement and capitulation to an obvious enemy.

This contest in which we are engaged is as old as man and as young as hope. The issue is over the God-given eternal principle of freedom—free agency, the right of choice. In this struggle it is not enough to be right—we must put strength and action back of that which is right.

In the conflict with socialistic communism we must have patience, courage, and wisdom. We must also have friends. Russia has hostages—we have friends—millions of them in temporary slavery back of the Iron Curtain, and millions more to be mobilized throughout the free world. In Russia people are unable to challenge the despotic godless dogmas forced on the people. We must take greater risks for freedom. We must dramatize American might and Soviet myth.

Let us awaken to our responsibilities and to our opportunities. . . . I quote Dr. Malik.

The civilization which has been blessed and transformed by Christ, needs only a mighty hand to shake it out of its slumber. And, once shaken, once really awakened to the world responsibilities which it and it alone can shoulder, there is nothing it cannot dare and do.

I love America. I know you do. God and our children will judge us for what we do with our land and our liberties. As Theodore Roosevelt said over half a century ago, we "hold in our hands the hope of the world, the fate of the coming years, and shame and disgrace will be ours if in our eyes the light of high resolve is dimmed, if we trail in the dust the golden hopes of men."

With God's help the light of high resolve in the eyes of the American people must never be dimmed. Our freedom must and will be preserved.

May God give us the wisdom to recognize the threat to our freedom and the strength to meet this danger courageously.

The alienation of some Americans from their own institutions is most profoundly evident in the growing split between Afro-Americans and a white majority. The social, economic, and political inequalities which persist in this era pose a two-pronged question as to the adaptability of democratic processes to a modern, pluralistic society: (1) is an inherited philosophic commitment to equality enough to merit the title, "democratic," or is democracy, by its very nature, dependent for vitality upon eternal expansion; and (2) can this society effectively confront and solve the glaring inequities resulting from three hundred years of racial discrimination, using democratic modes of action, before extremists—white and black—succeed in burning down the American political experiment? There can be no doubt that, as the McCone Commission warned following the Watts riot, "the existing breach, if allowed to persist, could in time split our society irretrievably."[1] The racial crisis in twentiety-century America is the most dramatic proof of all that great numbers of the people no longer trust the egalitarian professions of the government nor believe that the social and political value system which has been pieced together as the nation matured can or should continue to survive. Social scientists find enormous discontent amid the seeming affluence today; studies of the views of both rural and urban minorities reveal an "almost complete disassociation with government," rooted in that wasteland which divides the democratic promise and the realities of enforced disfranchisement and degradation.[2]

The massive unrest which seethes and boils over into destructive, bloody riots requires no scholarly investigation into causal factors. It can be measured at first-hand.[3] The sharecroppers' and migrant workers' country slums and the city ghetto dwellers' pestilential hell represent the residual effects of racial hatreds stretching back in time to the founding of European settlements in North America. White colonists were busily clearing the land of Indians and importing African slaves at the same time they were, as textbooks proudly record, hammering out an ideology which included concepts of human dignity, equality, and rationality. During the first half of the nineteenth century, Americans were as engrossed in institutionalizing a rigid, brutal slave system as in extending rights of suffrage and public education.[4] The hopes for true equality sparked by the Abolitionist crusade and fanned by Civil War and initial Reconstruction legislation were extinguished in the years after 1876 by the violent repressive acts of the Ku Klux Klan, insistent social pressures, and riots.[5] By the end of that century, legislation extending civil rights to all Americans, regardless of color, had been declared unconstitutional and segregation had acquired legality.[6] And the first years of the twentieth century offered little hope for change. The "progressivism" of Theodore Roosevelt and Woodrow Wilson stressed the importance of the "Forgotten Man," yet the truly forgotten racial minorities only suffered new indignities—the extension of Jim Crowism to federal services and facilities during the "New Freedom," and, in World War I (fought to extend democracy), military segregation.[7] The twenties witnessed a resurgent Klan, and even in the New Deal years, the extension of equality to ethnic groups proceeded very slowly, primarily on the economic front.[8] Afro-Americans found, in the Second World War, that the United States was far more interested in eradicating racism abroad than at home; the armed forces maintained segregation policies, and even blood for the wounded was segregated according to race by the Red Cross![9]

Racial minorities sought redress in amazingly cautious fashion. American Indians remained quietly on the small sections of land granted them as reservations or accepted the fixedly base social station accorded them in society at large. After the collapse of the IWW, migrant workers fell back on the paternalism of their employers. Black Americans, meanwhile, followed the conciliatory Booker T. Washington who urged temporary acceptance of social inequality while the black people mastered economic skills which, he hoped, would bring them eventual equality.[10] Despite repeated acts of white hostility, such as the riots in New York, Springfield, Ohio, Greensburg, Indiana, and Springfield, Illinois, Afro-American leaders hewed to a comparatively moderate course.[11] The Niagara movement of W. E. B. DuBois, aimed at such fundamental rights of citizenship as suffrage and desegregation, was labeled "radical."[12] DuBois' group grew into the National Association for the Advancement of Colored People and, emphasizing the protection and enlargement of civil rights through court actions, dominated the scene from its inception until the landmark Supreme Court decision overturning segregation in public schools in 1954.[13] This court victory spurred a rise in expectations which had begun in the New Deal years and had been nourished by President Truman's Fair Deal policies. "Ironically," as the members of President Johnson's Commission on Civil Disorder have observed, "it was the very successes in the legislatures and the courts that, more perhaps than any other single factor, led to intensified Negro expectations and resulting dissatisfaction with the limitations of legal and legislative programs."[14]

Legal and political successes gave Afro-Americans a new measure of self-respect, and with this self-respect came an aggressive call for full citizenship. They had come to "resent the cruel game of having to go into court or take to the sidewalks to prove again and again that their citizenship . . . [included] . . . the enjoyment of the most elemental human rights."[15] Furthermore, new organizations had appeared, equipped to wage the battle for civil rights on new fronts. The National Urban League sought equal employment opportunities through cooperation with business leaders; DuBois and A. Philip Randolph sought to galvanize black workers for concerted economic action.[16] The use of massive, nonviolent demonstrations, advocated by the Congress on Racial Equality after 1942, was applied spectacularly by Dr. Martin Luther King's Southern Christian Leadership Conference and great numbers of student volunteers at the end of the 1950's[17] Even the dramatic results achieved by these innovative, democratic techniques could not keep pace with the rising impatience of many Afro-Americans, however. The nineteenth-century Abolitionists had mistakenly believed that political equality would suffice to free the black people. It had not been enough then; manifestly, it was not enough in the twentieth century. Voting rights had no immediate impact, for example on widespread poverty, unemployment, illiteracy rates, or the stagnating environment of the urban ghettos.[18] To offer political rights which were long overdue without attacking the problems of ghetto existence only reinforced the conviction of many that American democracy was spurious.[19]

Racism had economic and social, as well as political and legal roots; the unemployment and wretched housing conditions of the ghettos required immediate attention, and self-help was not sufficient.[20] Once compressed into segregated areas, Afro-Americans were kept there by the color line. Unlike white immigrants, they could not overcome deprivation simply through hard work. Their skin color branded them as ghetto dwellers.[21] Nevertheless, the ferment for full citizenship, for all the neglected, accumulated grievances and a rhetoric of immediacy, has remained, at least to the present, an attempt to get inside, not to smash, American society. The black protest "has been firmly rooted in the basic values of American society, seeking not their destruction but their fulfillment."[22] A majority of active black civil rights workers still view their ultimate goal as "One race, one human race!"[23]

Yet the elements necessary for a final cleavage leading to savage racial revolution all are available; an accidental or planned coalescence of those elements is quite possible. The thousands of young, unemployed blacks form an easily exploitable "reservoir of hate."[24] Increasingly impatient leaders have found the martyred Dr. King's nonviolent road too long, too tortuous; some admit that they are "just past talking—there's simply no longer any point to it."[25] Urged on by demagogic, racist arguments and finding increasing support for extremism in the ghettos, a few black leaders have resurrected a dormant black nationalism and decreed an end to the peaceful but slow search for equality within the democratic framework.[26] The concepts of racism, separatism, and collective guilt are no longer preached solely by the Black Muslims. Cults dedicated to black nationalism and a violent racial confrontation are springing up in almost all the large urban centers.[27] Members of such groups as Uhuru, Black Flag, RAM, and Black Vanguard see no chance for a democratic solution to their plight; they store arms, drill in dark alleys, study diagrams of urban electrical and water systems, and manufacture crude but effective grenades for the inevitable war.[28] As one Black Muslim leader has promised, there will be "no torture—just annihilation. . . . We will not antagonize the white people. Some morning they will just wake up dead."[29] The presence of these terrorists in cities where rioting is on the increase is a clear danger. It is possible to understand the frustrations which lead to violence. Democracy's promise has not been fulfilled in areas where riots themselves express a deep distrust for a supposedly representative government.[30] Is violence, then, the answer? Are organizations like CORE or SNCC correct to sanction guerilla warfare and suggest that riots become revolutions?[31] The investigations of the President's Commission on Civil Disorder revealed that the actual results of the violence which has turned cities into jungles include: "increased distrust between blacks and whites, diminished interracial communications, and growth of Negro and white extremist groups."[32] As yet, the riots remain unorganized outbreaks, symptoms of a mortal disease in the political structure, shrieks of despair from violated human beings who want their rights.[33] Actual revolution, however, "is something more than the wild hallucinations of a relatively few angry black Napoleons."[34] Extremist cries for vengeance and organized terror form an "ugly background noise" in the current civil rights turmoil, and as one social commentator has written, "A revolution is underway in this country. . . . Whether it will be peaceful depends on . . . the capacity of the American people to recognize in time how urgent it is that all Americans be permitted to rise to the full dignity of liberty and equality."[35] The nation must, Berl Bernhard avows, "close the gap between the proclamation of freedom and its practice. *National survival cries for it."*[36]

NOTES

1. "Violence in the City—an End or a Beginning?," *A Report by the Governor's Commission on the Los Angeles Riots,* State of California, December 2, 1965, p. 7; Joseph P. Lyford, "Proposal for a Revolution—Part I," *Saturday Review,* 46 (October 19, 1963), pp. 19-22; *U.S., Report of the National Advisory Commission on Civil Disorders* (Washington, D.C.: Government Printing Office, 1968), p. 95.

2. Horatio Ulibari, "Social and Attitudinal Characteristics of Spanish-Speaking Migrant and Ex-Migrant Workers in the Southwest," *Sociology and Social Research,* 50 (April, 1966), p. 370; Emory S. Bogardus, "Stages in White-Negro Relations in the United States: An Outline," *Sociology and Social Research,* 45 (October, 1960), pp. 74-79; *Report on Civil Disorders,* p. 96.

3. Charlotte Devree, "The Young Negro Rebels," *Harpers Magazine,* 223 (October, 1961), p. 133.

4. John Hope Franklin, *From Slavery to Freedom: A History of Negro Americans* (3rd rev. ed.; New York: Alfred A. Knopf, 1967), pp. 71-241; *Report on Civil Disorders,* pp. 96-98.

5. Franklin, *From Slavery to Freedom,* pp. 324-343; Robert Goldston, *The Negro Revolution* (New York: Macmillan Company, 1968), pp. 123-140; *Report on Civil Disorders,* pp. 99-100.

6. *Report on Civil Disorders,* p. 100.

7. Eli Ginzberg and Alfred S. Eichner, *The Troublesome Presence: American Democracy and the Negro* (Glencoe: Free Press, 1964), pp. 265-290; *Report on Civil Disorders,* pp. 101-102.

8. *Report on Civil Disorders,* p. 102-103.

9. *Ibid.,* p. 104.

10. *Ibid.,* p. 101.

11. *Ibid.,* p. 100.

12. *Ibid.,* p. 101.

13. Franklin, *From Slavery to Freedom,* p. 556.

14. *Report on Civil Disorders,* p. 106; Franklin, *From Slavery to Freedom,* pp. 608-652; Harry A. Bailey, Jr., ed., *Negro Politics in America* (Columbus, Ohio: Charles E. Merrill Books, Inc., 1966), pp. iii-iv.

15. C. Eric Lincoln, "Extremist Attitudes in the Black Muslim Movement," *Journal of Social Issues,* 19 (April, 1963), p. 83.

16. *Report on Civil Disorders,* p. 102.

17. *Ibid.,* pp. 104-107.

18. *Ibid.,* p. 108.

19. Fredric Solomon and Jacob R. Fishman, "Youth and Social Action: Action and Identity Formation in the First Student Sit-in Demonstration," *Journal of Social Issues,* XX (April, 1964), pp. 36-45.

20. Michael Harrington, "The Economics of Racism," *Commonweal,* 74 (July 7, 1961), pp. 367-370.

21. *Ibid.; Report on Civil Disorders,* pp. 115-121.

22. John B. Turner and Whitney M. Young, Jr., "Who Has the Revolution, or Thoughts on the Second Reconstruction," *Daedalus,* (Fall, 1965), p. 1150; *Report on Civil Disorders,* p. 113.

23. Devree, "Young Negro Rebels," p. 135.

24. "Reservoir of Hate," *America,* 111 (September 5, 1964), p. 222.

25. Robert Penn Warren, "Two for SNCC," *Commentary,* 39 (April, 1965), pp. 38-48; Russell Sackett, "Plotting a War on 'Whitey'," *Life,* 60 (June 10, 1966), p. 100B.

26. George Dennison, "The Demagogy of LeRoi Jones," *Commentary,* 39 (February, 1965), pp. 67-70; Sackett, "Plotting a War on 'Whitey'," p. 100; *Report on Civil Disorders,* p. 111.

27. Albert B. Southwick, "Malcolm X: Charismatic Demagogue," *Christian Century,* 80 (June 5, 1967), p. 741; Lewis Bowman, "Racial Discrimination and Negro Leadership Problems: the Case of 'Northern Community'," *Social Forces,* 44 (December, 1965), pp. 173-186.

28. Sackett, "Plotting a War on 'Whitey'," pp. 100-101; "Negro Racists," *Nation,* 196 (April 6, 1963), p. 278.

29. Lincoln, "Black Muslim Movement," p. 81.

30. *Report on Civil Disorders,* p. 77.

31. *Ibid.,* p. 111.

32. *Ibid.,* p. 65.

33. *Ibid.,* p. 64.

34. Sackett, "Plotting a War on 'Whitey'," p. 100B; *Report on Civil Disorders,* p. 89.

35. *Report on Civil Disorders,* p. 93; "All, Here and Now," *Christian Century,* Vol. 78 (June 28, 1961), p. 788.

36. Berl I. Bernhard, "Equality and 1984: the Future Cannot be Delegated," *Vital Speeches,* 29 (July 15, 1963), p. 597.

U. S. Congress, Senate Committee on Government Operations. Permanent Sub-Committee on Investigations. *Hearings before the permanent SubCommittee on Investigations of the Committee on Government Operations.* 90th Cong., 2nd sess., March 21-22, 1968, Part 6. (Exhibit 82 made available through the courtesy of U. S. Senator Henry M. Jackson, Member, Committee on Government Operations.)

22

Revolutionary Action Movement Manifesto

ROBERT F. WILLIAMS

RAM was officially organized in the winter of 1963 by Afro-Americans who favored Robert F. Williams and the concept of organized violence. Through a series of workshop discussions, the group decided there was a need for a "Third Force" or movement that would be somewhere between the *Nation of Islam* (Black Muslims) and SNCC (Student Non-Violent Coordinating Committee).

Objectives:

1. To give black people a sense of racial pride, dignity, unity and solidarity in struggle.
2. To give black people a new image of manhood and womanhood.
3. To free black people from colonial and imperialist bondage everywhere and to take whatever steps necessary to achieve that goal.
4. To give black people a sense of purpose.

The motto was "One Purpose, One Aim, One Destiny," meaning:

One Purpose—To free black people from the universal slavemaster (slang for capitalist oppression).

One Aim—To develop black people through struggle to the highest attainment possible.

One Destiny—To follow in the spirit of black revolutionaries such as Gabriel Prosser, Toussaint L'Overture, Denmark Vesey, Nat Turner, Sojourner Truth, Harriet Tubman, Frederick Douglass, Marcus Garvey, Dr. DuBois, Robert F. Williams, and to create a new world free of colonialism, racism, imperialism, exploitation, and national oppression.

Thus RAM was officially organized as a movement. With rotating chairmen to develop leadership, RAM immediately plunged into action. It helped organize one of Philadelphia's largest black mass rallies for the NAACP over the issue of a "research project" designed by white liberals for the black community.

U. S. Congress, Senate Committee on Government Operations. Permanent Sub-Committee on Investigations. *Hearings before the permanent SubCommittee on Investigations of the Committee on Government Operations.* 90th Cong., 2nd sess., March 21-22, 1968, Part 6. (Exhibit 82 made available through the courtesy of U. S. Senator Henry M. Jackson, Member, Committee on Government Operations.)

We felt a need for "fresh, young and new ideas" to be discussed in the black community, so we began publishing a bimonthly *Black America*. RAM then organized several street meetings in the heart of the black ghetto to bring its program to our people, obtained an office, and began to hold free weekly African and *Afro*-American history classes. Through a free weekly publication, *Ram Speaks,* RAM attempted to raise the consciousness of the black community by the discussion of political issues.

RAM found, through its active involvement and living with the black masses, that one of the main reasons that we (black people) are unorganized is because we (black people) are politically unaware. RAM then reorganized its program to education in political revolution. We soon saw that the key to the black man's plight is his lack of revolutionary organization. We felt that this could best be brought about by the organization of a black political party. But we also felt that this black political party must have revolutionary objectives and not that of peaceful co-existence with the oppressor. In other words, we felt the need for a black revolution that could and would seize power.

In spreading revolutionary concepts throughout the community and especially among youth, RAM became a target for the power structure. When RAM demonstrated, along with many other groups over the racist-fascist police tactics used against unarmed women, children and men in Birmingham, the NAACP tried to oust RAM from a "united" picket line because of its sign stating, "We do not advocate non-violence in a police state." The more RAM pushed, the more the reformist leadership had to sound aggressive. When the NAACP decided to organize demonstrations over union discrimination on a school construction site, RAM played a major role. The racist-fascist police seized the opportunity to attack some RAM organizers and frame them on trumped-up charges of assault and battery, cutting, disorderly conduct, disturbing the peace, and conspiracy.

It soon became apparent that the NAACP and CORE were fighting to get headlines, so RAM ceased its public program and began to develop its members and those around them. RAM felt this was necessary since, in order to make our black revolt into a successful black revolution, we would have to train people in what real revolution means and what it is going to take.

To answer some questions raised by "orthodox black nationalists" and charges that RAM is an integrationist group, I will explain why we participated in the school construction site struggle.

As revolutionary black nationalists, we do not believe that standing on the street corners alone will liberate our people. Revolutionary black nationalists must act as a vanguard to show our people how to seize power so that they may gain some control over their lives. The main reason they are treated the way they are is that they are powerless. In the school construction site demonstration, our people saw the system denying them opportunity. As our struggle developed, they saw that the police who represent the state or state power were not on our side but on the side of those who uphold racism. This brought in the concept of government, protection of the community by a black people's police force, and the concept that we are at war with white America. Thus by our action, our people gained a vital lesson in the need for a revolutionary organization that has power by physical example and involvement.

RAM soon found that just being out in the streets was not enough and that national revolutionary organization was the key to victory of our revolution. RAM also shifted its program to an accent on youth. After careful analysis through action and study, RAM feels that black youth are the key to our revolution. We see youth all over the world leading the revolutions of our people. In the Angolan liberation army the soldiers' age range is 17-20; in the Congo's guerilla force called "Youth" the age range is 14-20; in the Viet Cong the age range is 14-19; in Kenya the Mau Mau was started by roving bands of youth. In Cuba Castro's forces were very young.

During the summer of 1963 RAM reorganized and sent field organizers throughout the North to help local groups organize demonstrations. Through our experience we have developed an organization on three levels of involvement: (1) *Field organizers,* who are full-time organizers with a period of orientation and training in the movement; (2) *Active members,* who cannot be full-time but actively support RAM by physical, financial and other help, and have also been through a period of orientation; (3) *Associate members,* who have been through a period of orientation but, for reasons approved by the movement, cannot give physical support but do pledge financial support. During the fall of 1963, RAM field organizers helped groups throughout the South develop a perspective beyond the limits of the integrationist movement. Also in Philadelphia, RAM's home base, RAM in 1962 and 1963 fought several cases of police brutality and in one case achieved unity among the young black militant groups for a brief period. RAM has recently been active in organizing demonstrations around the frame-up of Mae Mallory and the other Monroe defendants.

RAM philosophy may be described as revolutionary nationalism, black nationalism or just plain blackism. It is that black people of the world (darker races, black, yellow, brown, red, oppressed peoples) are all enslaved by the same forces. RAM's philosophy is one of the world black revolution or world revolution of oppressed peoples rising up against their former slavemasters. Our movement is a movement of black people who are coordinating their efforts to create a "new world" free from exploitation and oppression of man to man.

In the world today there is a struggle for world power between two camps, the haves (Western or white capitalist nations) and the have-nots (Eastern or newly independent nations struggling for independence, socialist nations). There are two types of nationalism. One type suppresses or oppresses, that is, a nation or particular group reaps profits or advances materially at the expense, exploitation, slavery or torture of another group or nation. In this nation and in the world today, this nationalism is considered "white nationalism" or the cooperation of the white Western nations to keep the new emerging oppressed world in bondage. This is capitalist or reactionary nationalism. The other type of nationalism is to liberate or free from exploitation. That is the binding force of a nation or particular group to free itself from a group or nation that is suppressing or oppressing it. In this country and in the world, this is considered black nationalism or revolutionary nationalism.

We can see that black nationalism is the opposite of white nationalism; black nationalism being revolutionary and white being reactionary. We see also that nationalism is really internationalism today.

While defining nationalism as a force towards black liberation, we define nationalism as black patriotism.

Nationalism is an identification and consciousness of our own kind and self. Knowledge of self is an integral part of nationalism. Knowledge of our own history of struggle is an essential part of nationalism. Love for our own people and not for the enemy is nationalism.

RAM feels that with the rise of fascism, the black man must not only think of armed self-defense but must also think aggressively.

Our black nation is still in captivity. RAM feels that the road to freedom is self-government, national liberation and black power. Our slogan is "Unite or perish." Our definition of revolution is one group's determination to take power away from another.

In ending this manifesto, we (RAM) say, "Think what you wish, but we shall accomplish what we will."

23

___

The Los Angeles War Cry, "Burn, Baby, Burn"
Purpose of the Revolutionary Nationalist

The purpose of the *Revolutionary Nationalist* is to clarify, give direction, program, methods of organization and to discuss problems of Revolutionary nationalists. The *Revolutionary Nationalist* functions as the internal bulletin of the May 1, 1964, Conference on Black Nationalism.

Revolutionary Nationalist is published by the permanent secretariat of the conference. The *Revolutionary Nationalist* will interpret and further develop the theories, aims, projects and actions of the May 1st Conference and events which are pertinent to the cause of liberation of our people. The *Revolutionary Nationalist* will also develop the philosophy of the conference—Pan African socialism, or what is publicly referred to as Revolutionary Nationalism—Black Internationalism.

13 Points from the May 1st Conference

1. Development of a permanent underground secretariat to carry out plans.

2. To push the Bourgeois reformist as far "up tempo" as fast as possible, while at the same time laying a base for an underground movement.

3. The Conference united with the African, Asian and Latin American Revolution

4. Adopt Robert F. Williams as leader in exile.

5. The achievement of Afro-American solidarity (to push the Restoration of the Revolutionary Spirit to Pan-Africanism).

6. Conference philosophy—Pan African Socialism.

7. The establishment of Internal Bulletin for Conference.

8. Construction of a Pan African Student Conference.

9. Secretariat contact all student Liberation Organizations around the world to develop rapport and coordination.

___

U. S. Congress, Senate Committee on Government Operations. Permanent SubCommittee on Investigations. *Hearings before the permanent SubCommittee on Investigations of the Committee on Government Operations.* 90th Cong., 2nd sess., March 21-22, 1968, Part 6. (Exhibit 88 made available through the courtesy of U. S. Senator Henry M. Jackson, Member, Committee on Government Operations.)

10. National Public organ, name: *Black America.*

11. Charge genocide against U. S. Imperialism before the United Nations.

12. Secretariat develop program for Revolutionary Black Nationalists.

13. Develop two Revolutionary Centers.

12. Secretariat develop program for Revolutionary Black Nationalists.

On the Eve of Black Revolution: Los Angeles Proves *"We Will Win"*

The National Rebellion Against Racist Oppression

The events in L.A. show we are at war with the United States government. With the national guard being called in to crush our peoples struggle for national liberation we see that we are in the same situation we were in over 102 years ago when the federal troops were called in to crush our slave revolts. This shows we are still slaves, i.e., colonial subjects, not citizens denied our rights.

In spite of the small number of weapons our people were still able to stand off the highly organized white right wing police of L.A. This shows when our people make up their minds to fight for their freedom they are uncontrollable. Also noted was the growing consciousness among our people of the nature of their situation. . ."This is the Negro revolution we want the world to know.". . ."we want to set fire right here (in L.A.) rather than to go to Vietnam and fight. We'd rather fight for the Negro here."

There was considerable comment that the people were leaderless but this was not true; the newspapers contradicted themselves by saying the youth were leading. Therefore the leaders in Los Angeles were the ghetto youth. These same youth who emerged to lead the struggle in L.A. are constantly categorized as criminal by the white society and are proven to be the most feared element among our people. The L.A. insurrection once again exposes the bankruptcy of the "responsible" leadership of the civil rights establishment. They had no control over our people although they made appeals for maintaining "whities" law and order over the radio.

As to the international ramifications of this revolt, it further exposes the U.S. as a racist colonialist prison for black people to the Bandung (colored) peoples of the world and shows that the African enslaved in America is not a satisfied "Uncle Tom" waiting to integrate with the racist imperialist beast society, and this also shows that we are victims of domestic (internal) colonialism. This latest insurrection shows that our people are learning through struggle, as witness the semi-gurrellia [sic] tactics of our people in L.A. If there are black troops among the ranks of the national guard they should turn their guns against their true enemy and not shot their own people for the white racist.

With the war of resistance against racist oppression and brutality spreading to Chicago and Springfield, Mass., we see that the African enslaved in America is involved in a para-military protracted war for national liberation. The semi-guerrilla tactics being used in L.A. is proving our people are beginning to learn how to use guerrilla tactics of applying ten against one and one against ten—that is using superior numbers against the enemies weakest point, constantly attacking, harrassing, annihilating and using one against ten as decoy to harass and demoralize the enemy.

The shooting of two brothers last weekend in Brooklyn, N.Y., by white racist police is the third shooting of a brother in Brooklyn this summer. The shooting represents a systematic play by the John Birch Society (which has successfully infiltrated the northern police force departments) of creating incidents in an attempt to annihilate revolutionary nationalists forces in urban areas before they have developed a sizeable organizational base. The recent proposed challenge by the power structure of the validity of Jesse Gray's petition for candidacy for Mayor of New York city shows that the white power structure will stop at nothing to keep black people from obtaining *BLACK POWER*. Such events lead black people to only one solution: the destruction of White America and the establishment of a Black peoples government having its own liberation army. The riot which occurred in Boston, Mass., that whitie tried to keep secret, between the black and white soldiers proves RAM's 'Revolutionary Action Movement' statement on July 4th, 1965 to the black soldiers to throw down their arms, to refuse to fight and to let their battle assignment be against white racist in the U.S.A. is the only alternative left for any sane Africanamerican in charlies! white racist yankee imperialist forces.

The current situation shows us that Africanamericans are at war against the U.S. government and in order for us to achieve liberation, it (the U.S. government) must become a thing of the past. With Congress passing a law making it a penality [sic] of five years in prison or $10,000 fine for burning draft cards the Africanamerican's situation is synonymous with his African brothers in another place called the U.S.A. (Union of South Africa) where they are also jailed for the burning of pass cards. Under these conditions no black man should join charlies army and go to Vietnam to fight his black brothers but should remain within racist America to fight for self-defense and survival. If he lives in the South he should join the Deacons for Defense and if he lives in the North he should join the Black Liberation Army (the developing guerrilla forces). Any thinking Africanamerican should see by now that conditions are developing into a racial war and the only way we can survive as a people is by developing an Africanamerican peoples liberation army. Such an army when its in the mobile guerrilla warfare stage should organize itself into small squads so that it can be extremely mobile and should develop guerrilla units of three to harass the enemy especially at night. When spontaneous action develops the guerrilla forces should use this as decoy against the enemy and should strike at the administrative operations of the enemy; i.e., police stations, city buildings, electric plants, etc. Up until recently the level of guerrilla warfare has been the destruction of property in the ghetto's [sic]. This does not bring severe damage to the enemy. Urban guerrillas should concentrate on the destruction of the enemies material—then the moral and the actual lives of his men [sic]. This would mean as rebellion breaks out within the black ghetto's [sic], guerrilla units would disperse themselves in the enemy's complex, usually downtown, destroying key buildings or, on the outskirts of the city destroying electrical plants and industry. Urban guerrillas main emphasis will be on the intangible thing called organization. The political prospective for the urban guerrilla would be to develop a dual front and dual organization. The dual front would be black people not participating in the war in Vietnam and a black united front of a war of resistance against racial oppression in the U.S. The dual organization would be a public and mass armed organization for the consolidation, expansion and development of black power and successful Black revolution coordinated with the development of an underground guerrilla force. Our message is *resist in the racists both home and abroad.* Fight tit for tat, an eye for an eye, tooth for a tooth, life for a life and use any means necessary to achieve justice and freedom in Johnson's great fascist racist society. *Unite* for a war of self-defense and survival or *Perish.*

Urban Guerrilla Warfare

by ROBERT F. WILLIAMS

We must defend ourselves. We must fight back. We must reject the unwritten committment that so-called Negro leaders have made guaranteeing our brutal oppressors immunity from retribution for their henious [sic] acts of violence against our defenseless people. Not only must we defend ourselves violently, but we must do it collectively. We must condition ourselves for defense, both physically and psychologically. We must become adept in the methods of massive defense.

There are those mercenary Uncle Toms and masochists among us, whose missions are to demoralize our people and encourage them to reject the first law of nature. They are quick to inform us that we cannot win any conflict that may degenerate into a state of massive violence. Why do they not tell the racist oppressors that they cannot win? Why do they not tell them that they constitute a minority in the world? The fact is that the racists are the ones who will lose such a conflict. America is too sensitive to withstand such a shock. The oppressors have more to lose than the dehumanized and oppressed in such a conflict. Our people have nothing to lose but their chains.

We prefer peaceful negotiations, but our oppressors have proved to us that they are not susceptible to such mild pressures for reform and that they will utilize massive violence to attempt to contain our struggle. When massive violence comes, the U.S.A. will become a bedlam of confusion and chaos. The factory workers will be afraid to venture out on the streets to report to their jobs. The telephone workers and radio workers will be afraid to report. All transportation will grind to a complete standstill. Stores will be destroyed and looted. Property will be damaged and expensive buildings will be reduced to ashes. Essential pipelines will be severed and blown up and all manner of sabotage will occur. Violence and terror will spread like a firestorm. A clash will occur inside the armed forces. At U.S. military bases around the world local revolutionaries will side with Afro G.I.'s. Because of the vast area covered by the holocaust, U.S. forces will be spread too thin for effective action. U.S. workers, who are caught on their jobs will try to return home to protect their families. Trucks and trains will not move the necessary supplies to the big urban centers. The economy will fall into a state of chaos.

This rascist imperialist oppressor will not be brought to his knees, simply because of the fighting ability and military power of Black Freedom Fighters and their allies inside the U.S., but because of the creation of economic, chaotic conditions, total disorganization, frustration of his essential and ultra vital organs of production, and adverse conditions created by the world-wide liberation struggle. Such a formidable enemy will fall prey to the new concept of revolution because of his ultra-modern and automated society and the lack of psychological conditioning of his forces. Our people have already been conditioned by almost 400 years of violence, terror and hunger.

The new concept of revolution defies military science and tactics. The new concept is lightning campaigns conducted in highly sensitive urban communities with the paralysis reaching the small communities and spreading to the farm areas. The old method of guerrilla warfare, as carried out from the hills and countryside, would be ineffective in a powerful country like the U.S.A. Any such force would be wiped out in an hour. The new concept is to huddle as close to the enemy as possible so as to neutralize his modern and fierce weapons. The new concept creates conditions that involve the total community, whether they want to be involved or not. It sustains a state of confusion and destruction of property. It dislocates the organs of harmony and order and reduces central power to the level of a helpless, sprawling, octopus. During the hours of day sporadic rioting takes place and massive sniping. Night brings all-out warfare, organized fighting and unlimited terror against the oppressor and his forces. Such a campaign will bring about an end to oppression and social injustice in the U.S.A. in less than 90 days and create the basis for the implementation of the U.S. Constitution with justice and equality for all people.

Of course, there would be great losses on the part of our people. How can we expect liberation without losses? Our people are already being admonished by the nonviolent forces to die for Freedom. We are being told to sacrifice our lives in situations of diminishing returns. If we must die, let us die in the only way that the oppressor will feel the weight of our death. Let us die in the tried and proven way of liberation. If we are going to talk about revolution, let us know what revolution means.

USA: The Potential of a Minority Revolution

by ROBERT F. WILLIAMS

The lesson of Monroe teaches that effective self-defense, on the part of our brutally oppressed and terrorized people, requires *massive organization with central coordination*. External oppressive forces must not be allowed to relieve the beseiged racist terrorists. The forces of the state must be kept under pressure in many places simultaneously. The white supremacy masses must be forced to retreat to their homes in order to give security to their individual families.

The weapons of defense employed by Afroamerican freedom fighters must consist of a poor man's arsenal. Gasoline fire bombs (Molotov cocktails), lye or acid bombs (made by injecting lye or acid in the metal end of light bulbs) can be used extensively. During the night hours such weapons, thrown from roof tops, will make the streets impossible for racist cops to patrol. Hand grenades, bazookas, light mortars, rocket launchers, machine guns and ammunition can be bought clandestinely from servicemen, anxious to make a fast dollar. Freedom fighters in military camps can be contacted to give instruction on usage.

Extensive sabotage is possible. Gas tanks on public vehicles can be choked up with sand. Sugar is also highly effective in gasoline lines. Long nails driven through boards and tacks with large heads are effective to slow the movement of traffic on congested roads at night. This can cause havoc on turnpikes. Derailing of trains causes panic. Explosive booby traps on police telephone boxes can be employed. High powered sniper rifles are readily available. Armor piercing bullets will penetrate oil storage tanks from a distance. Phosphorous matches (kitchen matches) placed in air conditioning systems will cause delayed explosions which will destroy expensive buildings. Flame throwers can be manufactured at home. Combat experienced ex-service men can easily solve that problem.

Techniques mentioned here are generalized and require a closer study, however, let the cynics take note that the mighty USA is not as smug and secure as it once was. Yes, a minority war of self-defense can succeed. The Afroamerican can win. We need not submit, passively to racist extermination and brutality. The race question is America's Achilles heel. America's great abundance is what makes America America, without it she would be a wretched land of chaos. Her economy is already under stress and her military might is spread out too thinly throughout the world.

The bourgeosie [sic] has very little stomach for massive blood and violence. They love their property, the source of their power and wealth. They are highly susceptible to panic. The majority white supremacists do not command the loyalty of the entire race. There are a few John Brown type students and militants.

Afroamericans must remember that such a campaign of massive self-defense should not be based upon a lust for sadistical gratification. It cannot be a campaign for vengeance, however, sweet and deserving vengeneance [sic] may be. Such a campaign of self-defense and survival must be based on the righteous cause of justice. It must not be anti-white but anti-oppression and injustice. Uncle Toms should be as much a target as racist whites.

When a brutally oppressed and dehumanized people are denied the peaceful channels through which to activate redress, and when their peaceful petitions are answered with ruthless violence, the only recourse left to them is to meet violence with violence.

We do not advocate the violent overthrow of the U.S. Government. We merely advocate self-defense for brutalized Afroamericans. If in the process of executing our Constitutional and God-given right of self-defense, the racist U.S. Government, which refuses to protect our people, is destroyed, the end result stems from certain historical factors of social relativity.

The Strategy and Tactics of Black Revolution, Sections 1 and 2

Section 1

Black revolutionists who are serious about revolution should study the oppressors' system very closely and learn how it operates inside and out. "Chuck's" weakness is his complexity and he can't stand simplicity because it is Eastern and because it is against his nature. With black people not having any power in this society the revolutionary nationalists must begin to see their ranks as an opposing nation or government and must see themselves and their ranks as "outlaws" of this society. Therefore, their government (ranks) is an outlaw government or government in exile.

The first thing revolutionary nationalists should be concerned with is the protection of power for their government (ranks). Therefore, their immediate concern would be the development of an army that could protect and liberate their nation. But what is more important is that revolutionary nationalists must know what to do with their armies of National Liberation once developed. In the process of revolution the mass communications system should be the first to go. Why? Because the enemy's populace and supporters relie on the mass communications system to know how to relate to events. By destroying the oppressor's communication system the revolutionary nationalists creates a vacuum in the oppressor's apparatus and isolates him from his machinery. Also, it sets the oppressor to a great disadvantage because he will have to attempt to rebuild his system in the middle of a battlefield. The electrical plants should be the first target, then radio and T.V. stations—after a revolutionary broadcast by seizing it, newspapers next—the destruction of newspaper buildings, including the press, etc. In urban areas transportation lines would be the number two target—sabotage of subway systems, derailing of trolleys or trains, etc. The destruction of airports, especially the tower, dents the beasts transportation system; telephone lines should be cut. In rural areas the roads leading in and out should be set up for ambush and traps for trucks, etc. In urban areas gasoline across highways, road blocks hold up traffic for hours.

With Wall Street, Madison Avenue, and half of the complex in Washington blown to bits the oppressor will have to function under wartime plans. The destruction of property (the concept of private property being the basis of his system) would be the chief concern of the revolutionary national liberation fighters. The demolition of industry would come after communication and transportation. The destruction of steel plants, auto plants, (the Detroit complex), chemical plants, oil fields and plants would divide the energies of the oppressor. The complex outside of cities like New York, Detroit, Chicago, Buffalo N.Y., Lansing, Michigan, Philadelphia, Cleveland, etc. are convenient for revolutionary nationalists. The destruction of such complexes could be achieved by stationary mortars or mortars from an automobile. The mayor's areas should also be completely demolished. This keeps the lower elite section of the capitalist ruling class isolated in the suburbs for days without communication with the outside world. Bombs on trains would stop the commuters system entirely; occasionally terror raids in the "super elite" sections killing important executives would create chaos in the oppressors isolated communities. The next phase would be taking power in the black communities, holding, maintaining and sustaining it. If psychological warfare is used with physical, then the oppressor's forces and supporters will be put at considerable disadvantage. We can see through phase one—destruction of communications system, destruction of transportation system, destruction of important property of the oppressor's (Wall St., Madison Ave., etc.) industrial complexes, steel, auto, iron, chemical, oil, gas industry, etc.—how the revolutionary nationalists, using the proper strategy and tactics can put the oppressor on the defensive. In section two we will discuss how they can keep the oppressor on the defensive.

Section 2

In section I we discussed the stage of mobile lightening guerrilla warfare of strike at night and run and hide during the day. Though section I described primarily the Northern front, this stage would take place simultaneously in the South. Birmingham Alabama is the main industrial complex in the South and would be the number 1 target for lightning guerrilla warfare in the South. Being that the social, economic and political structure is divided into two different categories, our partisan war of national liberation must have a dual front. The South is a rural area, but because of communication, terrain (basically flat) and transportation (highways) it takes on a semi-urban character. The North is highly industrialized being urban, almost super urban, on the East coast. The dual front of our forces would be a semi-urban campaign in the South and an urban campaign in the north. The struggle in the North would take a more terroristic and sabotage form because there is less area of mobility and potential supporters are outnumbered, even though they constitute a large section of the major cities. So emphasis in the North would be to wreck the oppressors political and economic apparatus—government buildings, assassination of government officials, state and city, police machinery, army, etc., business executives and business buildings. Strategic raids in certain suburbs at night, blowing up executive homes would be total social dislocation of major cities and will be the type of activity of the northern campaign. While in the South there will be semi-urban guerrilla warfare with more emphasis on occupying (liberating) certain areas establishing peoples governments and waging campaigns against the enemy. This type of warfare would take place within the Black Belt area—Louisiana, Mississippi, Georgia and South Carolina. In this area black people constitute near the majority and live in an area that extends from the Atlantic Coast to the Gulf of Mexico. Partisan warfare and the establishment of peoples liberation bases could cut the oppressors forces in half. Blacks constitute at least 45% of the population of Louisiana, 59% in Mississippi, 45% in Alabama, 40% in Georgia and 55% in South Carolina. The revolution would probably spread from the Northern cities to Southern cities then to Southern rural areas, then the initiative would fall on the rural area defeating the enemy in small campaigns while liberating the community. The Southern front would shift quickly from guerrilla to mobile warfare. At this time the oppressor would be forced to call in the National Guard and the Army battle forces would be divided because of internal descention due to the race issue. The National Guard and Army would be called in to crush mobile warfare in rural areas because it would be the most advanced form of guerrilla warfare. At this time guerrilla units in urban areas could engage the enemy in "mass ambush" while the enemy is preparing to mobilize against the Southern front. The elite of the mobile guerrilla Southern forces could wage an encirclement offensive on one of the major Southern work centers. At the same time the Northern guerrilla could wage a suburban offensive throwing the Northern military apparatus far into White America then the Southern mobile guerrilla could close the encirclement extending the war in a protracted manner splitting the enemies forces in two. The occupying of cities' black communities would be basically in the South where there are a great number of black people both within and out of the city. The play of movement would develop sabotage within a southern city with mass riot, assassination of racist leaders, then transforming the semi-rural areas (farm areas), taking over plantations, etc. Then the knocking out and taking over of roads leading into the city would be the next form of developing support on the outside with political cadres building support on the inside and returning to the city after engaging through small campaigns.

He will be forced to reinforce his weakening forces in the rural areas while waging a political struggle within. Therefore his force will be divided both inside and outside the city with the enemies forces suffering defeat their force will decrease, there will be mutiny among black soldiers who will come to join the black liberation front and also white soldiers will desert to protect their homes. Such a campaign will lead to total chaos and dislocation within the enemies forces that he will be unable to sustain his efforts against a protracted guerrilla war whether its 90 days, 9 years or a year.

Through this outline and perspective of a partisan war of survival we can see that the Afroamerican can and will win a protracted war of national liberation.

C. Intellectuals and the "Establishment"

Alienation has been an ever-present problem for American intellectuals. Living in a nation preoccupied from the first in conquering and exploiting the physical environment, where contemplation was considered a luxury, intellectuals have had to work out an uneasy truce with the utilitarian majority. Granted unprecedented freedom of expression by democratic society, intellectuals still had to fulfill their role as constructive critics of that society. Without an indigenous base, American intellectuals looked to Europe, and there found conclusions about the New World which were to remain the chief focal points for their own criticisms of their developing culture. To the European eye, the most novel (and therefore frightening) characteristics of the American experiment were the emphases on equalitarianism and material progress. Equating the continental view with sophistication, sensitive American writers and thinkers worried endlessly about the alleged exaltation of mediocrity and materialism in the United States. Throughout most of the nineteenth century, those fears were tempered by a deep sympathy for the democratic spirit, and provided a vision of humane values which helped soften the rough edges of popular thought and sanctioned political reform movements in the 1870's and at the turn of the century. Although seldom leading the public charge, intellectuals were instrumental in constructing the ideological supports for efforts at improving the economic and political status of the common man. Their insistence on a better society urged forward public education, the abolition of slavery, fair treatment for laborers, and periodic assaults on urban and industrial problems. Still, denied a prominent place in society and both distrusted and affronted by business leaders, the intellectuals drew close together, nursing their suspicion of equalitarianism and hatred for the entrepreneurs. Ironically, this growing isolation from the mainstream was hastened by the material plenty which not only threatened cultural excellence, but financed great universities and foundations and thus provided artists, writers, and scholars with a growing sense of importance. At the dawning of the twentieth century, the intellectuals had become an almost self-contained, estranged class.[1]

Having been driven, both in self-defense and in obedience to their role as social gadflies, into self-conscious solidarity, their traditional fears sometimes spilled over in bitter arraignments of the nation's customs, mores, and political practices. Intellectuals confronted an almost tragic dilemma: they tried "to be good and believing citizens of a democratic society and at the same time to resist the vulgarization of culture" they assumed democracy produced.[2] The new century offered no route of escape. Highly specialized clusters of expert social scientists uncovered data which tried their already strained loyalties to democratic assumptions, and

230

writers and political theorists agonized over the apparent inability of even democratic states to avoid war and imperial adventure. Many still found it possible to produce temperate, factual criticisms which were, in themselves, fresh affirmations of a social system rooted in at least the promise of human dignity. "The American system," wrote Herbert Croly in *The Promise of American Life,* "stands for the . . . hope that men can be improved without being fettered, that they can be saved without even vicariously being nailed to the cross."[3] Through two world wars, the Babylonian twenties, the anxious years of depression, and the brutal anti-intellectual climate of the 1950's, a majority of American intellectuals displayed a resilience (seldom cheerful) matched by few other elements in the population.

The more deeply alienated, on the other hand, displayed a furious desperation.[4] Borrowing here and there from Marx, Watson, Freud, and Einstein, they concluded that the common man was a presumptuous skinned ape in a world ruled by intractable forces. Since the social values they championed were not distinguishable throughout American society, they could argue that those whose values were in evidence held all the power, despite the appearance of political freedom.[5] They cheered Mencken's ridicule of middle-class democracy and reached for theories which seemed to support their long-standing conviction that the citizenry were pawns of a business elite. In their *Middletown* studies, Robert and Helen Lynd provided such a theory. They assumed, like most radicals, that politics was only a manipulative process. One could ignore political processes, then, to focus on the question, "Who *really* rules?"[6] The Lynds' answer was an "iron-clad, neatly formulated theory whose own self-confirming logic has the facility of proving almost anything it wants to."[7] According to the Lynds, a monolithic business elite ruled behind the scenes, rendering democracy a farce.[8]

The theory was redrawn and raised to greater prominence by C. Wright Mills, in *The Power Elite.* Written at the end of the 1950's, when many intellectuals still vividly recalled the academic and political purges unleashed by McCarthyism, *The Power Elite* proclaimed the existence of a "real" government comprised of command posts occupied by industrial and military leaders. Since, according to Mills's hypothesis, these men held the actual centers of power and influence, the democratic process was a cruel hoax, an enterprise useful only to perpetuate the *status quo.*[9] As one critic has noted, "the Populist imagery of power as closed conspiracy find[s] disturbing echo in Mills' book."[10] In fact, Mills's work, although clothed in sociological jargon, is a sarcastic moral indictment of American society, remarkable for its "empirical one-sidedness and distortion."[11] Mills *describes* a power elite, but does not bother to *demonstrate* its existence; assuming that power is all-important and secretly used, he proceeds to assume the existence of a cohesive bloc of manipulators.[12] The complexity and diversity of American politics are wholly ignored. For example, in assuming the monolithic nature of "real" authority, Mills fails to account for the difference between corporate management and corporate ownership, the long history of antipathy between big business and small business, the controls a supposedly servile political structure has imposed on business, the traditional hostility of business to government, or the vast number of significant and petty rivalries dividing the various branches of the American armed services.[13] Worst of all, Mills's simplistic assumptions about the nature and use of political processes act as a deterrent to involvement of intellectuals in those processes. The adherents of such a conspiracy theory, rather than view the future as "possibility, depending upon the decisions that are made and upon . . . collective intelligence," bow before a fatalism which "reinforces a sense of helplessness and belies the resources of a free society: the variety of interest conflicts, the growth of public responsibility, the weight of traditional freedoms . . . ."[14]

But alienated intellectuals have the same needs as others isolated from society. Long-term alienation can be rationalized as a requirement of the professional intellectual, much as the followers of political fundamentalism cast themselves in the role of a saving remnant and Black Nationalists counter white bigotry with a doctrine of black separatism. In such a context, rapprochement with society is not success but failure; to overcome alienation is to lose one's intellectual virginity.[15] As Richard Hofstadter has perceived, "many of the most spirited younger intellectuals are disturbed above all by the fear that, as they are increasingly recognized, incorporated, and used, they will begin merely to conform. . . ."[16] For them, an "establishment" theory has many-sided appeal. It is simple, compelling, dramatic, and "realistic."[17] "For individuals with a strong strain of frustrated idealism, it has just the right touch of hard-boiled cynicism."[18] It permits the radical to write off politics as futile and avoid the problems involved in democratic participation—the need and responsibility for devising tactics and ideals acceptable to at least a bare majority.[19] It releases angry young writers like Staughton Lynd from efforts to cope with all the trivia involved in pluralist democratic compromise, so that they may pursue that single Truth which they alone know.[20]

Lynd insists that action within the existing political structure is futile, that it places the intellectual in league with militarism and amounts to silent approval of past and present injustices. One could also argue that participation in any institutions in this tainted society—a university, for example—is coalitionism. To rule out coalition politics because it requires compromise is to invite continuation of the cycle of alienation: "defeat, political isolation, and powerlessness reinforce a sense of political alienation and lack of realism in the movement, while alienation and lack of realism in turn increase the likelihood that the movement . . . will remain politically isolated and powerless."[21]

A conspiracy theory which,. like communism and fascism, insists that democracy and capitalism are "so intertwined that the vices of one could be used as an indictment of the other"; the characterization of coalitionism as a dirty business; the demand for extralegal action—all smack of that "old and futile desire to close off the future with all its unexpected dangers and contingencies by enclosing it, by fixing it, in One Ideology."[22] It is a tragic irony that intellectuals such as Lynd, sincerely dedicated to the achievement of a just and peaceful world, are driven in desperation to demand a conformity of their choosing because they distrust or despair of the public will. "Full withdrawal and retreat are no longer possible," Eugene McCarthy has written. "Intellectual spolesmen and moral leaders are called upon today to prove the relevance of their ideas to life."[23] Perhaps now, as never before, the talented and committed must reject the temptations of elitism—the vision of a handful of the pure leading the masses into some final promised land. As Robert Dahl has phrased it, "among a people guided, even in their conflicts, by a talent for conciliation and a commitment to the principles and institutions of a democratic republic, both freedom and diversity might flourish."[24]

NOTES

1. Richard Hofstadter, *Anti-Intellectualism in American Life* (New York: Alfred A. Knopf, 1963), p. 408.

2. *Ibid.*, p. 407.

3. Herbert Croly, *The Promise of American Life* (New York: Macmillan Company, 1911), p. 12.

4. Hofstadter, *Anti-Intellectualism*, p. 419.

5. John H. Bunzel, *Anti-Politics in America* (New York: Alfred A. Knopf, 1967), pp. 110-111.

6. *Ibid.*, pp. 96, 112.

7. *Ibid.*, p. 99.

8. Robert Lynd, "Who Calls the Tune?" *Journal of Higher Education,* XIX (April, 1948), pp. 169-170; also, Lynd, *Knowledge for What? The Place of Social Science in American Culture* (Princeton: Princeton University Press, 1940), pp. 228-229; John H. Bunzel, "The Commitment to Power of Robert S. Lynd," *Ethics,* LXXI (January, 1961), p. 93.

9. Bunzel, *Anti-Politics,* pp. 95-96, 104; Jack L. Walker, "A Critique of the Elitist Theory of Democracy," *American Political Science Review,* LX (June, 1966), pp. 285-305.

10. Daniel Bell, "The Power Elite—Reconsidered," *American Journal of Sociology,* LXIV (November, 1958), p. 250.

11. Talcott Parsons, "The Distribution of Power in American Society," *World Politics,* X (October, 1957), p. 128; Bell, "The Power Elite—Reconsidered," p. 239.

12. Bunzel, *Anti-Politics,* p. 105; Robert A. Dahl, "A Critique of the Ruling Elite Model," *American Political Science Review,* 52 (June, 1958), p. 465.

13. Bunzel, *Anti-Politics,* p. 96; Parsons, "Distribution of Power," pp. 130, 134; Bell "The Power Elite–Reconsidered," p. 241.

14. Lynn White, Jr., "On Intellectual Gloom," *American Scholar,* 35 (Spring, 1966), pp. 223-226; Max Lerner, *et al., The Revolutionary Theme in Contemporary America* (Lexington: University of Kentucky Press, 1965), p. 6; Bell, "The Power Elite– Reconsidered," p. 250.

15. Hofstadter, *Anti-Intellectualism,* pp. 416-417.

16. *Ibid.,* p. 393.

17. Dahl, "Critique of the Ruling Elite Model," p. 463.

18. *Ibid.*

19. Bunzel, *Anti–Politics,* pp. 128-129.

20. *Ibid.,* pp. 107-110.

21. Robert A. Dahl, *Pluralist Democracy in the United States: Conflict and Consent* (Chicago: Rand McNally & Company, 1967), p. 452.

22. Alan P. Grimes, *American Political Thought* (New York: Henry Holt & Company, 1955), p. 434; William J. Newman, *The Futilitarian Society* (New York: George Braziller, 1961), p. 393.

23. Eugene J. McCarthy, "The Intellectual's Place in American Government," *Texas Quarterly,* 8 (Winter, 1965), p. 123; also, Hofstadter, *Anti-Intellectualism,* p. 420.

24. Dahl, *Pluralist Democracy,* p. 456.

The Power Elite
C. WRIGHT MILLS

Official commentators like to contrast the ascendancy in totalitarian countries of a tightly organized clique with the American system of power. Such comments, however, are easier to sustain if one compares mid-twentieth-century Russia with mid-nineteenth-century America, which is what is often done by Tocqueville-quoting Americans making the contrast. But that was an America of a century ago, and in the century that has passed, the American elite have not remained as patrioteer essayists have described them to us. The "loose cliques" now head institutions of a scale and power not then existing and, especially since World War I, the loose cliques have tightened up. We are well beyond the era of romantic pluralism.

The supremacy of corporate economic power began, in a formal way, with the Congressional elections of 1866, and was consolidated by the Supreme Court decision of 1886 which declared that the Fourteenth Amendment protected the corporation. That period witnessed the transfer of the center of initiative from government to corporation. Until the First World War (which gave us an advanced showing of certain features of our own period) this was an age of raids on the government by the economic elite, an age of simple corruption, when Senators and judges were simply bought up. Here, once upon a time, in the era of McKinley and Morgan, far removed from the undocumented complexities of our own time, many now believe, was the golden era of the American ruling class.

The military order of this period, as in the second, was subordinate to the political, which in turn was subordinate to the economic. The military was thus off to the side of the main driving forces of United States history. Political institutions in the United States have never formed a centralized and autonomous domain of power; they have been enlarged and centralized only reluctantly in slow response to the public consequence of the corporate economy.

In the post-Civil-War era, that economy was the dynamic; the "trusts"—as policies and events make amply clear—could readily use the relatively weak governmental apparatus for their own ends. That both state and federal governments were decisively limited in their power to regulate, in fact meant that they were themselves regulatable by the larger moneyed interests. Their powers were scattered and unorganized; the powers of the industrial and financial corporations concentrated and interlocked. The Morgan interests alone held 341 directorships in 112 corporations with an aggregate capitalization of over $22 billion—over three times the assessed value of all real and personal property in New England. With revenues greater and employees more numerous than those of many states, corporations controlled parties, bought laws, and kept Congressmen of the "neutral" state. And as private economic power overshadowed public political power, so the economic elite overshadowed the political.

Yet even between 1896 and 1919 events of importance tended to assume a political form, foreshadowing the shape of power which after the partial boom of the 'twenties was to prevail in the New Deal. Perhaps there has never been any period in American history so politically transparent as the Progressive era of President-makers and Muckrakers.

The New Deal did *not* reverse the political and economic relations of the third era, but it did create within the political arena, as well as in the corporate world itself, competing centers of power that challenged those of the corporate directors. As the New Deal directorate gained political power, the economic elite, which in the third period had fought against the growth of "government" while raiding it for crafty privileges, belatedly attempted to join it on the higher levels. When they did so they found themselves confronting other interests and men, for the places of decision were crowded. In due course, they did come to control and to use for their own purposes the New Deal institutions whose creation they had so bitterly denounced.

But during the 'thirties, the political order was still an instrument of small propertied farmers and businessmen, although they were weakened, having lost their last chance for real ascendancy in the Progressive era. The struggle between big and small property flared up again, however, in the political realm of the New Deal era, and to this struggle there was added, as we have seen, the new struggle of organized labor and the unorganized unemployed. This new force flourished under political tutelage, but nevertheless, for the first time in United States history, social legislation and lower-class issues became important features of the reform movement.

In the decade of the 'thirties, a set of shifting balances involving newly instituted farm measures and newly organized labor unions—along with big business—made up the political and administrative drama of power. These farm, labor, and business groups, moreover, were more or less contained within the framework of an enlarging governmental structure, whose political directorship made decisions in a definitely political manner. These groups pressured, and in pressuring against one another and against the governmental and party system, they helped to shape it. But it could not be said that any of them for any considerable length of time used that government unilaterally as their instrument. That is why the 'thirties was a *political* decade: the power of business was not replaced, but it was contested and supplemented: it became one major power within a structure of power that was chiefly run by political men, and not by economic or military men turned political.

The earlier and middle Roosevelt administrations can best be understood as a desperate search for ways and means, within the existing capitalist system, of reducing the staggering and ominous army of the unemployed. In these years, the New Deal as a system of power was essentially a balance of pressure groups and interest blocs. The political top adjusted many conflicts, gave way to this demand, sidetracked that one, was the unilateral servant of none, and so evened it all out into such going policy line as prevailed from one minor crisis to another. Policies were the result of a political act of balance at the top. Of course, the balancing act that Roosevelt performed did not affect the fundamental institutions of capitalism as a type of economy. By his policies, he subsidized the defaults of the capitalist economy, which had simply broken down; and by his rhetoric, he balanced its political disgrace, putting "economic royalists" in the political doghouse.

The "welfare state," created to sustain the balance and to carry out the subsidy, differed from the "laissez-faire" state: "If the state was believed neutral in the days of T.R. because its leaders claimed to sanction favors for no one," Richard Hofstadter has remarked, "the state under F.D.R. could be called neutral only in the sense that it offered favors to everyone." The new state of the corporate commissars differs from the old welfare state. In fact, the later Roosevelt years—beginning with the entrance of the United States into overt acts of war and preparations for World War II—cannot be understood entirely in terms of an adroit equipoise of political power.

We study history, it has been said, to rid ourselves of it, and the history of the power elite is a clear case for which this maxim is correct. Like the tempo of American life in general, the long-term trends of the power structure have been greatly speeded up since World War II, and certain newer trends within and between the dominant institutions have also set the shape of the power elite and given historically specific meaning to its fifth epoch:

I. In so far as the structural clue to the power elite today lies in the political order, that clue is the decline of politics as genuine and public debate of alternative decisions—with nationally responsible and policy-coherent parties and with autonomous organizations connecting the lower and middle levels of power with the top levels of decision. America is now in considerable part more a formal political democracy than a democratic social structure, and even the formal political mechanics are weak.

The long-time tendency of business and government to become more intricately and deeply involved with each other has, in the fifth epoch, reached a new point of explicitness. The two cannot now be seen clearly as two distinct worlds. It is in terms of the executive agencies of the state that the rapprochement has proceeded most decisively. The growth of the executive branch of the government, with its agencies that patrol the complex economy, does not mean merely the "enlargement of government" as some sort of autonomous bureaucracy: it has meant the ascendancy of the corporation's man as a political eminence.

During the New Deal the corporate chieftains joined the political directorate; as of World War II they have come to dominate it. Long interlocked with government, now they have moved into quite full direction of the economy of the war effort and of the postwar era. This shift of the corporation executives into the political directorate has accelerated the long-term relegation of the professional politicians in the Congress to the middle levels of power.

II. In so far as the structural clue to the power elite today lies in the enlarged and military state, that clue becomes evident in the military ascendancy. The warlords have gained decisive political relevance, and the military structure of America is now in considerable part a political structure. The seemingly permanent military threat places a premium on the military and upon their control of men, materiel, money, and power; virtually all political and economic actions are now judged in terms of military definitions of reality: the higher warlords have ascended to a firm position within the power elite of the fifth epoch.

In part at least this has resulted from one simple historical fact, pivotal for the years since 1939: the focus of elite attention has been shifted from domestic problems, centered in the 'thirties around slump, to international problems, centered in the 'forties and 'fifties around war. Since the governing apparatus of the United States has by long historic usage been adapted to and shaped by domestic clash and balance, it has not, from any angle, had suitable agencies and traditions for the handling of international problems. Such formal democratic mechanics as had arisen in the century and a half of national development prior to 1941, had not been extended to the American handling of international affairs. It is, in considerable part, in this vacuum that the power elite has grown.

III. In so far as the structural clue to the power elite today lies in the economic order, that clue is the fact that the economy is at once a permanent-war economy and a private-corporation economy. American capitalism is now in considerable part a military capitalism, and the most important relation of the big corporation to the state rests on the coincidence of interests between military and corporate needs, as defined by warlords and corporate rich. Within the elite as a whole, this coincidence of interest between the high military and the corporate chieftains strengthens both of them and further subordinates the role of the merely political men. Not politicians, but corporate executives, sit with the military and plan the organization of war effort.

The shape and meaning of the power elite today can be understood only when these three sets of structural trends are seen at their point of coincidence: the military capitalism of private corporations exists in a weakened and formal democratic system containing a military order already quite political in outlook and demeanor. Accordingly, at the top of this structure, the power elite has been shaped by the coincidence of interest between those who control the major means of production and those who control the newly enlarged means of violence; from the decline of the professional politician and the rise to explicit political command of the corporate chieftains and the professional warlords; from the absence of any genuine civil service of skill and integrity, independent of vested interests.

The power elite is composed of political, economic, and military men, but this instituted elite is frequently in some tension: it comes together only on certain coinciding points and only on certain occasions of "crisis." In the long peace of the nineteenth century, the military were not in the high councils of state, not of the political directorate, and neither were the economic men—they made raids upon the state but they did not join its directorate. During the 'thirties, the political man was ascendant. Now the military and the corporate men are in top positions.

Of the three types of circle that compose the power elite today, it is the military that has benefited the most in its enhanced power, although the corporate circles have also become more explicitly intrenched in the more public decision-making circles. It is the professional politician that has lost the most, so much that in examining the events and decisions, one is tempted to speak of a political vacuum in which the corporate rich and the high warlord, in their coinciding interests, rule.

It should not be said that the three "take turns" in carrying the initiative, for the mechanics of the power elite are not often as deliberate as that would imply. At times, of course, it is—as when political men, thinking they can borrow the prestige of generals, find that they must pay for it, or, as when during big slumps, economic men feel the need of a politician at once safe and possessing vote appeal. Today all three are involved in virtually all widely ramifying decisions. Which of the three types seems to lead depends upon "the tasks of the period" as they, the elite, define them. Just now, these tasks center upon "defense" and international affairs. Accordingly, as we have seen, the military are ascendant in two senses: as personnel and as justifying ideology. That is why, just now, we can most easily specify the unity and the shape of the power elite in terms of the military ascendancy.

But we always be historically specific and open to complexities. The simple Marxian view makes the big economic man the *real* holder of power; the simple liberal view makes the big political man the chief of the power system; and there are some who would view the warlords as virtual dictators. Each of these is an oversimplified view. It is to avoid them that we use the term "power elite" rather than, for example, "ruling class."

In so far as the power elite has come to wide public attention, it has done so in terms of the "military clique." The power elite does, in fact, take its current shape from the decisive entrance into it of the military. Their presence and their ideology are its major legitimations, whenever the power elite feels the need to provide any. But what is called the 'Washington military clique' is not composed merely of military men, and it does not prevail merely in Washington. Its members exist all over the country, and it is a coalition of generals in the roles of corporation executives, of politicians masquerading as admirals, of corporation executives acting like politicians, of civil servants who become majors, of vice-admirals who are also the assistants to a cabinet officer, who is himself, by the way, really a member of the managerial elite.

Neither the idea of a "ruling class" nor of a simple monolithic rise of "bureaucratic politicians" nor of a "military clique" is adequate. The power elite today involves the often uneasy coincidence of economic, military, and political power.

Even if our understanding were limited to these structural trends, we should have grounds for believing the power elite a useful, indeed indispensable, concept for the interpretation of what is going on at the topside of modern American society. But we are not, of course, so limited: our conception of the power elite does not need to rest only upon the correspondence of the institutional hierarchies involved, or upon the many points at which their shifting interests coincide. The power elite, as we conceive it, also rests upon the similarity of its personnel, and their personal and official relations with one another, upon their social and psychological affinities. In order to grasp the personal and social basis of the power elite's unity, we have first to remind ourselves of the facts of origin, career, and style of life of each of the types of circle whose members compose the power elite.

The power elite is *not* an aristocracy, which is to say that it is not a political ruling group based upon a nobility of hereditary origin. It has no compact basis in a small circle of great families whose members can and do consistently occupy the top positions in the several higher circles which overlap as the power elite. But such nobility is only one possible basis of common origin. That it does not exist for the American elite does not mean that members of this elite derive socially from the full range of strata composing American society. They derive in substantial proportions from the upper classes, both new and old, of local society and the metropolitan 400. The bulk of the very rich, the corporate executives, the political outsiders, the high military, derive from, at most, the upper third of the income and occupational pyramids. Their fathers were at least of the professional and business strata, and very frequently higher than that. They are native-born Americans of native parents, primarily from urban areas, and, with the exceptions of the politicians among them, overwhelmingly from the East. They are mainly Protestants, especially Episcopalian or Presbyterian. In general, the higher the position, the greater the proportion of men within it who have derived from and who maintain connections with the upper classes. The generally similar origins of the members of the power elite are underlined and carried further by the fact of their increasingly common educational routine. Overwhelmingly college graduates, substantial proportions have attended Ivy League colleges, although the education of the higher military, of course, differs from that of other members of the power elite.

But what do these apparently simple facts about the social composition of the higher circles really mean? In particular, what do they mean for any attempt to understand the degree of unity, and the direction of policy and interest that may prevail among these several circles? Perhaps it is best to put this question in a deceptively simple way: in terms of origin and career, who or what do these men at the top represent?

Of course, if they are elected politicians, they are supposed to represent those who elected them; and, if they are appointed, they are supposed to represent, indirectly, those who elected their appointers. But this is recognized as something of an abstraction, as a rhetorical formula by which all men of power in almost all systems of government nowadays justify their power of decision. At times it may be true, both in the sense of their motives and in the sense of who benefits from their decisions. Yet it would not be wise in any power system merely to assume it.

The fact that members of the power elite come from near the top of the nation's class and status levels does not mean that they are necessarily "representative" of the top levels only. And if they were, as social types, representative of a cross-section of the population that would not mean that a balanced democracy of interest and power would automatically be the going political fact.

We cannot infer the direction of policy merely from the social origins and careers of the policy-makers. The social and economic backgrounds of the men of power do not tell us all that we need to know in order to understand the distribution of social power. For: (1) Men from high places may be ideological representatives of the poor and humble. Men of humble origin, brightly self-made, may energetically serve the most vested and inherited interests. Moreover (3), not all men who effectively represent the interests of a stratum need in any way belong to it or personally benefit by policies that further its interests. Among the politicians, in short, there are sympathetic *agents* of given groups, conscious and unconscious, paid and unpaid. Finally (4), among the top decision-makers we find men who have been chosen for their positions because of their "expert knowledge." These are some of the obvious reasons why the social origins and careers of the power elite do not enable us to infer the class interests and policy directions of a modern system of power.

Do the high social origin and careers of the top men mean nothing, then, about the distribution of power? By no means. They simply remind us that we must be careful of any simple and direct inference from origin and career to political character and policy, not that we must ignore them in our attempt at political understanding. They simply mean that we must analyze the political psychology and the actual decisions of the political directorate as well as its social composition. And they mean, above all, that we should control, as we have done here, any inference we make from the origin and careers of the political actors by close understanding of the institutional landscape in which they act out their drama. Otherwise, we should be guilty of a rather simple-minded biographical theory of society and history.

Just as we cannot rest the notion of the power elite solely upon the institutional mechanics that lead to its formation, so we cannot rest the notion solely upon the facts of the origin and career of its personnel. We need both, and we have both—as well as other bases, among them that of the status intermingling.

But it is not only the similarities of social origin, religious affiliation, nativity, and education that are important to the psychological and social affinities of the members of the power elite. Even if their recruitment and formal training were more heterogeneous than they are, these men would still be of quite homogeneous social type. For the most important set of facts about a circle of men is the criteria of admission, of praise, of honor, of promotion that prevails among them; if these are similar within a circle, then they will tend as personalities to become similar. The circles that compose the power elite do tend to have such codes and criteria in common. The co-optation of the social types to which these common values lead is often more important than any statistics of common origin and career that we might have at hand.

There is a kind of reciprocal attraction among the fraternity of the successful—not between each and every member of the circles of the high and mighty, but between enough of them to insure a certain unity. On the slight side, it is a sort of tacit, mutual admiration; in the strongest tie-ins, it proceeds by intermarriage. And there are all grades and types of connection between these extremes. Some overlaps certainly occur by means of cliques and clubs, churches and schools.

If social origin and formal education in common tend to make the members of the power elite more readily understood and trusted by one another, their continued association further cements what they feel they have in common. Members of the several higher circles know one another as personal friends and even as neighbors; they mingle with one another on the golf course, in the gentlemen's clubs, at resorts, on transcontinental airplanes, and on ocean liners. They meet at the estates of mutual friends, face each other in front of the TV camera, or serve on the same philanthropic committee; and many are sure to cross one another's path in the columns of newspapers, if not in the exact cafes from which many of these columns originate. As we have seen, of 'The New 400' of cafe society, one chronicler has named forty-one members of the very rich, ninety-three political leaders, and seventy-nine chief executives of corporations . . . .

The sphere of status has reflected the epochs of the power elite. In the third epoch, for example, who could compete with big money? And in the fourth, with big politicians, or even the bright young men of the New Deal?

And in the fifth, who can compete with the generals and the admirals and the corporate officials now so sympathetically portrayed on the stage, in the novel, and on the screen? Can one imagine *Executive Suite* as a successful motion picture in 1935? Or *The Caine Mutiny?*

The multiplicity of high-prestige organizations to which the elite usually belong is revealed by even casual examination of the obituaries of the big businessman, the high-prestige lawyer, the top general and admiral, the key senator: usually, high-prestige church, business associations, plus high-prestige clubs, and often plus military rank. In the course of their lifetimes, the university president, the New York Stock Exchange chairman, the head of the bank, the old West Pointer—mingle in the status sphere, within which they easily renew old friendships and draw upon them in an effort to understand through the experience of trusted others those contexts of power and decision in which they have not personally moved.

In these diverse contexts, prestige accumulates in each of the higher circles, and the members of each borrow status from one another. Their self-images are fed by these accumulations and these borrowings, and accordingly, however segmental a given man's role may seem, he comes to feel himself a "diffuse" or "generalized" man of the higher circles, a "broad-gauge" man. Perhaps such inside experience is one feature of what is meant by "judgment."

The key organizations, perhaps, are the major corporations themselves, for on the boards of directors we find a heavy overlapping among the members of these several elites. On the lighter side, again in the summer and winter resorts, we find that, in an intricate series of overlapping circles; in the course of time, each meets each or knows somebody who knows somebody who knows that one.

The higher members of the military, economic, and political orders are able readily to take over one another's point of view, always in a sympathetic way, and often in a knowledgeable way as well. They define one another as among those who count, and who, accordingly, must be taken into account. Each of them as a member of the power elite comes to incorporate into his own integrity, his own honor, his own conscience, the viewpoint, the expectations, the values of the others. If there are no common ideals and standards among them that are based upon an explicitly aristocratic culture, that does not mean that they do not feel responsibility to one another.

All the structural coincidence of their interests as well as the intricate, psychological facts of their origins and their education, their careers and their associations make possible the psychological affinities that prevail among them, affinities that make it possible for them to say of one another: He is, of course, one of us. And all this points to the basic, psychological meaning of class consciousness. Nowhere in America is there as great a "class consciousness" as among the elite; nowhere is it organized as effectively as among the power elite. For by class consciousness, as a psychological fact, one means that the individual member of a 'class' accepts only those accepted by his circle as among those who are significant to his own image of self.

Within the higher circles of the power elite, factions do exist; there are conflicts of policy; individual ambitions do clash. There are still enough divisions of importance within the Republican party, and even between Republicans and Democrats, to make for different methods of operation. But more powerful than these divisions are the internal discipline and the community of interests that bind the power elite together, even across the boundaries of nations at war.

25

Coalition Politics or Nonviolent Revolution?

STAUGHTON LYND

Bayard Rustin's "From Protest to Politics: The Future of the Civil Rights Movement," an article which appeared in *Commentary* magazine for February 1965, has been widely criticized in radical publications. . . .

The gist of the radical critique of Rustin might be summarized as follows:

1. Rustin writes that "the objective fact is that Eastland and Goldwater are the main enemies." In so doing he exaggerates the liberalism of the Johnson coalition, even asserting that Big Business, forced into the Democratic Party by Goldwater, "does not belong there."

2. Not only does Rustin urge that direct action be abandoned for politics, he argues also that independent political action is only rarely appropriate.

The accurate perception that Negroes need white allies leads him to the conclusion that one must choose between existing aggregations of political forces: "The issue is which coalition to join and how to make it responsive to your program."

3. Thus, by exaggerating the Johnson coalition's capacity to solve fundamental social problems and by underestimating the need for independent action by Negroes, Rustin arrives at a stance which ... "leads to a dissolution of the old Rights movement, as well as assuring that any new Movement will not develop in a more radical fashion." The effect of his advice would be to assimilate Negro protest to the Establishment just as labor protest was coopted at the end of the 1930's, in each case leaving the poorest, least organized parts of the population out in the cold.

Fully to appraise Rustin's *Commentary* article, one must see it as the second in a series of three Rustin actions during the past year. First was his attempt to get the credentials committee offer of token seating accepted by the Mississippi Freedom Democratic Party delegates at Atlantic City (August 1964). Second was the article (February 1965). Third was the effort to undermine and stop the March on Washington against the war in Vietnam (March-April 1965). In this perspective, the most basic criticisms of his article should be these: 1. The coalition he advocates turns out to mean implicit acceptance of Administration foreign policy, to be coalition with the Marines; 2. The style of politics he advocates turns out to mean a kind of elitism which Bayard has been fighting all his life, in which rank-and-file persons would cease to act on their own behalf and be (in the words of "From Protest to Politics") "merely represented."

In opposing the March on Washington against the war in Vietnam Bayard Rustin has permitted himself to drift into that posture which once evoked epithets such as "labor lieutenant of capitalism." Exaggerated as such labels may have been, they designated something real. There were in Europe and there are now in America pacifists and socialists who always support their own government in its international confrontations when push comes to shove. Such Americans insist on condemning Washington and Moscow "equally," but end up supporting the U. S. government which "after all" and "on the whole" stands on the side of "freedom." They specialize in advising revolutionary movements overseas to be nonviolent, forgetting that American arms and aggression play a major role (as in Vietnam) in driving peaceful protest toward insurrection. They cultivate the concept that the President is a man of peace misled by his advisors, who if only one could reach him, would surely turn on the military-industrial complex and overcome. Theirs is the stance of telling Washington what *they* would do were *they* in power. If there is to be protest, so they say, let it be decorous protest which (as Norman Thomas said in his April 22nd letter to the *Times*) "goes off well," i.e., poses no serious embarrassment to the good man in the White House.

The basic error in this analysis seems to me the assumption that there now exists what Michael Harrington calls "*de facto* coexistence" between the United States and world revolution. Rustin and Harrington confine their analysis to domestic problems, as if believing that foreign affairs are frozen and can be forgotten. But as Harrington conceded in *Partisan Review:* " 'escalation' of the Vietnamese—or any other—crisis would . . . end talk of the War on Poverty, and of the Great Society." That escalation has occurred.

Coalitionism, then, is pro-Americanism. It is what Sidney Lens has called "two-and-a-half campism." It is a posture which subordinates foreign to domestic politics, which mutes criticism of American imperialism so as to keep open its channels to the White House, which tacitly assumes that no major war will occur. But war is occurring in Vietnam, major enough for the innocent people which it has killed. How can one reconcile virtual silence on Vietnam with the screams of Vietnamese women and children?

Coalitionism is also elitism. Its assumption is that major political decisions are made by deals between the representatives of the interests included in the coalition. Negro protest, according to the Rustin formula, should now take on the role of such an interest. And men like Rustin will become the national spokesmen who sell the line agreed-on behind doors to the faithful followers waiting in the street.

This was the meaning of Atlantic City. What was at stake, as it seemed to the S.N.C.C. people there, was not so much the question, Should the compromise be accepted? as the question, Are plain people from Mississippi competent to decide? Rustin, Martin Luther King and Roy Wilkins answered the latter question: No. The decision, they insisted, involved "national considerations." In some sense the destiny of America rested in the hands of those who made this decision. Hence it should be made wisely, by the leaders, and put over to the delegates from Mississippi.

But what those delegates and their S.N.C.C. associates learned at Atlantic City was simply no longer to trust these "national civil-rights leaders." They learned, as Mrs. Hamer put it on her return, that hypocrisy exists all over America. They learned, so Robert Parris told the *National Guardian* dinner in November, that the destiny of America was *not* in their hands, that they should seek their own objectives, "let the chips fall where they may."

So as some sunk deeper into the coils of coalitionism, S.N.C.C. people have joined with Students for a Democratic Society this winter in laying a new emphasis on "participatory democracy." Democracy, they say, means ordinary people making decisions for themselves. It means the staff of an organization making decisions rather than an executive committee, it means the organization itself working itself out of a job so that new popular organizations take over Freedom parties, Freedom schools.

All this Bayard Rustin used to believe. Direct action is inseparable from the idea that everyone involved in a movement has some ultimate responsibility and initiative. Decentralization was the hallmark of the early LIBERATION, which Bayard helped to found. Participatory democrats, as they move from direct action into politics, insist that direct action must continue along with politics, that there come into being a new politics which forces the representative back to his people, and politics back to life.

There is very little point in criticizing the coalition strategy suggested by Rustin unless one has an alternative to offer.

I think the time has come to begin to think of "nonviolent revolution" as the only long-run alternative to coalition with the Marines. The civil-rights movement, so often called a revolution, is thus far no more a revolution than the trade-union movement of the 1930's. Presumably the definition of a revolution is that the direction of society's affairs shifts from one group to another, and that the economic foundation of political power is transformed so as to make this shift permanent. A revolution in this sense—and not merely public works planning by an Administration whose power rests on private ownership and lack of planning—seems to me required both to prevent war and to satisfy the needs of the other America. But is talk of revolution merely what Rustin calls moral gesturing?

So long as revolution is pictured as a violent insurrection it seems to me both distasteful and unreal. The traditional alternative, the Social Democratic vision of electing more and more radical legislators until power passes peacefully to the Left, seems equally illusory. However, the events of the past year—the creation of the Mississippi Freedom Democratic Party and the protest against the war in Vietnam—suggest a third strategy. One can now begin to envision a series of nonviolent protests which would from the beginning question the legitimacy of the Administration's authority where it has gone beyond constitutional and moral limits, and might, if its insane foreign policy continues, culminate in the decision of hundreds of thousands of people to recognize the authority of alternative institutions of their own making.

Robert Parris has sketched out such a scenario as a possibility in Mississippi. What, he has asked, if Mississippi Freedom Democratic Party voters elected not only legislators but public officials as well? What if the Negroes of Neshoba County, Mississippi began to obey the instructions of the Freedom Sheriff rather than Sheriff Rainey? What if the Freedom Sheriff impanelled a Freedom Grand Jury which indicted Sheriff Rainey for murder?

The value of these imaginings is that they break up the concept of "revolution" as a monolithic, unitary event, and remind us that revolution begins as the decision of individuals to say, No, and take a first step. Even the most violent revolutions involved a larger component of nonviolent civil disobedience than is often recognized. Masses of poor men who defy constituted authority typically lack weapons, and succeed only when they convince the government's soldiers not to fire on them but to join them. Thus Trotsky presents the crux of the Russian Revolution as an encounter between mounted Cossacks and unarmed poor people rioting for bread; when the soldiers decided to join the rioters, the revolution was essentially won. St. Exupery, writing of the Spanish Civil War, describes two peasants, one in the Nationalist army and one in the Republican, whose units were stationed on opposite slopes of a valley and who as night fell hurled to each other across the great distance single words which sought to persuade: "Liberty," "Brotherhood." This is how real revolutions, as distinct from plots and insurrections, succeed or fail. Camus was wrong in presenting revolution and rebellion as mutually exclusive: no popular revolution is possible which is, not composed of hundreds of smaller rebellions. Thus the American Civil War, our closest approach to revolution, began with solitary decisions to defy Congress and the Supreme Court and to succor fugitive slaves.

Needless to say all this makes sense only if our situation is desperate. I think it is desperate. If it was desperate in Mississippi when perhaps two dozen people were murdered over a period of five years, what is it in Vietnam where a hundred thousand lives have needlessly been thrown away since 1954? If there are, in Camus' phrase, "limits" inherent in human nature to permissible government policy, what more can we do after what we have done in Vietnam? If Vietnam is permissible, can anything be forbidden? And how many more secret undebated Presidential decisions will it take to convince us that a constitutional crisis exists in America, that we have moved into a twilight zone between democratically delegated authority and something accurately called "fascism"? When the President sent troops into the Dominican Republic he called in Congressmen to tell them, he explained, before they read about it in the newspapers. As the New York

Times has pointed out, government management of the news, characteristic of previous temporary crises such as the U-2 and Bay of Pigs affairs, has in connection with Vietnam become settled public policy over a period of months and years. I believe we should have seen that America could not endlessly practice Seven Days in May in underdeveloped countries all over the world, making and unmaking governments at the behest of generals and C.I.A. agents, without these habits crossing the Rubicon between foreign and domestic politics to become our political style at home as well. I think the situation is desperate.

Yet nonviolence offers rational hope which can forestall desperation issuing in apathy or senseless violence. The situation of the Administration is more desperate than ours, and its present policy is the blind lashing-out of the cornered and frustrated, who see no orderly method to achieve their goals. On the other hand, few as we are our aspirations run along the grain of hopes and strivings of the majority of mankind. International public opinion constitutes some check even on an Administration which has determined to go it alone without friends. When suffragettes were over and over again imprisoned and mishandled on the streets of Washington during World War I, public opinion was aroused, some high government officials resigned, and women's suffrage was enacted into law. If students chained themselves to the Capitol this summer in wave after wave of massive civil disobedience, even the Johnson Administration would be constrained in its choice of means.

What then is to be done? Let me offer an imagined scenario, comparable to Parris' for Mississippi, which without presuming to define a "position" or lay down a "line" may help our thinking converge toward common action.

Suppose (I take this idea from Tom Hayden) there were convened in Washington this summer a new continental congress. The congresses of 1774 and 1775 came about on the initiative of committees of correspondence of the individual colonies. The continental congress of 1965 might stem from the initiative of the community union in a Northern ghetto, or the Freedom Party of a Southern state. Suppose, at any rate, that such a call goes out, saying in effect: This is a desperate situation; our government no longer represents us; let us come together at Washington to consult on what needs to be done.

Already there are in Washington Freedom Democratic Congresswomen who are, in a sense, tribunes of all the unrepresented people in America. As the actions of the Administration systematically exclude Congress from effective decision-making, the category of the unrepresented comes to include not only those (like 95 per cent of adult Mississippi Negroes) who cannot vote, but the rest of the American people who no longer have decision-makers that represent them. Although Mrs. Hamer and Mrs. Gray have held no "freedom legislative hearings" and introduced no "freedom bills," their presence is a symbol of the determination of the American excluded to have some say in what their government does.

The continental congress goes one step further. The act of convening it would stem from a conviction that even the victory of Mrs. Hamer and her colleagues would have little significance if the Congress which they joined no longer had effective power. The continental congress would be the coming-together of project and community union representatives who, were they one day to be elected to Congress, might refuse to go on the ground that Congress has given up its power.

Just as the American colonists organized Provincial Conventions and a Continental Congress to take the place of the colonial legislatures and the British Parliament, so the continental congress of 1965 would seriously and responsibly begin to debate the policies of the United States. The discussions which have failed to take place in the Senate about Vietnam, would take place here. Resolutions would be adopted and the form of treaties ratified; emissaries of the congress could seek to make direct contact with the people of other countries. In effect the continental congress would begin to govern.

The transfer of allegiance would apply, to begin with, only to specific acts. Those refusing to pay taxes might pay them to the continental congress. Those refusing to serve in the army might volunteer their labor to community projects under congress sponsorship. Some, with or without the explicit authorization of a congress majority, might initiate systematic civil disobedience in their own communities or in Washington (just so in 1774 Massachusetts moved out ahead of the Continental Congress and began to organize its own government and to prepare for war). Professors might organize a committee to hold foreign policy hearings, since the Senate Committee on Foreign Relations has failed to do so. Men of spiritual authority from all over the world might be convened as a parallel Supreme Court, to assess guilt and responsibility for the horror of Vietnam.

The pressures on American policy-makers suggest an iron drift toward more and more blatant repression at home and abroad. Yet even if this is so, all is not lost. Six months ago the air-conditioned nightmare seemed secure and invulnerable. Liberals congratulated themselves that American had turned its last corner, integrating the Negro into the happy permanent societal consensus. This was an illusion. America's situation was less secure,

Johnson was less rational, the American people were less brainwashed, than they seemed six months ago. Now we know: whom the gods would destroy they first make mad; but also: we can overcome.

At the April 17th march in Washington it was unbearably moving to watch the sea of banners and signs move out from the Sylvan Theater toward the Capitol as Joan Baez, Judy Collins and others sang "We Shall Overcome." Still more poignant was the perception—and I checked my reaction with many many others who felt as I did—that as the crowd moved down the Mall toward the seat of government, its path delimited on each side by rows of chartered buses so that there was nowhere to go but forward, toward the waiting policemen, it seemed that the great mass of people would simply flow on through and over the marble buildings, that our forward movement was irresistibly strong, that even had some been shot or arrested nothing could have stopped that crowd from taking possession of its government. Perhaps next time we should keep going, occupying for a time the rooms from which orders issue and sending to the people of Vietnam and the Dominican Republic the profound apologies which are due; or quietly waiting on the Capitol steps until those who make policy for us, and who like ourselves are trapped by fear and pride, consent to enter into dialogue with us and with mankind.

Epilogue

The Threat of the Garrison State

Epilogue

The Threat of the Garrison State

The twentieth century's social and intellectual turmoil reawakened old hostilities and contributed substantially to the widespread disbelief and alienation which comprise a formidable antidemocratic trend in the United States. Was it possible, then, that a people no longer convinced of democracy's meaning or strength or worth could keep freedom intact and, at the same time, support a defense posture such as that thrust upon the United States at the end of the Second World War? Could the nation engage in an international power struggle of indefinite duration without surrendering important portions of popular sovereignty to the encroachments of security needs and priorities?[1] Americans have nourished a traditional suspicion of the effects of military power and war; militarist elitism and the corrosiveness of standing armies have often been assigned primary roles in American analyses of totalitarianism. In an era of profoundly shifting, sometimes drifting, allegiances, the apparent necessity of maintaining enormous military forces might transform democratic equalitarianism into "the egalitarianism of the camp."[2] A blind grasping for survival might supplant liberty as a national goal. The American experiment in self-government might end in the erection of a "Garrison State."[3]

Those fearful of such an outcome cited three dangers stemming from the emphasis on military preparedness:

1. The reliance upon military expertise might erase the traditional supremacy of civilian power, opening the door to military interference in national policy-making and perhaps even a militarist dictatorship.

Such a threat was not new. Washington and Lincoln had confronted military challenges to civilian authority. Yet its seriousness in a time of total war could not be doubted. For example, when involvement in World War II appeared imminent, President Roosevelt, in attempting to prepare the governmental structure for the burden of defense, discovered that the Army-Navy Munitions Board had, during the 1930's, developed an industrial mobilization plan predicated on the assumption that during a modern war "almost any power could be had from Congress for the asking."[4] The military's plans, as an official government report later noted, would have conferred on a single individual vast powers over government organization and policy, which "would have constituted virtual abdication by the President and would have made him less able to meet his constitutional responsibilities."[5] Roosevelt blocked the plan by reviving the civilian-controlled Advisory Commission to the Council of National Defense in May, 1940, and placed the aggressive Donald Nelson in charge of the War Production Board.[6] The military "never gave up the effort to increase its control in these areas," however, seeking, in 1942, to place industrial mobilization under the supervision of the Joint Chiefs of Staff.[7]

Exceptions to the general rule of sullen compliance with civilian control were the post-war activities of two colorful, brilliant field commanders—Generals Douglas MacArthur and Edwin Walker. In command of United Nations forces during the Korean conflict, MacArthur found himself at odds with the Truman administration's concept of a limited war. Despite warnings from superior officers and the president, MacArthur issued public statements supporting policies contrary to the administration's and disconcerting to allied nations, finally providing one of Truman's sharpest partisan critics, House minority leader Joseph Martin, with a letter attacking official war objectives. The president, viewing MacArthur's acts as insubordinate, removed him from his command.[8] Walker, a dashing Texan with a fine record as commando leader in World War II and combat officer in Korea, but also a zealous right-wing extremist, came under scrutiny in 1961, after Senator William Fulbright brought Walker's "troop indoctrination program" to the attention of Secretary of Defense Robert McNamara.[9] Subsequent investigation revealed that Walker had attempted to urge ultraconservative congressional candidates upon troops in his 24th Division through editorials in the official unit newspaper, "seminars," and public speeches.[10] It was also found that, because of a vague National Security Council directive, not only Walker, but other military officers, were involved in "educating" armed services personnel and the public on the menaces of Communism—often through meetings cosponsored by groups of the far right.[11] An immediate uproar greeted this obvious military sortie into politics, and the Secretary of Defense assured investigating senators that he realized that it was "of vital importance that we protect the integrity of our military program by abstaining meticulously from partisan politics in any form and from attempting to make national policy."[12]

Still, the supposed "muzzling" of military officers by Pentagon censors, as well as Walker's insistence that he was a victim of the international communist conspiracy, served as issues for some who did not agree with McNamara that "the military establishment is an instrument, not a shaper of national policy."[13] In fact, the clamor which had followed the news of Walker's indiscretions was matched by a counterattack in the press and Congress led by Senator Strom Thurmond. Probably only a small minority of Americans supported Thurmond's advocacy of Walker and of the military's attempts to mold public opinion, but the popularity of such positions in some quarters emphasized the gravity of a second ground for suspicion of long-term preparedness:

2. *A society for which security was the chief goal might find the Bill of Rights an unnecessary nuisance.*

The institutionalized intolerance of dissent bred by war could be extended in periods of seemingly interminable world tension. It had happened in the 1920's, and the extreme right found it a convenient weapon again following World War II. As the Cold War stretched on, suspicion of anything except unanimity might become a habit.[14] The desire for national unity might stifle useful criticism. *The New York Times'* decision to remain silent in the national interest, rather than inform the public of the impending Bay of Pigs debacle, suggests how subtly intended patriotism can impinge on freedom, with unfortunate results. Far less subtle was the recent use of an instrument of national defense to silence criticism. However honest the motive, Selective Service Director Hershey's letter of October 26, 1967, to local draft boards, ordering the reclassification of known antiwar demonstrators, represented an attack upon the rights of free expression and free assembly.[15] Neither Hershey's defense of his act—"We cannot lose our home front to the lawless"—nor the argument of a congressional ally—"Let us not permit these malcontents to ... both destroy the draft law and America"—came to grips with the fact that an administrative agency was being used to punish dissent.[16] Despite the Justice Department's quiet effort to nullify Hershey's directive, that directive was a reminder of the inherent antidemocratic tendency of a survival psychology.

There was one other ground for grave concern:

3. *Massive government defense spending could lead to an economic addiction to military preparedness.*

It was not necessary to ascribe to Mills's power-elite theory to see that, for some industries and regions, prosperity seemed dependent already on permanent military spending.[17] Of course, large federal appropriations had been a constant factor in the American economy since the 1930's, and according to one critic, "it is defense expenditures and not welfare programs that have so greatly enlarged the federal government's role in the economy."[18] When veterans' benefits, atomic energy expenditures, and interest payments on a federal debt largely due to World War II were added to direct military spending, three-fourths of the federal budget could be labeled defense appropriations.[19] Without doubt, the American economy bore the unmistakable imprint of military demands. Some industries were almost wholly dependent on the federal defense budget: 94% of the aircraft industry's production; 61% of that of the shipping and boating industries.[20] Some observers claimed that a serious move toward disarmament would cripple the economies of states like Washington, where 28% of all manufacturing stemmed from defense industries.[21] Although outright adoption of a permanent war economy, like that espoused by Charles E. Wilson, appeared unlikely, there was always the possibility, as President Eisenhower warned in his farewell address, that the civil government might permit itself to be lobbied and frightened into placing long-range policy decisions in the hands of a military-industrial complex. [22]

NOTES

1. Wesley W. Posvor *et al., American Defense Policy* (Baltimore: Johns Hopkins Press, 1965), p. xiii; David M. Abshire and Richard V. Allen, *National Security: Political, Military, and Economic Strategies in the Decade Ahead* (New York: Frederick A. Praeger, 1963), *passim.*

2. Samuel P. Huntington, *The Soldier and the State: the Theory and Politics of Civil-Military Relations* (Cambridge: Belknap Press, 1957), p. 349.

3. *Ibid.,* pp. 345-346; Harold D. Lasswell, "The Garrison State," *American Journal of Sociology,* XLVI (January, 1941), pp. 455-468; Lasswell, *National Security and Individual Freedom* (New York: McGraw-Hill Book Company, 1950), pp. 23-49.

4. U.S., Bureau of the Budget, *The United States at War: Development and Administration of the War Program by the Federal Government* (Washington, D.C.: Government Printing Office, 1946), pp. 16, 23.

5. *Ibid.,* pp. 23-24.

6. *Ibid.,* p. 23.

7. *Ibid.,* pp. 129, 280; Ray F. Harvey, *The Politics of this War* (New York: Harper & Brothers, 1943), pp. 217-237.

8. U.S., Senate, *Hearings before the Committee on Armed Services and the Committee on Foreign Relations,* 82nd Cong., 1st Sess., (May-August, 1951), *passim.*

9. Fred J. Cook, *The Warfare State* (New York: Macmillan Company, 1962), p. 6; Jack Raymond, *Power at the Pentagon* (New York: Harper & Row, 1964), pp. 119-124.

10. Raymond, *Power at the Pentagon,* pp. 119-124; U.S., Senate, *Hearings before the Committee on Armed Services,* 87th Cong., 1st Sess., (1961), p. 11, and *passim.*

11. U.S., Senate, *Testimony and Statements of Edwin A. Walker before the Special Preparedness Subcommittee, Committee on Armed Services,* 87th Cong., 2nd Sess. (1962), pp. 1349-1394, 1406, 1409-1411.

12. Cook, *Warfare State,* pp. 5-6; U.S., Senate, *Hearings before the Committee on Armed Services,* 87th Cong., 1st Sess., (1961), p. 5.

13. *Ibid.*

14. *Cf.* Edward A. Kolodziej, *The Uncommon Defense and Congress, 1945-1963* (Ohio State University Press, 1966), pp. 20-22, 26-30.

15. *Selective Service,* vol. XVII (December, 1967), p. 4.

16. *Ibid.,* p. 2.

17. George A. Lincoln *et al.,* eds., *Economics of National Security* (New York: Prentice-Hall, Inc., 1950), pp. 228-249.

18. Julius Duscha, *Arms, Money, and Politics* (New York: Ives Washburn, Inc., 1964), p. 62.

19. *Ibid.;* Raymond, *Power at the Pentagon,* pp. 137-204.

20. Jules Backman *et al., War and Defense Economics* (New York: Rinehart & Company, Inc., 1952), p. 2; Duscha, *Arms, Money, and Politics,* p. 64.

21. Duscha, *Arms, Money, and Politics,* p. 64; Arthur Herzog, *The War-Peace Establishment* (New York: Harper & Row, 1963), pp. 100-121.

22. U.S., House of Representatives, *Supplemental Hearings Released From Executive Session Relating to Entertainment Furnished by the Martin Company of Baltimore, Maryland, of United States Government Officers,* Subcommittee for Special Investigations of the Committee on Armed Services, 86th Cong., 1st Sess., (September 10, 1959), *passim;* Duscha, *Arms, Money, and Politics,* pp. 86-113; Cook, *Warfare State,* pp. 9, 177.

26

WPB Aide Urges U.S. to Keep War Set-up

A full-fledged program of postwar preparedness, with American resources and energy geared to be thrown into war economy on a moment's notice, was advocated last night by Charles E. Wilson, executive vice chairman of the War Production Board, as this nation's best guarantee against any future Pearl Harbors.

Mr. Wilson, who characterized disarmament and unpreparedness as a "thoroughly discredited doctrine," placed his views on postwar military and naval necessities before the Army Ordnance Association at its annual dinner, held in the Waldorf-Astoria Hotel.

His audience included high Army and Navy officers as well as leading representatives of American industry, most of whom had attended round-table conferences earlier in the day devoted to ordnance problems.

Mr. Wilson observed that the United States had maintained a fleet "in being" ever since the days of Admiral Mahan, and asked his audience: "What is more natural and more logical than that we should henceforth mount our national policy upon the solid fact of an industrial capacity for war, and a research capacity for war that is also 'in being'? It seems to me that anything less is foolhardy." . . .

He agreed that thousands of management experts throughout the country had created miracles despite technical difficulties and inadequate equipment, then commented:

"But has it ever occurred to you that really good managers, in government or business, would never have allowed their own businesses to operate as haphazardly and spasmodically as has the business of defending the United States against its enemies?"

He said that in industry market trends were watched from year to year, always with an eye on future needs.

"Yet when it comes to the vastly important and tragic business of war," he said, "we shut our eyes and stop our ears until it is so late that top management has to perform miracles, and men die while waiting for them."

He asked his audience to consider, as an example, "the lives and money that could have been saved, and the perils averted, if the antisubmarine devices now available had been ready in the summer of 1940."

"Perhaps it is time for some fresh thinking on this matter of war and peace," Mr. Wilson remarked. "Instead of looking to disarmament and unpreparedness as a safeguard against war—a thoroughly discredited doctrine—let us try the opposite—full preparedness according to a continuing plan. The thought may be unpleasant, but through the centuries war has been inevitable in our human affairs, as a basic element in evolutionary peace. We have yet to learn that hard truth, apparently."

He cited the research applied to poison gas as a prime example of preparedness. Every nation in the world, he said, assigned its foremost chemists to the study of gas and its defensive complements after its terrifying appearance in the first World War.

As a result, he asserted, gas has been used in this war in only isolated instances and "no practical person attributes this to moral or humane reasons."

The WPB executive vice chairman declared that industry's cooperation with the Army and the Navy during the last two years had made a "very effective combination," one which he advocated be extended into the postwar period.

"Should the world know that we were in that position," he said, "that we were determinedly keeping the fires of scientific and developmental effort burning, and that we were ready to shift our industry quickly to the production of these thoroughly tested and proven superior weapons, the probabilities of another Hitler, Mussolini or Tojo undertaking to conquer the world will be much more remote."

The production front, under which is amassed twenty million workers, is "as deserving of a continuing general staff operation in peacetime as the Army and Navy," Mr. Wilson declared.

He told the industrialists in the audience that they, as much as generals and admirals, legislators and chiefs of state, were leaders of their country and that "their responsibility for postwar preparedness is certainly no less."

"The burden," he said, "is on all of us to integrate our respective activities—political, military and industrial—because we are in world politics to stay, whether we like it or not.

"Any latent ability we may have to procure for our children a durable peace will not be impaired by our ability to wage war victoriously and at a moment's notice."

He expressed his awareness that the sentiments such as those spoken by himself last night "have traditionally been met by the cry of 'war monger.' "

"To answer such views," he added, "I am convinced that had our country possessed this type of set-up, it would have been the most effective insurance against the Pearl Harbor attack. What I am here proposing is the harnessing of the technology and science of the services and of industry—for preparedness.

"The peaceful temperament of the American people is well known," he went on. "We can possess the mightiest and deadliest armaments in the world without becoming aggressors in our hearts because we do not have that intoxicating lust for blood and power which periodically transforms the German military caste."

Mr. Wilson submitted a "rough outline" of a program to carry through the ideas he advocated. He suggested that first of all the preparedness program be made the responsibility of the Federal Government, that it be a continuing program and "not the creature of an emergency," and that the program be "insured and supported" by Congress.

Industry's role, he said, should be to "respond and cooperate" and to be "allowed" to play its part unhampered "by political witch-hunts, or thrown to the fanatical isolationist fringe tagged with a 'merchants-of-death' label."

He recommended dividing industry's role into two parts: research and production. Great emphasis should be given, he continued, to the research activities of governmental agencies and the services as well as industry.

To develop this program of research, Mr. Wilson said he felt that competent, responsible civilian advisers should be named to institutional committees that could maintain liaison with industry and Government laboratories.

The chairmen of such committees, with ranking Army and Navy officers, then could compose a general committee for continuing postwar research and development, according to Mr. Wilson. It might even be wise, he suggested, for the Army and Navy to give reserve commissions to outstanding industrialists to insure their interest and build a closer bond between them and the services.

Out of the group of officers, he said, there might be chosen an "industrial coordinating committee" to serve in conjunction with the principal procurement officers of the services, thus providing a group that would carry into peacetime the consultative idea of the combined chiefs of staff.

"We have learned that our country has the strength and brains to do anything it needs to do," Mr. Wilson declared, "provided that it brings the strength and brains together and makes the proper use of them. As we love peace and long for its continuance, it is our responsibility to make sure that America's strength and brains, its craft and knowledge, are kept forever ready—not just ready for action, but in action."

The importance of his plan, according to Mr. Wilson, is that in keeping the United States "scientifically and technologically ready for war" it would not be necessary to maintain large armed forces, nor would it be expensive, or necessary to depend upon universal military service.

"It can fit into our peacetime way of living without difficulty," he said, "I believe with all my heart that it would guarantee that way of life.". . .

The round table on ordnance production, at which General Hayes presided, was also addressed by K. T. Keller, president of the Chrysler Corporation, who said the cooperation achieved between Army Ordnance and industry "will be a big factor not only in winning the war but in keeping the world at peace thereafter."

Examples of the close integration of resource and skills in industry were related by Roy T. Hurley, special assistant to the president of the Bendix Aviation Corporation. He cited manufacturers of carbines, who he said had exchanged more than 3,000,000 parts, as typifying the interchange of information in industry.

E. B. Yancey, general manager of the explosive department of E. I du Pont de Nemours & Co., told of the research conducted by his company in smokeless powder and other explosives.

Maj. Gen. Cladson M. Barnes, presiding over the conference on ordnance engineering, told of successful performances of certain American weapons.

Maj. Gen. Charles L. Scott, commanding general, Armored Force Replacement Training Center, Fort Knox, Ky., said proper operation, maintenance provisions for spare parts and replacement requirements could not be overemphasized. He added that our factories, engineers and shipping could not supply vehicles steadily unless the using troops operated them reasonably and cared for them continuously.

General Scott said he believed in the expenditure of material to save lives. He disclosed that for every tank knocked out only 20 percent of the crew were lost. This means, he said, that if you lose 1,000 tanks, you will save enough crews to man 800 replacement tanks. If the battle is won, he added, probably 80 percent of the tanks knocked out by the enemy can be picked up for salvage.

The various problems of ordnance training that arose when the nation was plunged into war in 1941 were presented by military and civilian leaders at a session in the Astor Gallery of the hotel. Brig. Gen. Harry R. Kutz, chief of the military training division of the Ordnance Department, presided.

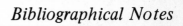

Bibliographical Notes

Bibliographical Notes

Students should be aware that indexes to periodicals, such as the *Reader's Guide*, the *Social Science and Humanities Index*, and the *New York Times Index* are excellent sources for contemporary material. Merely consulting the *Reader's Guide* under an appropriate subject heading such as "Democracy" indicates the misgivings some Americans had about representative government. General bibliographies of the United States which are useful include *Writings on American History*, an annual cumulation of books and articles beginning in 1902 (unfortunately none have appeared since 1958); Oscar Handlin et al. *Harvard Guide to American History* (Cambridge: Harvard University Press, 1955); and the Library of Congress, *Guide to the Study of the United States* (Washington, D. C.: Library of Congress, 1960); while the abstracting service, *America, History and Life*, is good for periodical articles. Congressional committee hearings and other publications of the federal government are listed and indexed in the *Monthly Catalog of United States Government Publications*. Brief biographical articles can be found in the *Dictionary of American Biography, Twentieth Century Authors*, and *Current Biography*, and references to sources of biographical information in the *Biography Index*.

Recommended general histories of the period are Arthur S. Link, **American Epoch: A History of the United States Since the 1890's*, 2nd ed. (New York: Knopf, 1963) and Forrest McDonald, **The Torch is Passed* (Reading, Mass.: Addison-Wesley, 1968). David Spitz, **Patterns of Anti-Democratic Thought* (New York: Macmillan, 1949) and John H. Bunzel, **Anti-Politics in America; Reflections on the Anti-Political Temper and Its Distortions of the Democratic Process* (New York: Knopf, 1962) are two excellent critical treatments of antidemocratic sentiment.

Babbit's *Democracy and Leadership* (New York: Houghton Mifflin, 1924) is illustrative of his thought, but his antagonism to democracy courses through all of his writings. Cram expressed his doubt for democracy in *The

*Works containing extensive bibliographies are noted with asterisk.

267

Nemesis of Mediocrity (Boston: Marshall Jones, 1917), *Convictions and Controversies* (Boston: Marshall Jones, 1935), and *The End of Democracy,* (Boston: Marshall Jones, 1937), John Higham, *Strangers in the Land: Patterns of American Nativism, 1860-1925* (New Brunswick: Rutgers University Press, 1955), Barbara Miller Solomon, *Ancestors and Immigrants: A Changing New England Tradition* (Cambridge: Harvard University Press, 1956), and E. Digby Baltzell, *The Protestant Establishment: Aristocracy and Caste in America* (New York: Random House, 1964) survey various aspects of the traditional scepticism about democracy in the United States.

In addition to *The Passing of the Great Race,* 4th ed., (New York: Scribner's Sons, 1921), see Grant's *The Conquest of a Continent,* rev. ed. (New York: C. Scribner's Sons, 1934). *Democracy and the Human Equation* (New York: E. P. Dutton, 1921), is a collection of articles containing the essence of Alleyne Ireland's thinking. Historical treatments of the Eugenics Movement include Mark Hughlin Haller, *Eugenics: Hereditarian Attitudes in American Thought* (New Brunswick: Rutgers University Press, 1963); Chapters 14 to 17 in Thomas F. Gossett, *Race: The History of an Idea in America* (Dallas: Southern Methodist University Press, 1963); and Garrett James Hardin, *Nature and Man's Fate* (New York: Rinehart, 1959). Charles C. Alexander, "Prophet of American Racism: Madison Grant and the Nordic Myth," *Phylon,* v. XXIII, No. 1 (Spring, 1962), pp. 73-90, contains a short account of Madison Grant's influence. Donald K. Pickens' doctoral dissertation, *American Eugenicists: Conservative Naturalists as Progressives* (Austin: University of Texas, 1964) and his article "The Sterilization Movement: the Search for Purity in Mind and State," *Phylon,* v. 28 (Spring, 1967), pp. 78-94 treat other aspects of scientism and democracy.

Robert M. Yerkes, "Psychological Examining in the United States Army," *Memoirs of the National Academy of Sciences,* Vol. 15 (1921), is a detailed study of the results of psychological testing during World War I. Percy E. Davidson, "The Social Significance of Army Intelligence Findings," *Scientific Monthly,* vol. 16 (1923) pp. 184-93, and Chapters I and VI in William C. Bagley's *Determinism in Education* (Baltimore: Worwich & York, 1925) are contemporary criticisms of the results of psychological testing, while a more recent reference is in Solomon, *Ancestors and Immigrants. The Subject Guide to Psychological Abstracts* as well as the *Reader's Guide* and *International Index,* contain many more references to the testing program. In addition to *How We Advertised America* (New York: Harper and Brothers, 1920), Creel's autobiography, *Rebel at Large* (New York: Putnam, 1947), is worth consulting. Creel's work with the Committee on Public Information is covered by Mark Sullivan in *Our Times: The United States* (New York: Charles Scribner's Sons, 1933), Vol. 5, pp. 433-440. An early analysis of the political implications of psychology is George Kibbe Turner, "Manufacturing Public Opinion; the New Art of Making Presidents by Press

Bureau," *McClure's Magazine,* Vol. 39 (July 1912), pp. 316-26. Bernays has written a number of books in which he discusses public relations, including his autobiography, *Biography of an Idea* (New York: Simon and Shuster, 1965). Stanley Kelley, **Professional Public Relations and Political Power* (Baltimore: John Hopkins University, 1956) is an objective analysis of the political use of public relations between 1949 and 1952, including a case study of a public relations firm's activities. James M. Perry **The New Politics: The Expanding Technology of Political Manipulation* (New York: Potter, 1968) is a journalist's account of more recent techniques of using professional political campaign firms and mass media in elections. Herbert M. Baus and William B. Ross, a political campaign management team, reveal their techniques in *Politics Battle Plan* (New York: Macmillan, 1968). **Richard La Piere, *The Freudian Ethic* (New York: Duell, Sloan, and Pearce, 1959), is an angry attack on the distortions of Freudian psychology in the United States. See also Daniel Bell, "Notes on Authoritarian and Democratic Leaders," in *Studies in Leadership* (ed. Alvin Gouldner, New York: Harper, 1950), pp. 395-408. Among Skinner's writings, *Walden Two* (New York: Macmillan, 1948), a utopian novel, is central to his thought, but *Science and Human Behavior* (New York: Macmillan, 1943) is important too. See the interesting exchange between Carl R. Rogers and B. F. Skinner, and Skinner's answers to some of his critics in "Some Issues Concerning the Control of Human Behavior: A Symposium," *Science,* Vol. 124, no. 3231 (Nov. 30, 1956), pp. 1057-1066. Besides Spitz and Bunzel, criticisms can be found in George Kateb, *Utopia and Its Enemies* (Glencoe: Free Press, 1963), and Daniel B. Stevick's brief review, * *B. F. Skinner's Walden Two* (New York: Seabury Press, 1968). John H. Schaar, **Escape from Authority; The Perspectives of Erich Fromm* (New York: Basic Books, 1961), and Bunzel, *Antipolitics in America,* have criticisms of Fromm's thinking.

James Burnham's *The Managerial Revolution* (New York: John Day, 1941) is an expanded version of the selection in the text. His essays "Is Democracy Possible?" in *Whose Revolution?* (ed. I. D. Talmadge, New York: Howell, Soskin, 1941), and "Coming Rulers of the U.S.," *Fortune,* Vol. 24 (Nov. 1941), pp. 100ff, are also worth consulting. Spitz, *Patterns of Antidemocratic Thought,* and Bunzel, *Antipolitics in America,* contain extensive treatments of Burnham's theory of the Managerial Revolution. Other critical studies are found in George Orwell, *Shooting an Elephant and Other Essays* (New York: Harcourt, Brace, 1950), pp. 122-48, and William H. Whyte, *The Organization Man* (New York: Simon and Schuster, 1956), pp. 277. Among the extensive body of literature endorsing technocracy, see Howard Scott's *Technocracy; Science vs. Chaos* (Chicago, 1933) and *Introduction to Technocracy* (New York: Technocracy Inc., 1938), and Harold Loeb's *Life in a Technocracy* (New York: Viking, 1933). Most libraries have at least one of Technocracy's periodicals. Apparently the only scholarly treatment of the Technocracy Movement is Henry Elsner, *The Technocrats; Prophets of Automation* (Syracuse: Syracuse University Press, 1967).

Haywood's autobiography, *Bill Haywood's Book* (New York: International Publishers, 1929), should be consulted. Reaction to radicalism, particularly the IWW, in the United States is found in William Preston, *Aliens and Dissenters; Federal Suppression of Radicals, 1903-1933* (Cambridge: Harvard University Press, 1963), but Paul F. Brissenden, *The I.W.W.; A Study of American Syndicalism,* 2nd ed. (New York: Russell and Russell, 1957), is considered the most significant study. Volume II of Donald Drew Egbert and Stow Persons,*Socialism and American Life* (Princeton: Princeton University Press, 1952), contains an excellent bibliography on the IWW. Daniel Aaron, *Writers on the Left* (New York: Harcourt, Brace & World, 1961), is a survey of the response of a selected group of writers to the idea of communism. Theodore Draper, *The Roots of American Communism* (New York: Viking, 1957), and Irving Howe and Lewis Coser, *The American Communist Party* (Boston: Beacon Press, 1957), are excellent histories of communism in the United States. A section of Thomas T. Hammond, ed., *Soviet Foreign Relations and World Communism* (Princeton: Princeton University Press, 1965), has an extensive list of books with annotations by and about communism in the United States. Over 300 radical periodicals, with annotations, are listed in Walter Goldwater, ed., *Radical Periodicals in America, 1890-1950* (New Haven: Yale University Library, 1966); this work includes a genealogical chart and a concise lexicon of the parties and groups which issued them.

Central to Coughlin's thought are his published speeches and issues of his magazine, *Social Justice.* In addition to *The Coming of American Fascism* (New York: Harper, 1936), Lawrence Dennis expressed his thinking in *The Dynamics of War and Revolution* (New York: The Weekly Foreign Letter,* 1940), and "Portrait of American Fascism," *American Mercury,* Vol. 36 (1935), pp. 404-413. James Madole's writings have been limited to his National Renaissance Party's *National Renaissance Bulletin.* Raymond G. Swing, *Forerunners of American Fascism* (New York: Messner, 1935), is an early and highly colored description of fascist sentiment, while Seymour Martin Lipset *"Three Decades of the Radical Right; Coughlinites, McCarthyites and Birchers," The Radical Right* (ed. Daniel Bell, New York: Anchor Books, 1962), discusses the persistence of a right-wing authoritarian attitude. Charles J. Tull, *Father Coughlin and the New Deal* (Syracuse: Syracuse University Press, 1965), is a recent treatment of Coughlin, although Tull is reluctant to charge Coughlin with embracing fascism. Fascism is one of the topics in George Thayer *The Farther Shores of Politics* (New York: Simon and Schuster, 1967), a comprehensive survey of contemporary political extremism in the United States.

An early, substantial study of the Ku Klux Klan is John M. Mecklin, *The Ku Klux Klan: A Study of the American Mind* (New York: Harcourt Brace, 1924). Among the recent books are William Pierce Randel, *The Ku Klux Klan; A Century of Infamy* (Philadelphia: Chilton Books, 1965), and Charles C. Alexander, *The Ku Klux Klan in the Southwest* (Lexington: University of Kentucky, 1965). Joseph McCarthy's thinking can be found in *McCarthyism: the Fight for America* (New York: Devin-Adair, 1952), and *America's Retreat from Victory: The Story of General George C. Marshall* (New York: Devin-Adair, 1952), but his speeches in the *Congressional Record* and the transcripts of his investigative committee hearings should be consulted. Richard Rovere's *Senator Joe McCarthy* (New York: Harcourt, Brace, 1959) is a useful biography, while Michael Paul Rogin, *The Intellectuals and McCarthy: The Radical Specter* (Cambridge: MIT Press, 1967), is a recent interpretative study. See current issues of *The Cross and the Flag* for more of Gerald L. K. Smith's thought. Benson expressed his fears of internal subversion and conspiracy in *The Red Carpet* (Salt Lake City: Bookcraft, Inc., 1962). However, Robert Welch, founder of the John Birch Society, has been the most influential exponent of "political fundamentalism"—consult *The Politician* (privately printed, 1958), the *Blue Book* (Belmont, Mass.: 1959), and his collection of speeches, *The New Americanism* (Boston: Western Islands, 1966). For further insight see issues of *American Opinion,* the magazine of the John Birch Society. Many writers have probed the elements of political fundamentalism; besides Bell and Thayer, see Harry and Bonaro Overstreet, *The Strange Tactics of Extremism* (New York: Norton, 1964). A right-wing group has compiled a *First National Directory of "Rightist" Groups' Publications and Some Individuals in the United States,* 5th ed. (Los Angeles: Alert American Association, 1965); according to the editors, "the single thing in common with these listings is that they all represent a protest of some sort against prevailing leftist political and/or social trends." The 1965 edition has 3406 entries ranging from the most paranoid of groups to the *Wall Street Journal.* Another (presumably impartial) list is Group Research, Inc., *Directory* (Washington, D.C.), a subscription service having information on groups, individuals, and publications. Robert H. Muller, ed., *From Radical Left to Extreme Right: Current Periodicals of Protest Controversy, or Dissent— U.S.A.* (Ann Arbor: Campus Publishers, 1967), is "a bibliography containing dispassionate summaries of content samples to guide librarians and other educators through the polemic fringe."

Among the growing body of literature on the Afro-American protest movement, the most influential have been Malcolm X's collection of speeches, *Malcolm X Speaks* (ed. George Breitman, New York: Merit Publishers, 1965), and Stokely Carmichael and Charles V. Hamilton, *Black Power: The Politics of Liberation in America* (New York: Random House,

1967). E. D. Cronon, *Black Moses* (Madison: University of Wisconsin Press, 1955), is a biography of Marcus Garvey, a leader of an early withdrawal movement. For accounts of the present situation, see C. Eric Lincoln, *The Black Muslims in America* (Boston: Beacon Press, 1961), and E. Essien-Udom, *Black Nationalism: A Search for an Identity in America* (Chicago: University of Chicago Press, 1962). A recommended book on "Black Power" is Nathan Wright, *Black Power and Urban Unrest* (New York: Hawthorn Books, 1967). Daniel T. Williams and Carolyn L. Redden, *The Black Muslims in the United States: A Selected Bibliography* (Tuskegee Institute, 1964) (mimeographed), and Elizabeth W. Miller, *The Negro in America: A Bibliography* (Cambridge: Harvard University Press, 1966), are useful. Floyd B. Barbour, ed., *The Black Power Revolt* (Boston: Porter Sargent, 1968), contains an excellent bibliography, as well as essays by advocates and critics of "Black Power."

G. William Domhoff and Hoyt B. Ballard have compiled a useful anthology of criticisms of the power-elite theory, *C. Wright Mills and The Power Elite* (Boston: Beacon Press, 1968), representing what the editors call "liberal," "radical" and "high brow" points of view. Also included is Mills's answer to his critics, and a review by Domhoff of criticisms, especially those that have appeared since Mills's death. See also pages 360-365 of James H. Meisel, *The Myth of the Ruling Class: Gaetana Mosca the Elite* (Ann Arbor: Ann Arbor Paperbacks, University of Michigan Press, 1962). Lynd is an editor of *Liberation* and has written numerous books and articles illustrative of his thinking. Paul Jacobs and Saul Landau, *The New Radicals; A Report with Documents* (New York: New American Library, 1966), and Jack Newfield, *A Prophetic Minority* (New York: New American Library, 1966), are two of the numerous books on the radical left.

Many people, including President Eisenhower in his farewell address, have expressed concern over the coming of a "Garrison State." See Marc Pilisuk and Thomas Hayden, *"Is There a Military Industrial Complex Which Prevents Peace?: Consensus and Countervailing Power in Pluralistic Systems," Journal of Social Issues,* Vol. XXI, No. 3 (July, 1965), pp. 67-117, for a critical analysis of the literature as well as a proposal for deploying countervailing forces for peace.

Finally, for surveys of fiction that reflect the strain upon American democracy in this century, see Harlan Hatcher, *Creating the Modern American Novel* (New York: Russell and Russell, 1965), Gordon Milne, *The American Political Novel* (Norman: University of Oklahoma Press, 1966), and Walter B. Rideout, * *The Radical Novel in the United States, 1900-1954* (Cambridge: Harvard University Press, 1956).